POVERTY AND
SOCIAL PROTECTION
IN INDONESIA

THE SMERU RESEARCH INSTITUTE

The SMERU Research Institute, which was established in 2001, is an independent institution that undertakes research and policy studies on socioeconomic matters concerning Indonesia, especially those related to poverty. SMERU also conducts research on governmental matters, including the implementation of regional autonomy and decentralisation policies and their impact on the provision of public services. SMERU's most recent research includes participatory poverty assessments, social protection program evaluations, and studies of direct and conditional cash transfer programs and pro-poor budgeting. Through formal and informal networking with various institutions and agencies, SMERU has participated in policy development and has endeavoured to ensure that the policies produced are relevant to real conditions in Indonesia.

The **Institute of Southeast Asian Studies (ISEAS)** was established as an autonomous organization in 1968. It is a regional centre dedicated to the study of socio-political, security and economic trends and developments in Southeast Asia and its wider geostrategic and economic environment. The Institute's research programmes are the Regional Economic Studies (RES, including ASEAN and APEC), Regional Strategic and Political Studies (RSPS), and Regional Social and Cultural Studies (RSCS).

ISEAS Publishing, an established academic press, has issued almost 2,000 books and journals. It is the largest scholarly publisher of research about Southeast Asia from within the region. ISEAS Publishing works with many other academic and trade publishers and distributors to disseminate important research and analyses from and about Southeast Asia to the rest of the world.

POVERTY AND SOCIAL PROTECTION IN INDONESIA

Edited by Joan Hardjono, Nuning Akhmadi, and Sudarno Sumarto

ISEAS

Institute of Southeast Asian Studies
Singapore

LEMBAGA PENELITIAN
SMERU
RESEARCH INSTITUTE

The SMERU Research Institute
Jakarta, Indonesia

First published in Singapore in 2010 by ISEAS Publishing
Institute of Southeast Asian Studies
30 Heng Mui Keng Terrace
Pasir Panjang
Singapore 119614
E-mail: publish@iseas.edu.sg
Website: <http://bookshop.iseas.edu.sg>

Jointly with
The SMERU Research Institute
Jl Pandeglang 30 Menteng
Jakarta 10310
Indonesia
E-mail: smeru@smeru.or.id
Website: < http://smeru.or.id>

The responsibility for facts and opinions in this publication rests exclusively with the authors and their interpretations do not necessarily reflect the views or the policy of the publishers or its supporters.

ISEAS Library Cataloguing-in-Publication Data

Poverty and social protection in Indonesia / Joan Hardjono, Nuning Akhmadi, and Sudarno Sumarto.
   1. Poverty—Indonesia.
   2. Indonesia—Social conditions.
   I. Sumarto, Sudarno.
   II. Hardjono, Joan.
   III. Akhmadi, Nuning
HC450P6P88   2010

ISBN 978-981-230-939-6 (soft cover)
ISBN 978-981-230-952-5 (E-Book PDF)

Photo Credit: Fourth grade children in a village school in Kronjo, Tangerang District, Banten. Photo courtesy of the SMERU Research Institute, Jakarta.

Typeset by Superskill Graphics Pte Ltd
Printed in Singapore by Photoplates Private Limited

*To the memory of the late Wenefrida Dwi Widyanti (1969–2008).
Her tireless dedication did much to help SMERU develop into a
prominent research institute.*

CONTENTS

List of Tables   ix

List of Figures   xiii

Preface   xv

Postscript: The 2008 Financial Crisis   xxi

Acknowledgements   xxiii

Glossary and Acronyms   xxv

The Editors   xxx

The Contributors   xxxi

1. A Brief Overview of Growth and Poverty in
   Indonesia during the New Order and after
   the Asian Economic Crisis   1
   Thee Kian Wie

Part One: Trends in Poverty and Technical Issues of Measurement

2. The Impact of the Economic Crisis on Consumption
   Expenditures and Poverty Incidence   17
   Asep Suryahadi and Sudarno Sumarto

3. Poverty and Vulnerability in Indonesia Before and
   After the Economic Crisis   36
   Asep Suryahadi and Sudarno Sumarto

4. Short-term Poverty Dynamics in Rural Indonesia
   during the Economic Crisis   63
   *Asep Suryahadi, Wenefrida Widyanti,
   and Sudarno Sumarto*

5. The Evolution of Poverty during the Crisis
    in Indonesia   81
    Asep Suryahadi, Sudarno Sumarto, and Lant Pritchett

Part Two: Poverty Alleviation Policies and Programs

6. Designs and Implementation of the Indonesian Social
    Safety Net Programs   111
    Sudarno Sumarto, Asep Suryahadi,
    and Wenefrida Widyanti

7. Safety Nets or Safety Ropes? Dynamic Benefit Incidence
    of Two Crisis Programs in Indonesia   149
    Sudarno Sumarto, Asep Suryahadi, and Lant Pritchett

8. New Approaches to the Targeting of
    Social Protection Programs   190
    Asep Suryahadi, Wenefrida Widyanti,
    Daniel Suryadarma, and Sudarno Sumarto

9. Post-crisis Social Protection Programs in Indonesia   218
    Sudarno Sumarto and Asep Suryahadi

10. Conclusion: Coping with the Crisis   234
    Sudarno Sumarto and Asep Suryahadi

Bibliography   247

Index   261

LIST OF TABLES

Table 1.1   Headcount Measure of Poverty, 1970–1996   4

Table 1.2   Headcount Measure of Poverty, 1996–2007   13

Table 2.1   Sensitivity of Real Consumption Changes
to Deflator Used   21

Table 2.2   Median Household Real Consumption
Expenditures per Person in 10 Districts
from Rounds of the 100 Village Survey   21

Table 2.3   Changes in Median Consumption
Expenditures (Nominal and Real) for
the Entire 12,000 Sample of Households   27

Table 2.4   Poverty Incidence in the 100 Village Survey
Sample with Three Benchmarks   30

Table 3.1   Population Distribution across Poverty
Categories, 1996 and 1999   43

Table 3.2   Poverty Categories by Province, 1996   48

Table 3.3   Poverty Categories by Province, 1999   49

Table 3.4   Changes in Poverty Categories by
Province, 1996–99   50

Table 3.5   Poverty Categories by Urban and
Rural Areas, 1996 and 1999   52

Table 3.6   Poverty Categories by Occupational Sector
of Household Heads, 1996 and 1999   54

Table 3.7   Poverty Categories by Educational Level of Household Heads, 1996 and 1999   57

Table 3.8   Poverty Categories by Gender of Household Heads, 1996 and 1999   59

Table 4.1   Income, Consumption, and Poverty   69

Table 4.2   Income and Consumption Quintile Transition Matrices   70

Table 4.3   The Pattern of Changes in Household Poverty Status   73

Table 4.4   Poverty Movements   74

Table 4.5   Poverty Categories   75

Table 4.A1   (Appendix) Poverty Lines for Selected Provinces   79

Table 5.1   Sensitivity of Change in "Real" Expenditures between February 1996 and February 1999 to Deflator Used to Deflate Nominal Expenditures   85

Table 5.2   Sensitivity of Headcount Poverty to the Poverty Line   88

Table 5.3   Changes in Poverty Rates Using Various Food Shares and Prices   93

Table 5.4   Differences in Inflation Rates between the Consumer Price Index (CPI) and SUSENAS Unit Prices   94

Table 5.5   Estimates of Poverty Rates Calculated from Primary Data   100

Table 5.6   Estimates of Poverty Rates Calculated from Secondary Data   102

Table 6.1   Areas and Major Programs of the Indonesian
             Social Safety Net   113

Table 6.2   Targeting Mechanisms in the Social
             Safety Net Programs   118

Table 6.3   Evaluating Targeting Outcomes   121

Table 6.4   Calculation of the Implementation Ratio,
             Targeting Expenditure Ratio, and Coverage
             Ratio of the Social Safety Net Programs   133

Table 6.5   Distribution of Households by Participation
             in JPS Programs and Quintile of per Capita
             Expenditure   136

Table 6.6   Budget Allocation of the Social Safety Net
             Programs   140

Table 6.A1   (Appendix) Comparison of Mean per
             Capita Expenditures in Core SUSENAS and
             Consumption Module SUSENAS   143

Table 6.A2   (Appendix) Coverage of Various Social
             Safety Net Programs by Quintiles of
             per Capita Expenditures   145

Table 7.1   Number of Households in 100 Village Survey
             Data by Quintile of per Capita Household
             Expenditures in May 1997 and Quintile of
             per Capita Household Expenditure Changes
             between May 1997 and August 1998   162

Table 7.2   Households in 100 Village Survey Data who
             Received *Sembako* (rice) in the Three Months
             Prior to December 1998, by Quintile of
             per Capita Household Expenditures in
             May 1997 and Quintile of per Capita
             Household Expenditure Changes between
             May 1997 and August 1998   165

Table 7.3   Households in 100 Village Survey Data
               that Participated in any *Padat Karya*
               (Employment Creation) Work in the Three
               Months Prior to December 1998, by Quintile
               of per Capita Household Expenditures in
               May 1997 and Quintile of per Capita
               Household Expenditure Changes between
               May 1997 and August 1998   168

Table 7.4   Targeting of *Sembako* (Rice) Relative to
               Padat Karya (Employment Creation)
               Programs: Ratio of Proportion Receiving
               in Each Cell Relative to the Cells of
               Poorest Quintile, Worst Shock for
               the Two Programs   170

Table 7.5   Receipts and Budget Shares   175

Table 7.6   Choices over Programs   179

Table 8.1   The Ten Variables with the Greatest
               Weight in CBMS Pilot Project Villages   204

Table 8.2   Characteristics of the Richest and
               Poorest Families in Cibulakan Village   206

LIST OF FIGURES

Figure 3.1   Poverty and Vulnerability Categories   40

Figure 3.2   Cumulative Distribution Function of
              Vulnerability to Poverty   45

Figure 4.A1   (Appendix) Selected Macroeconomic
              Indicators, August 1998 – November 1999   78

Figure 5.1   The Engel Curve and Poverty Line   95

Figure 5.2   Consistent Estimates of Poverty Rates,
              February 1996–February 2002   103

Figure 6.1   Coverage of Various Social Safety Net
              Programs   126

Figure 6.2   Coverage of Various Social Safety Net
              Programs by Quintiles of per Capita
              Expenditure Relative to Q1   132

Figure 6.3   Coverage Ratio (CR) of Various Social
              Safety Net Programs   135

Figure 6.4   Coverage of the Subsidized Rice Program
              at District Level   137

Figure 6.5   Coverage of the Medical Services Program
              at District Level   138

Figure 7.1   Household Participation in Subsidized Rice
              Program by Quintiles of Level and
              Changes in per Capita Consumption   166

Figure 7.2   Household Participation in Employment
               Creation Programs by Quintiles of Level
               and Changes in per Capita Consumption   167

Figure 7.3   Probability of the Poorest Households
               in 1997 Receiving Subsidized Rice and
               Participating in Employment Creation
               Programs, by Quintile of Shock   171

Figure 7.4   Probability of Middle-Quintile Households
               in 1997 Receiving Subsidized Rice and
               Participating in Employment Creation
               Programs, by Quintile of Shock   172

Figure 8.1   Poverty Map of East Kalimantan by
               District/City, Subdistrict and Village   195

PREFACE

The present volume consists of papers that describe the findings of research conducted by the SMERU Research Institute, Jakarta, Indonesia. The papers share a common theme in that they deal with various aspects of poverty in Indonesia. Most were written in connection with the effects on the poor of the Indonesian economic crisis of 1997–98 and the response of the Indonesian Government to those effects. Many of the papers have appeared in journals and other publications and are reproduced here with permission from the publishers. In some cases they have been edited to avoid the repetition of similar material.

The papers in the present volume fall into two groups. Chapters 2, 3, 4, and 5 deal with trends in poverty and the measurement of poverty, while Chapters 6, 7, 8, and 9 describe the major poverty alleviation policies and programs introduced by the Indonesian Government since early 1998. Chapter 1, which is the only paper in the present volume not written by SMERU researchers, gives a brief overview of the economic situation in Indonesia before and after the crisis and describes the general context in which most of the papers were written. Absolute poverty had been quite high in Indonesia in the early and mid-1960s, prior to the political upheaval that led to a change of government in 1966. During the thirty-two years of economic growth under the New Order government (1966–98), great progress had been made in social development and the incidence of absolute poverty in both urban and rural areas had declined steadily. In mid-1997, however, Indonesia was struck by a financial, economic, and political crisis whose full impact was felt only in 1998 and the following years. As the economy contracted, the poverty rate rose once again, presenting immense challenges to the post-New Order government.

The economic crisis had a major impact on consumption expenditures. Chapter 2 uses these expenditures, which reflect the actual changes that took place in living standards and which can serve as a measurable proxy for income changes, to examine the extent of poverty in the years immediately after the crisis. In doing so, it tracks changes in the headcount measure of poverty, that is, in the number and proportion of individuals whose consumption at that time was below a defined poverty line.

Vulnerability to poverty, that is, the risk that a household will become poor in the near future, is examined in Chapter 3. It is always possible that people who are not poor at a certain point in time may fall below the poverty line in days to come. At the same time it is possible for people who are currently poor to move out of poverty. In comparing the levels of vulnerability to poverty before and after the crisis, the writers use a method specifically developed for estimating vulnerability. It involves the use of cross-sectional data from household surveys to estimate different categories of poverty and vulnerability by combining information on consumption levels, estimates of vulnerability to poverty, and estimates of expected consumption levels.

During the economic crisis, the headcount poverty rate in Indonesia changed quickly over short periods of time, which suggests that a large number of people moved in and out of poverty frequently and experienced relatively short spells of poverty. Chapter 4 demonstrates that the changes occurring at the household level were in fact even greater than the changes indicated by aggregate figures. An examination of only the changes in total poverty rate might therefore give a misleading impression of the actual poverty dynamics of households.

Chapter 5 discusses the most suitable method by which to compare changes in poverty over time and presents a consistent series of estimated poverty rates in Indonesia from various sources for the period February 1996 to February 2002. The poverty rate increased from its lowest point of around 15 per cent in mid-1997 to its highest point of around 33 per cent near the end of 1998. This increase of 18 percentage points implies that around 36 million additional people were pushed into absolute poverty by the crisis. After reaching its peak, the poverty rate started to decline again and reached the pre-crisis level of around 15 per cent at the end of 1999, suggesting that the economic crisis delayed progress in the alleviation of poverty by around two and a half years.

The Indonesian Government responded to the social consequences of the economic crisis by introducing a social safety net that consisted of programs designed to protect real incomes and to ensure that the poor had access to social services. Chapter 6 reviews these programs and discusses the difficulties involved in designing and implementing programs that provide cash or in-kind transfers in a developing country as large and diverse as Indonesia. It looks specifically at the problems of undercoverage, where social protection programs do not reach many of the poor, and of leakage, where the non-poor enjoy a large proportion of social protection benefits.

While some safety net programs were designed to benefit only currently poor households, others were designed to mitigate shocks by providing transfers to those households whose incomes had fallen and who were vulnerable to poverty, irrespective of whether or not they had fallen below an absolute poverty threshold. Calculations of the benefit incidence and the targeting effectiveness of safety net programs have usually examined only the relationship between a household's current expenditures and program participation. Chapter 7 looks at the relationship between program benefits and changes in household expenditures. It compares the static and dynamic benefit incidence of two of the social safety net programs, one of which (subsidized rice) used administrative criteria as the basis of targeting, while the other (a set of public employment schemes) was based on self-selection targeting.

The benefits of accurate targeting in social protection programs are substantial because they enable public expenditures to be concentrated on those households most in need of assistance. In the absence of better alternatives, implementation of the social safety net programs involved targeting methods developed for other purposes by Statistics Indonesia (BPS) and the National Family Planning Coordinating Board (BKKBN). This inevitably resulted in a certain amount of mistargeting, since in situations where poverty indicators are determined prior to data collection, data can easily be manipulated. Furthermore, since poverty is a localized phenomenon in which the characteristics of the poor differ among regions and even villages, the use of uniform indicators for the whole country introduces bias. Chapter 8 describes two recent attempts to develop more effective targeting tools than those used previously. It looks first at poverty mapping as a way to improve geographic targeting and then at community based monitoring systems as a means of ensuring better individual targeting.

After describing the modifications made in the original social safety net programs and the gradual phasing-out of these programs after the year 2000, Chapter 9 outlines the social protection initiatives that have replaced them. The government has designed the new programs in such a way that the shortcomings of the original social safety net programs may hopefully be avoided. These new programs have been introduced in the context of the government's focus on regaining economic stability and ensuring economic progress. Because national policies have included reductions in fuel subsidies on a number of occasions, the new social protection programs have been founded on the concept of compensation for fuel price increases and have included unconditional cash transfers targeted at poor households.

Chapter 10 sums up the strengths and weaknesses of the social safety net programs and highlights the main lessons learned from the Indonesian economic crisis about poverty alleviation and the targeting and management of social protection initiatives.

It is our hope that this volume will form a useful reference for those who are interested in poverty alleviation and social protection programs in Indonesia.

Joan Hardjono
Nuning Akhmadi
Sudarno Sumarto
Editors

POSTSCRIPT
The 2008 Financial Crisis

Even though the sources, magnitude and complexity of the 2008 global financial crisis differ from those of the 1997–98 Asian financial crisis, the impact on the Indonesian economy and on the economies of many other developing countries will most probably be very much the same, particularly in terms of reduced economic growth, shrinking employment opportunities and a worsening of socioeconomic development. We live in an interconnected world where the current crisis, triggered by the slump in the U.S. housing market and the simultaneous escalation of international oil and food prices, could have an immense effect on economies in the developing world. Thus the subsequent burden will be borne not only by the poor living in wealthy countries but also by the billions of poor and vulnerable people in low-income countries that include Indonesia.

Much has been written in the press and in academic circles arguing that the current global financial crisis will lead to an economic recession in developed countries, particularly the United States and Europe. This would reduce demand for exports from developing countries like Indonesia, and could be exacerbated if the United States and Europe adopt trade protectionism as their response to the crisis. Furthermore, foreign aid and direct foreign investment are likely to be cut since international mobile capital will most probably be secured in the safe havens of the United States and Europe.

Indonesia will face extensive economic problems, some of which are already being felt with the volatility of the stock market, the liquidity crunch in the banking sector, and a rapid weakening of the exchange rate pressuring the balance of payments and liquidity in the financial system. Even though the impact on current exports has been minimal so far and has resulted in relatively small account deficits, many observers predict that the full impact on the real sector will start to be felt in the first quarter of 2009. This is attributed to factors such as the falling demand for Indonesian commodities from developed economies, which may lead to fewer employment opportunities for the poor and the non-poor alike.

The articles in this book are very timely as they include research findings on the 1997–98 economic crisis. In particular, they offer an assessment of the social impact of that crisis and the implementation of social safety nets introduced by the Indonesian Government to help the chronic poor and the new poor to cope with the economic shocks generated by the crisis. The lessons learned, also discussed in this book, will hopefully provide direction to policy-makers in Indonesia and in other developing countries on how to establish an effective response package to address the impact of economic crises on the poor and vulnerable. At the same time, already scarce resources should be allocated efficiently in a manner that does not jeopardize the prospect of achieving future economic growth.

Sudarno Sumarto
Director
The SMERU Research Institute
November 2008

ACKNOWLEDGEMENTS

This book is a collection of studies conducted between 1998 and 2006 by researchers at the SMERU Research Institute (known until the end of 2000 as the Social Monitoring & Early Response Unit, Jakarta). Its contents represent the tireless work of many people and for that reason we would like to thank all current and former SMERU researchers for their participation and contributions. In particular, we wish to express our thanks to Daniel Perwira, Yusuf Suharso, Sulton Mawardi, and Amalia Firman for their excellent assistance.

We benefited from many invaluable contributions during the preparatory stages of the original articles. We are grateful to Statistics Indonesia (BPS) for access to data used in various chapters in this book. Among the many individuals to whom we are indebted for valuable suggestions and comments on the original articles are Lisa Cameron, Shubham Chauduri, John Maxwell, Menno Pradhan, Peter Rosner, Emmanuel Skoufias, and Frank Wiebe. Our thanks are also due to Mark Baird, Tubagus Feridhanusetyawan, Scott Guggenheim, Mohamad Ikhsan, Chris Manning, Martin Ravallion, Hadi Soesastro, and the late M. Sadli for discussions on many of the topics covered in this book.

We would also like to express our appreciation to SMERU's donors — especially the Australian Agency for International Development (AusAID), the Ford Foundation, and the Department for International Development (DFID) in the United Kingdom for their financial support. Their assistance has enabled the SMERU Research Institute to undertake the socioeconomic and policy studies upon which the articles in this book are based.

Finally, allow us to express our thanks to Hal Hill, Suzanne Siskel, and Thee Kian Wie for their full encouragement of the idea of compiling this volume. We also wish to acknowledge the careful editing done by Joan Hardjono and Nuning Akhmadi, as well as the technical assistance provided by Mona Sintia. Last but not least, we wish to thank Triena Ong and her staff at the Institute of Southeast Asian Studies for their support in the publication of this volume.

Sudarno Sumarto, Director
The SMERU Research Institute
September 2008

GLOSSARY AND ACRONYMS

ASEAN	Association of Southeast Asian Nations
Askes	*Asuransi Kesehatan* (Health Insurance)
Askeskin	*Asuransi Kesehatan* untuk Masyarakat Miskin (Health Insurance for the Poor)
AV	average vulnerability
Bapel	*Badan Pelaksana* (Management Unit)
BAPPENAS	*Badan Perencanaan Pembangunan Nasional* (National Development Planning Board)
BAPPEDA	*Badan Perencanaan Pembangunan Daerah* (Regional Development Planning Board)
BBM	*Bahan Bakar Minyak* (fuel, i.e., gasoline/petrol, diesel fuel, and kerosene)
BKKBN	*Badan Koordinasi Keluarga Berencana Nasional* (National Family Planning Coordinating Board)
BKM	*Bantuan Khusus Murid* (Special Assistance for Students)
BKS	*Bantuan Khusus Sekolah* (Special Assistance to Schools)
BLT	*Bantuan Tunai Langsung* (Direct Cash Assistance)
BOS	*Bantuan Operasional Sekolah* (School Operational Assistance)
BPS	*Badan Pusat Statistik* (Central Bureau of Statistics, now known as Statistics Indonesia)
BULOG	*Badan Urusan Logistik* (State Logistics Agency)

CBMS	Community Based Monitoring System
CCT	conditional cash transfer
CDF	cumulative distribution function
CP	chronically poor
CPI	consumer price index
CR	coverage ratio
CRRA	constant relative risk aversion
DAU	*Dana Alokasi Umum* (General Allocation Funds)
DBO	*Dana Bantuan Operasional* (School Operational Assistance Funds)
DOLOG	*Depot Logistik* (district-level Logistics Depot)
DPRD	*Dewan Perwakilan Rakyat Daerah* (Regional Representative Council)
FPL	food poverty line
FGD	focus group discussion
FGLS	feasible generalized least squares
GDP	gross domestic product
GIS	geographical information system
GLS	generalized least squares
gotong royong	self-help
GDRP	gross domestic regional product
HPAEs	high-performing Asian economies
HVC	high variability of consumption
IDT	*Inpres Desa Tertinggal* (Presidential Instruction for Underdeveloped Villages)
IHK	*Indeks Harga Konsumen* (Consumer Price Index)
IMF	International Monetary Fund
IFLS	Indonesia Family Life Survey
Inpres	*Instruksi Presiden* (Presidential Instruction)
IR	implementation ratio

Jabotabek	the Jakarta, Bogor, Tangerang, and Bekasi conurbation
JPK-Gakin	*Jaminan Pelayanan Kesehatan untuk Keluarga Miskin* (Health Service Insurance for Poor Families)
JPS	*Jaring Pengaman Sosial* (Social Safety Net)
JPS-BK	*Jaring Pengaman Sosial — Bidang Kesehatan* (Social Safety Net Program in the Health Sector)
kabupaten	administrative district
kecamatan	subdistrict
KKN	*Korupsi, Kolusi dan Nepotisme* (Corruption, Collusion and Nepotism)
kota	administrative city or town
KPS	*keluarga pra-sejahtera* (pre-prosperous family)
krismon	*krisis moneter* (monetary crisis)
KS	*keluarga sejahtera* (prosperous family)
KTP	*Kartu Tanda Penduduk* (identification card)
KUD	*Koperasi Unit Desa* (Village Unit Cooperative)
LKMD	*Lembaga Ketahanan Masyarakat Desa* (Village Community Resilience Institution)
LLC	low level of consumption
LR	leakage ratio
Menpangan	*Menteri Negara Pangan dan Hortikultur* (Minister of State for Food and Horticulture)
NFA	non-food allowance
NGO	non-governmental organization
NTB	*Nusa Tenggara Barat* (West Nusa Tenggara)
NTT	*Nusa Tenggara Timur* (East Nusa Tenggara)
OPK	*Operasi Pasar Khusus* (Special Market Operation or Cheap Rice Program)

PAD	*pendapatan asli daerah* (locally derived revenue)
padat karya	labour intensive
PCA	principal component analysis
PDF	probability density function
perda	*peraturan daerah* (regional regulation)
PKB	*Pajak Kendaraan Bermotor* (Motorized Vehicle Tax)
PL	poverty line
PODES	*Potensi Desa* (Village Potential)
PDM-DKE	*Pemberdayaan Daerah Mengatasi Dampak Krisis Ekonomi* (Regional Empowerment Program to Overcome the Impact of the Economic Crisis)
PDPSE — BK	*Penanggulangan Dampak Pengurangan Subsidi Energi — Bidang Kesehatan* (Program to Handle the Impact of Energy Subsidy Reductions — Health Sector)
PKPS-BBM	*Program Kompensasi Pengurangan Subsidi Bahan Bakar Minyak* (Program to Compensate for Fuel Subsidy Reductions)
posyandu	*pos pelayanan terpadu* (integrated health service post)
PPK	*Program Pengembangan Kecamatan* (Kecamatan Development Program)
PPM — Prasarana	*Program Pemberdayaan Masyarakat — Prasarana* (Community Empowerment Program and Infrastructure)
puskesmas	*pusat kesehatan masyarakat* (community health centre)

Raskin	*Beras untuk Keluarga Miskin* (Rice for Poor Families)
RE	real expenditure
SAKERNAS	*Survei Tenaga Kerja Nasional* (National Labor Force Survey)
SD	*Sekolah Dasar* (primary school)
SKTM	*Surat Keterangan Tidak Mampu* (Letter giving poverty status, issued at village level)
SMP	*Sekolah Menengah Pertama* (junior secondary school)
SMA	*Sekolah Menengah Atas* (senior secondary school)
SSD	*Survei Seratus Desa* (the 100 Village Survey)
SWF	social welfare function
sembako	*sembilan bahan pokok* (nine basic necessities, which include rice, sugar, cooking oil and flour)
SUSENAS	*Survei Sosial Ekonomi Nasional* (National Socio-Economic Survey)
TER	targeting expenditure ratio
TP	transient poor
TVG	total vulnerable group
UCT	unconditional cash transfer

THE EDITORS

Joan Hardjono is a senior freelance researcher living in Bandung and a member of SMERU's Board of Trustees.

Nuning Akhmadi, editor and publications coordinator of the SMERU Research Institute from 2001 to 2006, is currently SMERU's External Affairs Officer.

Sudarno Sumarto was the Director of the SMERU Research Institute from 2001 to 2009. Since August 2009, he has been a Senior Research Fellow at SMERU and is currently a Visiting Fellow at the Walter H. Shorenstein Asia Pacific Research Center, Stanford University for 2009–2010.

THE CONTRIBUTORS

Asep Suryahadi has been Research Deputy and senior researcher at the SMERU Research Institute since 2001.

Daniel Suryadarma has been a researcher at the SMERU Research Institute since 2003. He is currently a PhD student in Economics in the Research School of Social Sciences, the Australian National University, Canberra.

Lant Pritchett is Professor of the Practice of International Development, John F. Kennedy School of Government, Harvard University.

Thee Kian Wie is Senior Economist at the Economic Research Centre of the Indonesian Institute of Sciences (LIPI), Jakarta.

The late **Wenefrida Widyanti** was a quantitative researcher at the SMERU Research Institute from 2001 to May 2008.

Chapter 1

A BRIEF OVERVIEW OF ECONOMIC GROWTH AND POVERTY IN INDONESIA DURING THE NEW ORDER AND AFTER THE ASIAN ECONOMIC CRISIS

Thee Kian Wie

The Asian economic crisis of 1997–98 had devastating effects on Indonesia's poor and near poor, the numbers of whom increased rapidly as a result. This development was particularly tragic since much progress had been made in poverty alleviation during thirty-two years of rapid and sustained economic growth under the New Order government (1966–98). To put adverse developments, particularly the rise in the incidence of poverty, in proper perspective, it might be helpful to have a brief historical overview of Indonesia's economic development and its impact on poverty during the three decades preceding the onset of the crisis and in the decade following it.

1 ECONOMIC GROWTH AND POVERTY ALLEVIATION DURING THE NEW ORDER 1966–98

As a result of political turmoil and the utter neglect of sound economic policies after the late 1950s, the Indonesian economy in the early 1960s experienced steadily rising inflation. As a consequence of the unrestrained printing of money to finance the rising government budget deficit, this spiraled into hyperinflation, which had reached almost 600 per cent by 1965. The economy had stagnated during the 1961–64 period; the modest growth that occurred in 1965 reflected only a good agricultural season (Hill 1996: 2). Since population growth exceeded economic growth in the early 1960s, per capita income declined during this period, particularly in 1962–63, with the economy contracting by three per cent in 1963 (World Bank 1998: 2.1).

With the deterioration in economic conditions, absolute poverty was quite high in the mid-1960s. In Java, 61 per cent of the population was very poor, while outside Java the very poor accounted for 52 per cent of the population. In 1961 no less than 68 per cent of the total population had no schooling at all, while only 0.1 per cent had enjoyed a tertiary education (Hill 1996:5). The available evidence also shows that per capita income in Indonesia in the mid-1960s was well below that of other Southeast Asian economies for which reliable data are available, and below even that of India. Indonesia's real per capita GDP in 1966 is estimated to have been only 535 international dollars (1985 prices), compared with US$650 in India (Booth 2000: 74).[1]

After recovering from the serious economic crisis and the traumatic political dislocations of the mid-1960s, the Indonesian economy under the New Order government embarked on a period of rapid growth that averaged around seven per cent annually and was sustained for three decades. Rapid industrialization transformed Indonesia's economy from one that was agricultural to one in which the manufacturing sector became increasingly important, to the point where it overtook agriculture in the mid-1990s. In view of this impressive economic performance, Indonesia was classified in 1993 as one of the eight "high-performing Asian economies" (HPAEs) by the World Bank in its well-known and controversial report *The East Asian Economic Miracle* (1993a). The World Bank classified these eight East Asian countries as HPAEs because since 1960 (in the case of Indonesia, the late 1960s) these economies had grown more than twice as fast as those of the rest of East Asia, roughly three times as fast as those of Latin America and South Asia and five times faster than those of countries in Sub-Saharan Africa. They also significantly outperformed the advanced industrial economies and the oil-rich Middle East-North Africa region (World Bank 1993a: 1–2).

As in the other HPAEs, rapid economic growth in Indonesia was accompanied by significant advances in social development, indicated by steadily increasing educational enrollments at all levels but particularly at the primary level, an improved adult literacy rate, and improved nutritional intake, as well as improvements in various indicators of health status such as infant mortality rate, life expectancy at birth, and per capita daily calorie supply (Thee 2002: 201–3). By East Asian standards, however, some of Indonesia's social indicators continued to lag somewhat (Hill 1999: 5). The likely reason for this lag is that in Indonesia, as in most other developing countries, social development followed in the wake of economic development. The fact that Indonesia started its economic development about one decade later than its ASEAN neighbours and the East Asian Tigers (South Korea, Taiwan, Hong Kong, and Singapore) helps to explain why Indonesia's social development was in general behind that of these other countries (Thee 2002: 203).

A more striking aspect of Indonesia's social development, however, was its success in poverty alleviation. As in the other HPAEs, Indonesia's rapid and sustained economic growth was accompanied by a decline in the incidence of absolute poverty in both urban and rural areas. According to Indonesia's Central Bureau of Statistics (BPS), absolute poverty had steadily decreased from 53.6 per cent in urban areas and 38.7 per cent in rural areas in 1970 to 9.7 per cent and 12.3 per cent respectively in 1996 (Booth 2000: 78). For Indonesia as a whole, the incidence of absolute poverty declined from 40.1 per cent of the total population in

1976 to 11.3 per cent in 1996 (Table 1.1). The corresponding number of people in poverty fell from around 54 million in 1976 to less than 23 million in 1996 (BPS 1998: 576).

The sharp reduction in poverty during the New Order was remarkable when compared to the rate in most other developing countries. A comparative study by the World Bank on poverty alleviation in several developing countries found that over the 1970–1987 period Indonesia had been the most successful in reducing absolute poverty, as indicated by its achievement of the highest annual reduction in the two key indicators of poverty, namely, the headcount index and the under-five mortality rate (World Bank 1990: 45).

Thus in Indonesia no "immiserizing growth" took place during the New Order, since people did not become poorer as growth proceeded, as some critics have alleged. Indonesia's success in reducing absolute poverty can be attributed to the government's

TABLE 1.1
Headcount Measure of Poverty, 1970–1996

Year	Percentage below Poverty Line			Numbers in Poverty (millions)		
	Urban	Rural	Total	Urban	Rural	Total
1970	53.6*	38.7*	na	...	...	...
1976	38.8	40.4	40.1	10.0	44.2	54.2
1978	30.8	33.3	33.3	8.3	38.9	47.2
1980	29.0	28.4	29.6	9.5	32.8	42.3
1981	28.1	26.5	26.9	9.3	31.3	40.6
1984	23.1	21.2	21.6	9.3	25.7	35.0
1987	20.1	16.4	17.4	9.7	20.3	30.0
1990	16.8	14.3	15.1	9.4	17.8	27.2
1993	13.5	13.8	13.7	8.7	17.2	25.9
1996	9.7	12.3	11.3	7.2	15.3	22.5

Note: * The 1970 estimates were derived from a poverty line based on 1976 BPS poverty lines.
Source: Booth (2000, Table 3; based on BPS data)

commitment to a broad-based rural development strategy, which targeted the rural areas where most of Indonesia's poor were living and working. The emphasis on rural and agricultural development, particularly during the first two decades of the New Order, led to rapid expansion in agricultural production, particularly of rice. This rapid agricultural growth in the 1970s and early 1980s stemmed from the successful dissemination of new production technologies in the food crop sector, which created new employment opportunities in agricultural processing, transport, and commerce and also contributed to the rapid growth of the construction and manufacturing sectors in both rural and urban Java. Higher wage incomes contributed to higher household incomes and thus reduced poverty (Booth 1992: 639).

The steep decline in the incidence of absolute poverty in Indonesia's rural areas during the 1970s was an outstanding achievement, particularly by comparison with the experiences of other oil-exporting countries with large agricultural sectors. Although this decline cannot be attributed solely to government policy, the oil boom did lead to increased government expenditure, although little of this increase was explicitly targeted at the poor. Similarly, the regional development grants (*Instruksi Presiden* or *Inpres* grants) were not specifically designed to alleviate poverty but rather were intended to give provincial and district governments a better opportunity to implement much needed rehabilitation and development of infrastructure. In fact, after the mid-1970s the employment generated by *Inpres* programs fell steadily. After the mid-1970s, however, the sharp decline in poverty was due in part to the successful stabilization of food prices which meant, particularly in Java, that the poor experienced a lower rate of inflation than the rich (Booth 2000: 80–1).

Although the end of the oil boom in 1982 forced the Indonesian Government to cut its budget expenditures severely, the greatest cuts were carried out in the more capital-intensive sectors and programs, including energy, transmigration, and subsidies to state-owned enterprises. As they did not have a large adverse effect on employment (Booth 2000: 85), there was no impact on poverty. Rapid economic growth resumed after 1987 and was sustained up to the time of the Asian economic crisis, in response to a series of deregulation measures designed to increase non-oil exports. But in spite of the resumption of rapid growth, absolute poverty declined more slowly during the 1987–1996 period.

Three hypotheses have been advanced by Professor Booth to account for this slowdown. First, after 1987 development policies became less pro-poor since the manufacturing and modern services sectors received greater policy emphasis and thus emerged as the main engines of growth. The agricultural sector on the other hand was relegated to a secondary role in policy debates. Secondly, policy-makers held that the persistence of poverty was due to the fact that poverty was mainly located outside of Java and in isolated poverty traps, which in turn meant that the poor in these regions were not able to benefit from the rapid manufacturing growth taking place in Java. Thirdly, in spite of the rapid growth in educational enrollments at all levels in Indonesia, access to good quality secondary education and in particular to high quality tertiary education was still severely limited in the late 1980s and early 1990s, so the rents were not dissipated through increased supply (Booth 2000: 89–90).

Despite the slower decline in the incidence of poverty in the 1980s and early 1990s, the available data show a clear downward trend in poverty throughout the New Order up to the time of the Asian economic crisis. It should be borne in mind, however, that the poverty estimates based on the official poverty line, at least in a comparative sense, understate the incidence of absolute poverty. For instance, Indonesia's official poverty line is not only lower than that of the Philippines, which has about the same per capita income as Indonesia, but is also lower than those of some of the poorest countries in the world (Booth 1992: 637). Even so, higher poverty lines for Indonesia would still show a clear downward trend in the incidence of absolute poverty, although a higher poverty line, such as the one developed by the World Bank, would naturally show a higher incidence of absolute poverty than Indonesia's official poverty line does.

2 GROWTH AND POVERTY AFTER THE ASIAN ECONOMIC CRISIS 1997–2007

2.1 The Onset of the Crisis

During the early 1990s the Indonesian economy was performing quite well. The economy was growing at an average annual rate of 7.7 per cent, while inflation was only 6.6 per cent, a sizable fiscal surplus was maintained, and approved domestic and foreign direct investment and foreign exchange reserves were growing rapidly. Moreover, large prepayments of high-interest, public external debts were continued (McLeod 1998: 6–10; World Bank 1997: xxi). For this reason the World Bank, in its annual report on the Indonesian economy in May 1997, released a fairly upbeat assessment of the economy, projecting, with some qualifications, that it would continue to achieve a robust growth of 7.8 per cent for the remainder of the 1990s (World Bank 1997: 29). In fact, a year earlier Indonesia's good economic performance had also been hailed by Professor Jeffrey Sachs of Harvard University who, in a report on economic competitiveness released at the World Economic Forum in May 1996, ranked Indonesia fifteenth, up from thirtieth a year earlier and slightly outranking China and Thailand (Sadli 1999: 16).

By July 1997, however, only two months after the release of this report, the Indonesian economy suddenly experienced a severe shock when, in the wake of the depreciation of the Thai baht in July 1997, the Malaysian ringgit, the Philippine peso, and the Indonesian rupiah also started to depreciate steadily through the "contagion" effect. As in the other Southeast Asian countries, foreign creditors to Indonesian corporations and foreign investors scrambled to reduce their exposure by withdrawing their funds from Indonesia (Thee 2003: 186).

When the rupiah continued to depreciate even after Bank Indonesia had widened its intervention band, Bank Indonesia abandoned the band and floated the rupiah on 14 August 1997 while also tightening monetary policy. For a while the rupiah strengthened, but it soon resumed its downward slide. Demand for foreign exchange rose sharply as corporations sought to get dollars to cover their unhedged exposure, while new private capital inflows dried up. As the panic rose, the rupiah depreciated to around Rp 3,500 to the U.S. dollar (Sadli 1999: 17).

Increasingly concerned about the continuing depreciation of the rupiah, the Indonesian Government turned to the International Monetary Fund (IMF) for financial assistance in late October 1997. In return for a large stand-by loan offered by the IMF, the Indonesian Government in its Letter of Intent (LOI) to the IMF pledged to implement a comprehensive reform program, involving sound macroeconomic policies, a restructuring of the financial sector, and structural reforms, including the disbandment of various monopolies sanctioned by the government. It was hoped that, with the availability of the IMF loan backed by a credible reform program, confidence in the rupiah would be restored (Sadli 1999: 17).

The involvement of the IMF, however, failed to stem the downward slide of the rupiah and the ensuing economic crisis, as the Indonesian Government seemed unwilling to implement the agreed-upon reform program, particularly the structural reforms, in a vigorous manner. The inability of the Indonesian Government to deal effectively with the financial and economic crisis led to a serious political crisis that forced President Soeharto to step down after a reign of thirty-two years. Thus, within a time span of only one year, Indonesia had turned from a booming economy, extolled by the international aid community and many foreign economists as a development model worthy of emulation, into a "melted-down" economy that was dependent for its very survival on the charity of the international aid community and its bilateral donors.

2.2 The Socioeconomic Impact of the Crisis

Although the financial crisis had hit Indonesia in mid-1997, its full economic impact was felt only in 1998 when the economy contracted by an unprecedented 13.1 per cent, with manufacturing, construction, the financial sector and business services, trade, hotels and restaurants, and transport and communications recording the sharpest declines. Only the agricultural sector and public utilities recorded slight growth. This economic contraction was much worse than the one that had occurred in 1963, when the economy had contracted by 3.0 per cent (World Bank 1998: 2.1).

Besides the severe financial and economic crisis, which became known as the *krismon* (from the words *krisis moneter*, or "monetary crisis"), Indonesia was also affected by an extremely bad drought caused by the El Nino of 1997 and 1998. The drought was not only severe but occurred twice, first in July/August 1997 and again in March 1998 (World Bank 1998: 1.11). Because of this drought, total rice production fell by 4 per cent in 1997, causing the agricultural sector to grow by only 0.6 per cent in that year (Johnson 1998: 16–7). To make matters worse, during this period the international price of oil also experienced a sharp decline, which hurt Indonesia's exports and government revenues.

By 1999, however, macroeconomic stability was slowly being restored, as inflation, the exchange rate, and interest rates all responded well to tight monetary policies (World Bank 1999: 1.1–2.1). As a consequence the economy began to recover slightly in 1999, when it recorded a positive, albeit minuscule, growth rate of 0.8 per cent. In the next few years economic growth picked up, with the economy growing at 4.8 per cent in 2000, 3.8 per cent in 2001, 4.3 per cent in 2002, 4.8 per cent in 2003, 5.1 per cent in 2004, 5.6 per cent in 2005, and 6.1 per cent in 2006.

The severe economic crisis of 1998 had a devastating effect on the welfare of the Indonesian population. The socioeconomic effects of this crisis were transmitted through two channels. First, there was the impact of capital outflows, the steep depreciation of the rupiah, and the contractionary effects of tight monetary and fiscal policies on the economy. The sharp contraction of sectors located in urban areas, including the manufacturing, construction, and financial sectors, led to many lay-offs. Second, there were shifts in relative prices when the prices of tradable goods such as manufactured products rose steeply vis-à-vis non-tradable goods and services as a result of the steep depreciation of the rupiah, which in turn led to a sharp increase in inflation (Daimon and Thorbecke 1999: 2).

The adverse impacts passed on through these two channels suggest that the urban population was affected more severely than the rural population. First, the sectors hit hardest by the crisis were mostly located in urban areas, which adversely affected employment in these areas. Second, the sharp rate of inflation adversely affected net purchasers of foodstuffs (mostly urban dwellers) because of the steep increase in food prices in 1998 (Daimon and Thorbecke 1999: 2–3). Thus urban households may have suffered more than rural households, particularly farm households growing their own food. As the impact of the economic crisis intensified in the course of 1998, many workers in the formal sector, particularly in the urban-based manufacturing, construction, and modern services sectors, were indeed laid off. Nevertheless, the open unemployment rate increased only slightly to around six per cent, since the informal labour market was much better able to absorb those who were laid off in the formal sector (Cameron 1999: 15).

In both urban and rural areas the numbers of employed workers classified as "family workers" increased, which seems to confirm the assumption that people who had lost their wage jobs as well as new entrants to the labour force who were unable to find wage employment were absorbed into jobs in family enterprises (Booth 1999: 4.1).

Data from the National Socio-Economic Survey (SUSENAS) of February 1998 show that employment in manufacturing had fallen by 13 per cent, in finance by 7 per cent, and in electricity by 27 per cent. But as some sectors such as finance were employing only a small part of the labour force, even a large reduction in employment in these sectors had only a relatively small impact on employment (Poppele, Sumarto, and Pritchett 1999: 20). Employment in agriculture and in the urban informal sector expanded because the labour market and the social structures in these sectors were sufficiently flexible to reabsorb the workers laid off in formal sector activities.

The loss of jobs in the formal sector, the shift to low income activities in the informal sector, and the hyperinflation of 1998, which was accompanied by a drop in purchasing power, all led to a significant increase in the incidence of absolute poverty in both urban and rural areas. As a result, poverty rose from 17.6 per cent in 1996 (according to the revised method of estimating poverty used by BPS) to 23.4 per cent in 1998 (World Bank 2006: ix).

Nevertheless, with a gradual but steady economic recovery from 1999 onwards and the restoration of macroeconomic stability in 2000, the poverty rate declined steadily from its peak in 1999 to 16.0 per cent in February 2005 (World Bank 2006: ix), which was lower than the pre-crisis rate of 17.6 per cent. This sharp decline in the poverty rate was primarily due to rising incomes and a decline in food prices, particularly of rice. By March 2006, however, the poverty rate had gone up again to 17.8 per cent, corresponding to an increase in the number of poor people from 35 million to 39 million over this period. This rise in early 2006 was the second time since the crisis that poverty had increased again after experiencing a steady decline in the preceding period.

The poverty level, which had increased by over one third during the crisis, was back to the pre-crisis level by early 2006 (Table 1.2). In fact, although the crisis had made millions of Indonesians poor again and turned Indonesia into a low-income country once more as in the early and mid-1960s, the recent economic recovery has made Indonesia once again one of the world's emerging middle-income countries (World Bank 2006: ix).

The data in Table 1.2, however, also show that while the poverty level had declined from 17.8 per cent in 2006 to 16.6 per cent in 2007, there were still 37.2 million people living in absolute poverty in that year, which is almost three million more than in 1996. Moreover, despite the steady decline in the poverty level, a large percentage of the population remains vulnerable to poverty, since a large number of households are clustered around the poverty line. Hence, small price changes in the basic wage goods such as rice have a disproportionate effect on the proportion of households classified as poor (World Bank 2007: 19).

According to a recent World Bank study of poverty, three quarters of the additional four million people who fell below the poverty line in early 2006 did so as a consequence of the 33 per cent rise in rice prices between February 2005 and March 2006 (World Bank 2006: ix) rather than the jump in fuel prices in October 2005, as has been asserted by some politicians and a number of economists belonging to the "Indonesia Awakes Team" (*Tim Indonesia Bangkit*) (Basri and Patunru 2006: 308). Meanwhile, the increase in rice prices was caused mainly by the ban on rice imports (World Bank 2006: x).

The World Bank view of the ban on rice imports is supported in a study by Peter Warr, who has used a general equilibrium model to analyse food policy and poverty in Indonesia (Warr 2005: 429, 445). Warr's quantitative analysis found that a rice import ban

TABLE 1.2
Headcount Measure of Poverty, 1996–2007

Year	Population under Poverty Line (%)	Number of People under Poverty Line (millions)
1996*	17.6	34.5
1999	23.5	48.4
2001	19.0	37.3
2002	18.4	38.4
2003	18.2	37.3
2004	17.4	36.1
2005	16.0	35.0
2006	17.8	39.0
2007	16.6	37.2

Note: *As of 1996, BPS has used a revised method to estimate absolute poverty (referred to as the "new" definition of poverty), which resulted in a higher estimate of the incidence of poverty than the poverty figure for that year, as recorded in Table 1.1 above.
Source: World Bank 2005 Table 1 derived from BPS data and World Bank 2007, Fig. 12.

raises the domestic price of rice relative to the import price by an amount equivalent to a 125 per cent tariff. As a result of this import ban, the poverty rate rises by a little under one per cent of the population, with an increase occurring in both urban and rural areas. Among farmers, only the richest gain from the rice import ban, since they have smaller shares of rice in their total expenditures and are less reliant on their own labour as a source of income. Hence they are less affected by the increase in the price of rice and the decline in real wages that this causes.

3 CONCLUSION

This brief historical account of economic growth and the evolution of absolute poverty in Indonesia indicates that, despite the progress achieved over the past four decades, absolute poverty is still a major national problem and is in fact the most serious problem facing Indonesia. During times of severe economic stress, as during the Asian economic crisis, the number of poor people increases, since many people who are just above the poverty line — that is, the near poor — will fall below the poverty line.

For that reason, at the start of its term in late 2004 the current government set an admirable target of reducing absolute poverty from 18.4 per cent in 2002 to 8.2 per cent by late 2009, when its term ends. The government is unlikely to achieve its stated target, however, since the growth elasticity of poverty in Indonesia is estimated at only 0.7 (Balisacan et al. 2003: 346). Assuming that this figure still holds in the next two years, an average annual growth rate of 6 per cent would lead the poverty rate to fall to 15.7 per cent by late 2009 (Lindblad and Thee 2007: 29–30). Even if economic growth were to increase to 7 per cent in 2008 and 2009 (an unlikely prospect because of the adverse effects of the steep rise in oil prices in the world oil market and the predicted global economic slowdown because of the sub-prime crisis), the poverty rate is very unlikely to decline to 8.2 per cent by late 2009.

Note

1. Real per capita GDP figures in international dollars means that the figures have been adjusted for differences in purchasing power parities across countries. They are also adjusted for changes in the terms of trade (Booth 2000: 97).

Part One

TRENDS IN POVERTY AND TECHNICAL ISSUES OF MEASUREMENT

Chapter 2

THE IMPACT OF THE ECONOMIC CRISIS ON CONSUMPTION EXPENDITURES AND POVERTY INCIDENCE

Asep Suryahadi and Sudarno Sumarto

1 INTRODUCTION

The economic crisis that began in mid-1997 had an overwhelming social impact on the Indonesian population, whose living standards deteriorated as the *krismon* increasingly affected their incomes. In examining this social impact, the present chapter focuses on changes in real household consumption expenditures, as they reflect actual changes in living standards and form a measurable proxy for income changes due to the crisis. At the same time, the use of consumption expenditures enables the evolution of poverty to be examined by tracking changes in the headcount measure of poverty.

The data used in this chapter are from the consumption expenditures module of the 100 Village Survey (*Survei Seratus Desa* or SSD), which was sponsored by UNICEF and carried out by Statistics Indonesia (*Badan Pusat Statistik* or BPS) in May 1997, August 1998, and December 1998.[1] The Survey covered one hundred villages located in ten administrative districts (*kabupaten*) spread across eight provinces. The present analysis is based on three rounds of the Survey.[2]

2 THE 100 VILLAGE SURVEY

In December 1998, the 100 Village Survey collected data from 12,000 households, many of which had previously been surveyed in August 1998 and May 1997. It surveyed 120 households in each of the 100 villages in each round. The selection of households was somewhat complicated. In the May 1997 round, 120 households were chosen randomly from two enumeration areas within the villages. The general method in the August 1998 round was to add a new enumeration area. Forty new households were then chosen randomly from this new enumeration area. In the two enumeration areas used in the previous survey, eighty households were chosen to be re-interviewed in return visits to the same dwellings. If the households could not be identified at those dwellings, other households from the original 120 interviewed in 1997 were selected and added to keep the sample size at 120.[3] This was the planned methodology but it appears that there were some deviations from this sampling procedure in the field: in some villages more than eighty households were matched and in other villages many fewer than eighty households were matched. Meanwhile, in December 1998 all 120 households from the August 1998 round were supposed to be re-interviewed. Unidentified households were replaced by new, randomly selected households.

The sample, while quite large, was not designed to be statistically representative of the country. The 100 villages are geographically quite concentrated, being located in only ten of the over 300 districts in the country. Until these data can be matched with national data, it is impossible to say how representative these areas might be of the impact of the crisis. On the one hand, the survey areas were chosen in 1994, before the crisis, based on a purposive sampling approach that was meant to capture villages representative of various parts of the rural economy. Since the areas were chosen before the crisis, there is no reason to suspect that sampling could have been influenced by the crisis. On the other hand, since the survey was meant to focus on rural and relatively poor areas, we already know that it is not representative of the entire country. It is in fact impossible to know how representative it is of the changes due to the crisis. For this reason we focus first on the district-by-district analysis. All aggregate conclusions are for this sample only.

One very important caveat is that while the sample covers some urban areas, the major urban areas on Java such as the Jabotabek area[4] or Surabaya and the major cities off Java such as Medan and Makassar are not included in the survey. Since the crisis hit mainly through the modern sector, the indications from the samples used here say nothing about these major urban areas where, with ongoing financial and corporate restructuring, things may get worse before they get better.

The survey instrument includes much more than just the expenditure items that we focus on in this chapter. It contains a modified version of the Core SUSENAS (*Survey Sosial Ekonomi Nasional,* or National Socio-Economic Survey),[5] including questions on the demographic, educational, and health characteristics of the households, as well as a limited PODES *(Potensi Desa,* or Village Potential)[6] questionnaire, which collects information on village and community infrastructure and access to services. The December 1998 round[7] contains a module on the knowledge of, and participation in, the social safety net programs introduced in 1998.[8]

3 THE DEFLATOR ISSUE

Once a survey has measured actual household expenditures (including imputations for home production or market goods, for example, food and housing) in current prices, it is necessary to purge these nominal expenditures of the changes in money expenditures that have occurred due to inflation so that they may be used to compare changes in standards of living. This involves constructing a basket of goods that can be priced in each period to form a price index. This price index then deflates nominal expenditures so that any change in income shown in these deflated or real currency units indicates a change in real purchasing power.

If relative prices do not change or if all consumers consume exactly the same basket of goods, then this problem of deflation is straightforward, if not trivial. However, over this period in Indonesia, neither of these conditions holds true. First, the share of total expenditures that goes to food is very high for the poor and much lower for the rich. This means that the food share of the "average" consumer used in a consumer price index will be much lower than the share of food in the expenditures of someone near the poverty line. Second, for a variety of reasons, food prices rose much faster than non-food prices over the period studied. From May 1997 to December 1998, food prices increased by 136 per cent while non-food prices rose by only 72 per cent.

These two facts mean that any analysis of changes in real consumption and especially in poverty incidence will be extraordinarily sensitive to the choice of deflator used. Table 2.1 shows the sensitivity of the percentage change in real consumption between May 1997 and December 1998 to various deflators.[9] With near-equal accuracy, one could say that in this sample of households, real median consumption expenditures per capita either increased by 3 per cent or decreased by 10 per cent.

Five deflators are used in Table 2.1. An explanation of each will elucidate the problem, both in measuring the real income of this sample and in measuring changes in poverty. All the deflators are based on exactly the same set of prices: the desegregated price series from the Consumer Price Index (CPI). The only difference is the weights that are used for aggregating these prices into an index. The five deflators are:

TABLE 2.1
Sensitivity of Real Consumption Changes to Deflator Used

	CPI	Consumption Basket of 100 Village Survey Sample (1997)	Consumption Basket of bottom 30%, SUSENAS 1996	Food Share at the Poverty Line of Ikhsan (1999)	
				Urban	*Rural*
Food share (%)	40	68	70	55	62
Inflation rate from May 1997 to Dec. 1998 (%)	89	116	117	107	112
Percentage change in median real consumption	3	−10	−10	−6	−8

Note: This table is illustrative and is built from a food price inflation rate of 136 per cent and a non-food price inflation rate of 72 per cent from May 1997 to December 1998.
Source: 100 Village Surveys, SUSENAS 1996, Ikhsan (1999)

- The CPI, or *Consumer Price Index* (*Indeks Harga Konsumen*, or IHK), for which weights are based on the average expenditures of the population in 1996. The food share was around 40 per cent.[10] It should be kept in mind that, since this is an expenditure-weighted basket, the consumption of the rich counts not per household but per rupiah, which means that the mean food share is even higher than the food share of the median household.
- The *100 Village Survey index*, which is a price index based on the actual 1997 consumption shares of the households in the Survey, for which the food share was 68 per cent (this includes alcohol and tobacco). This suggests that households in the 100 Village Survey were substantially less well off before the crisis than the Indonesian population at large.

- The *bottom 30 per cent index*, in which the consumption shares used are based on the actual expenditure shares of the bottom 30 per cent of households (when ranked by nominal expenditures per person) of the 1996 SUSENAS.
- *Ikhsan's Poverty Line index* (urban and rural). This deflator is based on an aggregate of food and non-food price indices. The food share is based on expenditures that are just sufficient to purchase a nutritionally adequate food bundle (at the average expenditure per calorie of a poor household). This follows the poverty-line methodology recommended in Ravallion and Bidani (1994) as implemented for urban and rural areas in 1998 by Ikhsan and Wikarya (1999).

Table 2.1 reveals two points. First, the extent of inflation and hence the extent of change in real expenditure for any given change in nominal expenditures boil down to the food share: the higher the food share in a deflator, the higher the inflation rate implied by the deflator and hence the bigger the fall in real expenditures. For example, if the increase in nominal expenditures in the aggregate 100 Village Survey sample is deflated by the nationwide CPI, median real expenditures actually increase by 3 per cent from their pre-crisis levels to December 1998. But if the price index is based on the consumption shares of the Survey sample, which had a food share of 68 per cent and hence a much faster increase in the cost of the basket, then median real expenditures fall by 10 per cent.[11]

The second point revealed in Table 2.1 is that, in order to get an appropriate price deflator for the change in the poverty line, a food share of around 70 per cent is needed. This emerges from using either the consumption shares of the bottom 30 per cent of households or Ikhsan's poverty-line calculations (which are actually a little lower) and suggests that the Survey's 1997 consumption basket deflator is a reasonably appropriate deflator for use in the analysis of poverty. Hence, the whole of the present analysis is based on the 100 Village Survey index. We use the same deflator for all regions and not region-specific deflators based exclusively on the urban price series of BPS.

4 THE REGIONAL EVOLUTION OF CONSUMPTION EXPENDITURES

We shall first show the evolution of median real consumption expenditures (using the 100 Village Survey index) during the crisis in each of the districts included in the Survey.[12] Table 2.2 reveals the enormous regional heterogeneity that developed as a result of the crisis. In one district median expenditures rose by 6.6 per cent, while in another they fell 23 per cent — a 30 percentage point difference.

Based on the patterns of changes in consumption during the crisis period, we have divided the districts into three classes. The first consists of the two recovered districts, that is, those whose expenditures were higher in December 1998 than in May 1997. The second takes in the rebound districts, that is, those in which a substantial fall in real consumption expenditures occurred during the period from May 1997 to August 1998 but that experienced an increase in consumption in the later period from August to December 1998. Five districts fall into this category. The third class consists of districts that experienced continuously falling consumption during the whole period. Of the three districts in this category, two are located in Java.

Recovered. There are two districts in which median real income rose. Each, however, has its own pattern. In Indragiri Ilir (Riau) expenditures did not fall at all between May 1997 and August 1998 but in fact rose substantially (11 per cent), while from August to December 1998 this rise was moderated and the total "pre-crisis to most recent" change was 6.6 per cent. By contrast, median expenditures in Kendari (Southeast Sulawesi) also rose,

TABLE 2.2
Median Household Real Consumption Expenditures per Person in 10 Districts from Rounds of the 100 Village Survey

District/Province	Levels: Median Real per Capita Consumption, May 1997 (Rp)			Percentage Changes		
	May 1997	August 1998	December 1998	May '97–Aug. 1998	Aug. '98–Dec. 1998	May '97–Dec. 1998
Recovered:						
Indragiri Ilir, Riau	55,391	61,560	59,020	11.1	-4.1	6.6
Kendari, Southeast Sulawesi	34,044	32,070	35,267	-5.8	10.0	3.6
Rebound:						
Karangasem, Bali	52,958	40,863	47,343	-22.8	15.9	-10.6
Pandeglang, West Java	45,816	37,809	43,510	-17.5	15.1	-5.0
Rembang, Central Java	47,085	42,635	46,878	-9.5	10.0	-0.4
South Lampung, Lampung	37,957	32,024	34,790	-15.6	8.6	-8.3
Kupang, East Nusa Tenggara	34,441	25,358	26,520	-26.4	4.6	-23.0
Continuous fall:						
Sumedang, West Java	56,781	47,610	45,995	-16.2	-3.4	-19.0
Kutai, East Kalimantan	66,501	58,186	56,168	-12.5	-3.5	-15.5
Banjarnegara, Central Java	34,971	33,620	30,297	-3.9	-9.9	-13.4

Note: The deflator used is the 100 Village Survey index, deflating to the mid-points of the survey months.
Source: 100 Village Survey

by 3.6 per cent (although mean expenditures fell by 2 per cent). In this case, however, there was an initial 5.8 per cent fall from May 1997 to August 1998, followed by a 10 per cent recovery from August to December 1998.

Rebound. In five of the districts there was a dramatic fall in measured expenditures from the pre-crisis (May 1997) to the August 1998 data, with all five recording falls of between 10 and 26 per cent. In many of these areas, however, the data also record a substantial rebound in real consumption expenditures, by amounts ranging from 15 percentage points in Pandeglang and Karangasem to only 5 percentage points in Kupang. These are substantial rebounds as the changes took place over only a four-month period. In all of these areas, however, real expenditures remained lower in December 1998 than at eighteen months earlier. In some areas the fall was modest (just 0.4 per cent in Rembang and 5 per cent in Pandeglang). In other areas, however, even though there was some bottoming out and expenditures were no longer falling, they were down substantially under pre-crisis levels. In Kupang the modest rebound of 4.6 per cent still left median expenditures down by 23 per cent.

Continuous fall. In three of the districts, real expenditures fell from May 1997 to August 1998 and again from August to December 1998. In these locations the crisis appeared not to have abated. Real expenditures were down substantially under their pre-crisis levels, by 13 to 19 per cent. Two of the three continuous-fall locations are on Java (although there are other locations on Java in the rebound category).

The fact that seven out of ten districts were in either the recovered or rebound category and were spread across seven different provinces probably indicates that large parts of the country, especially in the rural areas represented in the sample, were already past the worst phase of the crisis. This micro evidence of some recovery since August 1998 is consistent with the macroeconomic evidence of the stabilized price of rice, stabilization and strengthening of the rupiah, and reductions in the rate of inflation after that month. Since, however, there was a significant number of districts that continued to experience falling consumption or were impacted by the crisis only in the latter period, enormous caution is warranted. In some areas at least, things could deteriorate still further.

5 AGGREGATE CONSUMPTION EVOLUTION

Although the 100 Village Survey was not designed to be nationally representative, it is still useful to see the consumption evolution for the aggregate of the whole sample (without weighting the sample areas to represent population shares). Table 2.3 aggregates the findings for all 12,000 households in the sample for nominal and real consumption. The numbers show clearly that nominal consumption continued to increase during the crisis and that it increased by almost 100 per cent. This increase in nominal consumption is a consequence of inflation and would hardly be worth mentioning if it were not for the fact that some calculations in other studies have been based on an assumption of unchanged nominal consumption.

But the increase in nominal consumption in the earlier period lagged behind the aggregate price increase. Therefore, real consumption in August 1998 was significantly lower than in May 1997. In the subsequent period the increase in nominal consumption somewhat caught up with the price increase. As a result, the regional pattern of a rebound in real consumption after August 1998 is also shown in aggregate, albeit in much weaker form. Real consumption in December 1998, however, was still significantly lower than in May 1997 when measured using the weights price index of the 100 Village Survey. Nevertheless, the

TABLE 2.3
Changes in Median Consumption Expenditures (Nominal and Real) for the Entire 12,000 Sample of Households

	Levels (median real per capita consumption, May 1997 rupiah)			Percentage Changes		
	May 1997	August 1998	December 1998	May 1997– Aug. 1998	Aug. 1998– Dec. 1998	May 1997– Dec. 1998
Nominal consumption expenditures	46,685	78,559	91,200	68.3	16.1	95.4
Real consumption expenditures (using 100 Village Survey deflator)	46,685	40,287	42,222	–13.7	4.8	–9.6
Real consumption expenditures (using CPI)	46,685	44,636	48,254	–4.4	8.1	3.4

Source: See Table 2.2

results still suggest that the impact of the crisis on household welfare was easing in the second half of 1998.

With these aggregate figures in mind, it is worth revisiting the question of whether real expenditures increased or decreased. The typical calculation of deflating by the CPI to convert from nominal to real rupiah would lead to the conclusion that real expenditures were higher in December 1998 than before the crisis began. If, however, a deflator specific to the sample is used, the conclusion is different, namely, that because households spent a greater fraction of their budget on food, their loss in purchasing power was greater when measured by the 100 Village Survey index than when gauged by the CPI, and that real expenditures *for this sample* fell significantly.

6 CHANGES IN THE INCIDENCE OF POVERTY

We now consider the changes in absolute poverty from May 1997 to December 1998.[13] We do not do a full-blown calculation of a poverty basket to establish the appropriate poverty line for the benchmark in 1997. Rather, since we are principally interested in the *changes* in poverty, we choose a conventional figure for the poverty line for the initial year to match with other sources of data and then update the poverty line by an appropriate deflator to measure changes. In this calculation the poverty line is updated using the 100 Village Survey price index; that is, the cost of the basket that constitutes the "poverty line" is assumed to increase by the same percentage as the increase in prices weighted by the Survey index. As shown in Table 2.1 above, these results would be approximately the same if any of the other deflators based on food shares in a poverty basket (such as the bottom 30 per cent or Ikhsan's poverty line indices) was used.

We do this in two ways. First, we choose as the poverty line the eleventh percentile of the 1997 consumption expenditures.[14] Using this poverty line, the proportions of households whose real consumption in August and December 1998 was below the poverty line are then calculated for the aggregate. The resulting percentage point changes and percentage changes are presented in the first row of Table 2.4. As expected from the analysis of the evolution of median expenditures, poverty first rose substantially by 7 percentage points from May 1997 to August 1998 — a 63.6 per cent increase in poverty incidence. From August to December 1998 poverty incidence declined by 2.8 percentage points or 15.6 per cent. The overall change in poverty incidence between May 1997 and December 1998 was an increase of 4.2 percentage points or a 38.2 per cent increase in poverty.[15] Assuming that the poverty rate in this sample was 11 per cent in May 1997, it had risen to 18 per cent by August 1998 but fell back to 15.2 per cent by December 1998.

While the present analysis assumes that the poverty rate was 11 per cent in 1997 as a convenient benchmark (since it makes comparisons with other poverty rate changes easier), the sample households in the 100 Village Survey are relatively poorer than the general population. An indication of this can be found in the proportion of households classified as pre-prosperous by the National Family Planning Coordinating Board (BKKBN).[16] The December 1998 Survey data show that 49 per cent of households in the sample were classified as pre-prosperous. Meanwhile, the BKKBN data for September 1998 indicate that nationally only around 16 per cent of households were pre-prosperous. Therefore, to calculate poverty incidence in another way it is probably appropriate to rescale the benchmark of poverty incidence from the 11 per cent national level to (49/16)*11 per cent or 34 per cent to match the characteristics of the 100 Village Survey sample.

Using this adjusted benchmark for the poverty rate in 1997, poverty incidence in August and December 1998 is recalculated for the aggregate level. The resulting percentage-point changes and percentage changes in poverty incidence are shown in the second row of Table 2.4. Although the levels of poverty incidence

TABLE 2.4
Poverty Incidence in the 100 Village Survey Sample with Three Benchmarks

Benchmark of Poverty Incidence	Percentage Point Change			Percentage Change		
	May 1997 – Aug. 1998	Aug. '98– Dec. 1998	May '97– Dec. 1998	May '97 – Aug. 1998	Aug. '98 – Dec. 1998	May 1997– Dec. 1998
Original (chosen to match the national poverty rate in 1997)	7.0	–2.8	4.2	63.6	–15.6	38.2
Adjusted (chosen to match poverty in the 100 Village Survey sample)	12.2	–4.3	7.9	35.9	–9.3	23.2
Backward (start from poverty rate in December 1998)	9.2	–3.7	5.5	49.2	–13.3	29.4

Note: The benchmark of poverty incidence is 11 per cent in May 1997 for the original analysis, 34 per cent in May 1997 for the adjusted, and 24.2 per cent in December 1998 for the backward.

Source: See Table 2.2

shown with the adjusted benchmark are much higher during the whole period than with the original benchmark, Table 2.4 shows that the changes in poverty incidence are slightly greater in terms of percentage-point changes but smaller in terms of percentage changes. With the original benchmark there is a 4.2 percentage-point or 38.2 per cent increase in poverty incidence between May 1997 and December 1998. With the adjusted benchmark, there is a 7.9 percentage point or 23.2 per cent increase. This indicates that the changes in poverty incidence suggested by Table 2.4 are reasonably robust whatever the choice of poverty incidence benchmark; that is, the bounds of absolute and percentage changes show a fairly robust pattern of changes no matter what the starting point is. If we begin from a higher base in this case (34 versus 11) the *percentage-point* increase in poverty is greater (7.9 versus 4.2) but the *percentage* change is smaller (23 per cent versus 38 per cent).

We can reverse this and compare the changes going back in time from any conventional figure for the latest data. An example of this is presented in the third row of Table 2.4. Suppose, for instance, that the poverty rate in December 1998 is assumed to have been 24.2 per cent. Then by our method the poverty rate in August 1998 would have been 27.9 per cent while in May 1997 it would have been 18.7 per cent. This implies a pre-crisis to December 1998 change in the poverty rate of 5.5 percentage points or an increase of 29.4 per cent. Again, the level is less important than the change.

7 CONCLUSION

The above discussion has provided further perspectives on the social welfare impacts of the Indonesian crisis as measured by consumption levels and poverty incidence. If a deflator based on the higher food share in consumption of this sample is used to deflate nominal consumption expenditures, the evidence suggests that some easing off of the crisis impacts took place after August 1998. Real consumption expenditures increased and poverty incidence decreased between August and December 1998. Since this followed a massive deterioration during the crisis period from May 1997 to August 1998, nearly all areas are still worse off than before the crisis. Caution regarding these results is warranted, however, considering that some regions were still experiencing continuous deterioration, even after August 1998.

Notes

This paper was originally published as a SMERU Working Paper, "Update on the Impact of the Indonesian Crisis on Consumption Expenditures and Poverty Incidence: Results from the December 1998 Round of 100 Village Survey", August 1999.

1. The 100 Village Survey was part of a much larger capacity-building exercise. It aimed to integrate quantitative and qualitative indicators, tracked over time, into policy-making in the social sectors and to provide a more dynamic and integrated family-based picture of poverty.
2. The first round of the 100 Village Survey was conducted in May 1994 but is not included in this analysis.
3. This means that the sample in 1998 suffered from attrition bias as the eighty re-interviewed households were not a random sample but a sample of those who could be re-interviewed.
4. Jabotabek is the name given to the conurbation of Jakarta and the surrounding districts of Bogor, Tangerang, and Bekasi.
5. SUSENAS is a nationally representative household survey covering all areas of the country. A part of the SUSENAS is conducted annually, collecting information on the characteristics of over 200,000 households and over 800,000 individuals, including information on aggregated values of household consumption expenditures. This part of the SUSENAS is known as the "Core" SUSENAS. Another part of the SUSENAS is conducted every three years and specifically collects information on very detailed consumption expenditures

from approximately 65,000 households that are a randomly selected subset of the 200,000 households of the Core SUSENAS sample of the same year. This consumption module part of SUSENAS is known as the "Module" SUSENAS. In addition, other modules on special topics are also conducted as parts of the SUSENAS on an occasional basis.

6. PODES is a complete enumeration of villages throughout Indonesia. The information collected through PODES includes only village characteristics such as size, population, infrastructure, and local industries. The questionnaires are completed by local village officials responsible for collecting statistics. Information is obtained from official village documents as well as interviews with village officials. The PODES survey is conducted three times in every ten years, usually prior to and as preparation for a full census. A PODES survey was conducted in 1996 preceding the economic census of that year, while another PODES survey was conducted in 1999 in preparation for the 2000 Population Census. The 1996 PODES dataset contains 66,486 villages, while the 1999 PODES set contains 68,783 villages.

7. The December 1998 questionnaire breaks down household consumption by source: market, own production, and gifts. In the two previous rounds, however, only total consumption was asked about. This might have caused under-reporting in the earlier rounds, particularly for rice, because respondents might have reported only market-sourced consumption. To test this, the proportion of rice consumption from total food consumption for landowners, where own production is important, was examined. The results show that the proportion of rice consumption in August 1998 was 37 per cent, while in December 1998 it was 41 per cent, of which 25 per cent was from the market, 14 per cent from own production, and 2 per cent from gifts. These results suggest that total consumption in the August round is commensurate with total consumption in the December round, implying that under-reporting does not constitute a significant problem.

8. The social safety net programs are discussed in Chapters 6 and 7.

9. All the inflation rates in this chapter are calculated on a mid-monthly basis.

10. The actual food share in the revised CPI is only 38.5 per cent. This is much lower than the average food share in consumption expenditure in the 1996 SUSENAS — 55 per cent.

11. The food share in the poverty line is not the food share of those at the poverty line. This is a major difference between using a deflator to update a poverty line and using a method to recalculate a poverty line in two periods.

12. The median is the point of a distribution where half are above and half are below. As distributions of expenditures are typically skewed to the right (some people are very rich while there is a lower limit to how poor a person can be), the mean or average expenditures are higher than median expenditures. Since some data suggest that there have been substantial changes in the distribution of income that would alter the relationship between the mean and median, we use the median as the indicator of the central tendency of the distribution.

13 In the present chapter only the headcount poverty ratio is examined. Analysis of other data has suggested an expansion in the poverty gap and an increase in inequality among those below the poverty line (although inequality of nominal expenditures appears to have fallen).

14. The BPS data indicate that the proportion of the population living below the poverty line in 1996 was 11.34 per cent. The benchmark figure of 11 per cent poverty incidence in 1997 is a conservative estimate, considering the economic growth rate of 7.8 per cent in 1996 and 4.9 per cent in 1997.

15. The simultaneous occurrence of increasing real expenditures when deflated using the CPI and rising poverty suggests a shift in relative prices against the poor.

16. The National Family Planning Coordinating Board (*Badan Koordinasi Keluarga Berencana Nasional*, or BKKBN) divides Indonesian households into several socioeconomic categories, of which "pre-prosperous" is the lowest. In this sample, 49 per cent are "pre-prosperous" households, although in reality the same districts have only 26 per cent "pre-prosperous" households. A household is defined as pre-prosperous if it fails to satisfy one of the following five conditions: (i) all household members are able to practise their

religious principles, (ii) all household members are able to eat at least twice a day, (iii) all household members have different sets of clothing for home, work, school, and visits, (iv) the largest floor area of the house is not made of dirt, and (v) the household is able to seek modern medical assistance for sick children and family planning services for contraceptive users.

Chapter 3

POVERTY AND VULNERABILITY IN INDONESIA BEFORE AND AFTER THE ECONOMIC CRISIS

Asep Suryahadi and Sudarno Sumarto

1 INTRODUCTION

In the middle of 1997 Indonesia was hit by a major economic crisis. The social impact of the large economic contraction that occurred was very substantial, reversing many of the improvements in the social sector that had been achieved in previous decades. In the labour market, although the open unemployment rate only slightly increased from 4.7 per cent in 1997 to 5.5 per cent in 1998, real wages fell by approximately one-third (Feridhanusetyawan 1999; Manning 2000). The national headcount rate of poverty, according to one estimate, increased from 15.7 per cent in 1996 to 27.1 per cent in 1999 (Pradhan et al. 2001). Another study, which tracked the poverty rate over the course of the crisis, estimated that the poverty rate increased by 164 per cent from the onset of the crisis in mid-1997 to the peak of the crisis at the end of 1998 (Suryahadi et al. 2000).

It is obvious that poverty increased rapidly along with the worsening of the crisis, implying that there were large numbers of households moving into poverty in a short period of time (Suryahadi et al. 2000; Skoufias et al. 2000). In contrast to the static concept of the headcount rate of poverty, the fact that the poverty rate changed relatively quickly over short periods of time following the crisis shows that, in reality, the state of poverty is dynamic.

Although the dynamic nature of poverty only recently gained wide attention, it is not a new concept. It was already well known that, over time, households enter into and exit from poverty (Bane and Ellwood 1983). This means that there is always a chance that people who are currently not poor will fall below the poverty line and at the same time that the poor will move out of poverty at some time in the future. This leads to the concept of "vulnerability to poverty", defined as the risk that a household will be poor in the near future.

The economic crisis brought severe multiple shocks to Indonesian households. The present study is an attempt to assess what happened to poverty and vulnerability to poverty in Indonesia before and after the economic crisis. The analysis is based on a method specifically developed for estimating vulnerability to poverty using cross-sectional data.

2 METHODOLOGY

2.1 Definition of Vulnerability

A household's vulnerability to poverty is measured as a risk or probability that the household will be poor in the near future, implying that households have greater or lesser degrees of vulnerability. Vulnerability to poverty affects everybody and can be caused by various events such as a bad harvest, a lost job, an unexpected expense, an illness, and the many other risks and shocks of life. Because the future is uncertain, the degree of vulnerability rises with the time horizon, so vulnerability over the next week is quite low, over the next year it is higher, and over several years higher still (Pritchett et al. 2000). In general, risks and shocks can be classified by (i) the level at which they occur (that is, individual, community or country), (ii) the nature of the event (for example, natural, health, social, economic, political, and environmental), and (iii) their severity and frequency (World Bank 2000).

2.2 Method for Estimating Vulnerability

The key to estimating a household's vulnerability to poverty is to obtain an estimate of the household's variance in consumption expenditures. A reliable estimate of consumption expenditure variance can be obtained from panel data collected over a sufficiently long period of time. Most household survey data available to date, however, are cross-sectional and cannot be used for this purpose (Jalan and Ravallion 2000). Hence, there is clearly a need to develop a method for estimating the consumption expenditure variance of households from cross-sectional data. Such a method was developed by Chaudhuri (2000) and is briefly discussed below.

Suppose that for household h the stochastic process generating consumption is:

$$\ln c_h = X_h \beta + \varepsilon_h \tag{3.1}$$

where c_h is per capita consumption, X_h is a vector of household characteristics, β is a vector of parameters, and ε_h is idiosyncratic shocks. Then the probability that a household with characteristics X_h will be poor is:

$$\hat{v}_h = \hat{\Pr}\left(\ln c_h < \ln \underline{c} | X_h\right) = \Phi\left(\frac{\ln c_h - X_h \hat{\beta}}{\hat{\sigma}}\right) \tag{3.2}$$

where v_h denotes vulnerability to poverty, that is, the probability that the per capita consumption level (c_h) will be lower than the poverty line ($\underline{c}$) conditional on household characteristics (X_h). Meanwhile, $\Phi(.)$ denotes the cumulative density of the standard normal distribution and σ is the standard error of equation 3.1.

A three-step feasible generalized least squares (FGLS) procedure (Amemiya 1977) can be used to estimate the vulnerability to poverty of household h empirically through the generalization of equation 3.2.

2.3 Poverty and Vulnerability Categories

As a result of the estimation, each household in the sample can be assigned an estimated degree of vulnerability to poverty (that is, the risk or probability of each household falling into poverty in the near future). To classify households into those that have high and low vulnerabilities to poverty, a threshold of 0.5 vulnerability to poverty is used.[1]

In addition to the estimated degree of vulnerability to poverty, the results of the estimation also provide each household's expected consumption $X_h\hat{\beta}$. Using a combination of (i) the poverty and vulnerability status of households based on their current consumption levels, (ii) the estimated degree of vulnerability of households to poverty, and (iii) their estimated expected consumption levels, households can now be grouped into several poverty and vulnerability categories as illustrated in Figure 3.1.

In particular, there are five overlapping groups of households: (i) the poor, (ii) the non-poor, (iii) the high vulnerability group, (iv) the low vulnerability group, and (v) the total vulnerable group. The poor group consists of the chronic poor and the transient poor. The high vulnerability group is differentiated into two subgroups based on the cause of high vulnerability: low level of consumption and high variability of consumption. The non-poor can be disaggregated into the high vulnerability non-poor and the low vulnerability non-poor.

Finally, the total vulnerable group is defined as a combination of the high vulnerability group and the currently poor. This means that the total vulnerable group includes all the people who are

FIGURE 3.1
Poverty and Vulnerability Categories

		Current Consumption (c)			
		$c < \underline{c}$	$c \geq \underline{c}$		
Vulnerability to poverty (v)	$v \geq 0.5$	A	D	$E[c] < \underline{c}$	*Expected consumption (E[c])*
		B	E		
	$v < 0.5$	C	F	$E[c] \geq \underline{c}$	

Notes:
Poor = A + B + C (chronic poor = A; transient poor = B + C)
Non-poor = D + E + F (high-vulnerability non-poor = D + E;
      low-vulnerability non-poor = F)
High vulnerability group = A + B + D + E
      (low level of consumption = A + D;
      high variability of consumption = B + E)
Low vulnerability group = C + F
Total vulnerable group = A + B + C + D + E

Source: Compilation by the authors

currently poor plus the people who are currently non-poor but who have a relatively large chance of falling into poverty in the near future. Hence, while vulnerability to poverty is defined as the risk or probability of falling below the poverty line, the definition of the total vulnerable group is based on both this risk and the initial poverty status.[2]

More detailed poverty categories, as depicted in Figure 3.1, rather than the common approach of simply dividing households into the poor and the non-poor are useful as they demonstrate that the poor and the vulnerable actually consist of heterogeneous groups. Each of these groups may respond differently to particular policies aimed at reducing poverty. Hence it might be necessary to devise different policies for different groups (Jalan and Ravallion 2000).

2.4 Measurement Error

Data collected through household surveys most likely contain measurement errors. In estimating vulnerability, measurement error cannot be ignored because it tends to overstate the variance of consumption (Luttmer 2000; Pritchett et al. 2000). Fortunately, in the method described above the measurement error in consumption is eliminated in the estimation process (Chaudhuri 2000). Hence, despite measurement error, the method will result in a consistent estimate of the true variance of consumption.

If, however, the measurement error varies systematically with certain household characteristics, then the estimate of consumption variance will in fact still be contaminated by the measurement error. For example, because rural households consume some of their own production (which is harder to measure than purchased market goods), there is a possibility that the measurement error will vary systematically across urban-rural areas. To overcome this problem, it is necessary to perform separate estimates for urban and rural areas. This suggests that the method must be implemented at a disaggregated level, as far as the data permit (Chaudhuri 2000).

3 DATA

The data analysed in this study are a combination of the National Socio-Economic Survey (SUSENAS)[3] and the Village Potential (PODES)[4] datasets, which were both collected by Statistics Indonesia (*Badan Pusat Statistik*). The periods analysed are 1996 (the latest Consumption Module SUSENAS that was conducted before the crisis) and 1999 (the first Consumption Module SUSENAS conducted after the crisis).

In the present study, a dataset is created by merging the three datasets for each year. The created dataset has a combination of: (i) information on household consumption from the Consumption Module SUSENAS; (ii) household characteristics from the Core SUSENAS; and (iii) village-level community variables from the PODES dataset. The 1996 dataset had 57,724 household observations located in 3,619 villages, while the 1999 dataset had 57,921 household observations in 3,483 villages.

4 THE POOR AND THE VULNERABLE BEFORE AND AFTER THE CRISIS

Using the method specified in Section 2 above, the merged dataset, discussed in Section 3, is used to estimate the degree of vulnerability to poverty across households in Indonesia. The poverty lines used in the estimation are taken from Pradhan et al. (2001). The estimation was performed by region, defined as a combination of province and urban-rural areas. Because at the time there were twenty-six provinces in Indonesia, while the capital Jakarta was an entirely urban area, estimations were conducted for a total of fifty-one regions.

The household characteristics used in the estimation were: (i) household size and its square; (ii) the dependency ratio in the household; and (iii) a set of characteristics of the household head, including marital status, age and its square, educational level (less than primary, primary, lower secondary, upper secondary, and tertiary), gender, and occupation (agriculture, industry, trade, services and "receiving transfers").

In addition, community characteristics at the village level are used as controlling variables. These include (i) population density; (ii) proportions of agricultural households, officially poor households, and houses with electricity; (iii) dummy variables for whether the village has a hospital, a polyclinic, a community health centre, a medical doctor who resides in the village, a transport facility, a vocational course facility, an upper secondary or tertiary education institution, an industry, a trade facility, a bank, a cooperative and/or a public communication facility; (iv) dummy variables for whether there are households in the village that use liquid petroleum gas or kerosene as the energy source for cooking, use piped or pumped water for their water supply, and have their own toilet; and (v) the educational level of the village head (less than upper secondary, upper secondary, and tertiary).

4.1 The Poor and the Vulnerable at National Level

It is now well known that the crisis caused the poverty rate in Indonesia to increase very significantly, as the results of the estimation confirm. Table 3.1, which shows the distribution of households across poverty categories in 1996 and 1999, indicates

TABLE 3.1
Population Distribution across Poverty Categories,
1996 and 1999 (%)

Poverty Category	1996	1999	Change
Poor:			
Transient Poor	12.4	17.9	5.5
Chronic Poor	3.2	9.5	6.3
Total	15.6	27.4	11.8
High vulnerability group:			
Low level of consumption	4.8	13.4	8.6
High variability of consumption	2.2	5.0	2.8
Total	7.0	18.4	11.4
Total vulnerable group	18.3	33.7	15.4
Average vulnerability to poverty	16.6	27.2	10.6

Source: SUSENAS, PODES

that the headcount poverty rate in Indonesia increased from 15.6 per cent in 1996 to 27.4 per cent in 1999 — a change of 11.8 per cent or 76 per cent from the initial rate.[5]

Disaggregation of the poor category indicates that the proportions of both transient poor and chronic poor within the total population rose significantly. The transient poor increased from 12.4 per cent in 1996 to 17.9 per cent in 1999, while the chronic poor jumped from 3.2 per cent to 9.5 per cent during the same period. This means that, while the headcount rate of transient poverty increased by only 5.5 per cent (that is, an increase of less than one-half from the original rate), the headcount rate of chronic poverty increased by 6.3 per cent or double the original rate, so the proportion of chronic poor almost tripled. This means that the bulk of the increase in the number of the poor occurred mostly among the chronic poor. As a result, the chronic poor, who made up only approximately 20 per cent of the total poor before the crisis, constituted about 35 per cent of the total poor in 1999.

Similarly, the proportion of those in the high vulnerability group rose significantly. In total, this group increased from 7 per cent in 1996 to 18.4 per cent in 1999 (an increase of more than 160 per cent over the original rate). This rise in the proportion of the high vulnerability group in the population was driven by increases in the proportions of those who had low levels of consumption as well as those who had a high variability of consumption. The latter more than doubled from 2.2 per cent in 1996 to 5 per cent in 1999, while the former is even more worrying since the number almost tripled from 4.8 per cent in 1996 to 13.4 per cent in 1999.

As a result of increases in the proportions of the population who were poor and who had high vulnerability to poverty, the total vulnerable group in the population increased very significantly from 18.3 per cent in 1996 to 33.7 per cent in 1999.

FIGURE 3.2
Cumulative Distribution Function of Vulnerability to Poverty

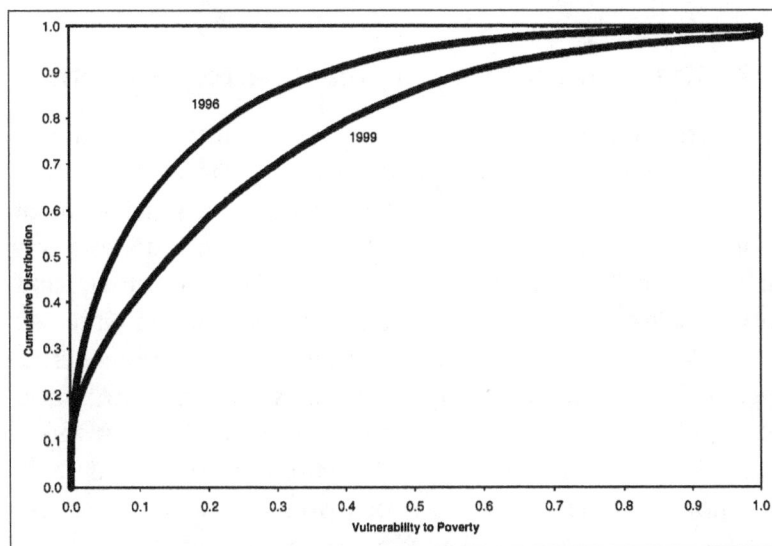

Source: Compilation by authors

This was an increase of 15.4 per cent or proportionally almost 85 per cent over the original rate.[6]

Similarly, the average vulnerability to poverty across households, that is, the mean of estimates of $\hat{v}_h$ in equation 3.2 above, also increased significantly from 16.6 per cent in 1996 to 27.2 per cent in 1999 an increase of almost two-thirds from the original vulnerability rate. Figure 3.2 graphs the cumulative distribution functions (CDF) of vulnerability to poverty in 1996 and 1999. The figure shows that the 1999 CDF lies to the right of the 1996 CDF with no crossings, implying that the 1996 CDF stochastically dominates the 1999 CDF. This means that the proportion of the high vulnerability group in the population is always higher in 1999 than in 1996, no matter what "vulnerability threshold" is chosen. In other words, vulnerability to poverty among Indonesian households after the crisis unambiguously increased from the pre-crisis level.

4.2 The Poor and the Vulnerable across Regions

Indonesia is a large and heterogeneous country. According to the 2000 Population Census, the country's total population stood at over 206 million in that year and was made up of more than 300 ethnic groups. Administratively, Indonesia was divided into 26 provinces, 341 districts, 4,044 subdistricts, and 69,065 villages in 1999. The national aggregate figures discussed in the previous section certainly mask large variations across regions and population groups. Table 3.2 shows the distribution of population by poverty categories across provinces in 1996, Table 3.3 shows the post-crisis distribution in 1999, and Table 3.4 shows the changes between the two periods. In these tables provinces are ranked from the lowest to the highest incidence of the total vulnerable group.

Tables 3.2 and 3.3 show that the proportions of the poor and the vulnerable groups in the population vary greatly across provinces. In 1996, the total vulnerable group ranged from less than 1 per cent of the population in the capital Jakarta to almost 70 per cent in the province of East Nusa Tenggara. Table 3.2 indicates that, in this pre-crisis period, there was practically no incidence of chronic poverty in Jakarta, West Sumatra, and Aceh. Very low incidences of chronic poverty were observed in Central Kalimantan, Riau, and South Kalimantan. Meanwhile, low proportions of the high vulnerability group were observed in Jakarta, West Sumatra, Central Kalimantan, Riau, and Aceh.

In contrast, approximately half of the people of East Nusa Tenggara and Papua were poor and, worse still, most of them were in the chronically poor category. In addition, the high vulnerability group in these provinces made up more than half of the population. As a result, the total vulnerable groups in these provinces were almost 70 and 60 per cent respectively. Other provinces with similarly high proportions of poor and vulnerable households were West Nusa Tenggara and Maluku. These two provinces had poverty rates greater than 30 per cent and proportions of the total vulnerable group that exceeded 40 per cent.

In 1996 most provinces had incidences of chronic poverty that were much lower than transient poverty levels. There were only three exceptions: Papua, East Nusa Tenggara, and Maluku. The worst incidences of chronic poverty were found in Papua and East Nusa Tenggara, where around 40 per cent of the population was chronically poor. Meanwhile, the highest incidence of transient poverty was found in West Nusa Tenggara, where almost a quarter of the population was in that category.

In 1999, as Table 3.3 shows, Jakarta and East Nusa Tenggara retained the highest and the lowest ranks respectively but both had experienced significant increases in the incidence of both poverty and vulnerability. In Jakarta the proportion of the total vulnerable group increased from 0.8 per cent in 1996 to 3.7 per cent in 1999, while in East Nusa Tenggara the proportion rose from 69.2 per cent to 75.4 per cent. In fact, no single province was spared the negative impact of the crisis in terms of increases in the proportions of the poor and the vulnerable.

Table 3.4 shows that the province of Lampung suffered the highest increase in the total vulnerable group, in terms of percentage-point increase. The proportion of the total vulnerable group in this province increased from 19.6 per cent in 1996 to 48.1 per cent in 1999 — an increase of 28.1 per cent and almost 150 per cent more than the original proportion. Only two other provinces, namely, Central Sulawesi and West Java, experienced an increase of 20 per cent or more in the proportion of the total vulnerable group.

Meanwhile, Jakarta experienced the lowest increase in the total vulnerable group in terms of percentage-point increase.

TABLE 3.2
Poverty Categories by Province, 1996 (%)

No.	Province	Poor			High Vulnerability Group			TVG	AV
		TP	CP	Total	LLC	HVC	Total		
1.	Jakarta	0.8	0.0	0.8	0.0	0.0	0.0	0.8	2.0
2.	West Sumatra	2.9	0.0	2.9	0.1	0.0	0.1	3.0	3.7
3.	Central Kalimantan	3.8	0.1	3.9	0.1	0.3	0.3	4.1	5.6
4.	Riau	5.1	0.2	5.3	0.2	0.2	0.4	5.5	7.1
5.	Aceh	6.2	0.0	6.2	0.3	0.2	0.5	6.7	5.7
6.	East Kalimantan	5.3	0.7	6.0	1.5	1.3	2.8	7.6	7.6
7.	Jambi	7.0	0.9	7.9	1.2	0.4	1.6	8.6	7.8
8.	North Sumatra	7.8	0.5	8.3	0.6	0.5	1.1	8.7	9.3
9.	Bali	7.2	1.5	8.7	1.6	0.4	2.0	8.9	9.1
10.	South Kalimantan	8.7	0.3	9.0	0.6	1.0	1.6	9.7	10.6
11.	Bengkulu	9.7	0.7	10.4	1.2	2.2	3.4	11.7	11.3
12.	West Java	10.8	1.0	11.8	1.7	1.3	2.9	13.0	12.7
13.	South Sumatra	7.9	1.2	9.1	3.8	2.8	6.6	13.9	14.6
14.	South Sulawesi	11.3	3.3	14.6	5.5	1.8	7.4	17.5	16.2
15.	Yogyakarta	14.6	1.6	16.2	3.0	1.8	4.8	18.6	15.7
16.	Lampung	16.2	1.0	17.2	2.5	1.7	4.2	19.6	17.7
17.	Central Sulawesi	15.0	1.7	16.7	3.7	2.7	6.3	20.4	17.1
18.	East Java	16.5	2.2	18.7	3.3	2.7	6.1	21.3	19.2
19.	Central Java	18.4	2.6	21.0	3.9	4.2	8.1	24.4	22.2
20.	North Sulawesi	12.3	7.3	19.6	12.2	3.9	16.1	25.9	20.8
21.	West Kalimantan	13.1	7.0	20.1	12.1	2.0	14.1	26.2	21.3
22.	Southeast Sulawesi	15.2	10.1	25.3	14.1	4.0	18.1	32.0	24.9
23.	Maluku	12.1	21.8	33.9	29.0	2.4	31.4	42.4	33.8
24.	West Nusa Tenggara	22.9	13.5	36.4	19.5	6.6	26.1	45.1	33.8
25.	Papua	6.2	40.9	47.1	50.4	3.1	53.6	58.5	48.8
26.	East Nusa Tenggara	14.9	38.5	53.4	51.8	6.0	57.8	69.2	53.4

Note: TP, transient poor; CP, chronic poor; LLC, low level of consumption;
HVC, high variability of consumption; TVG, total vulnerable group;
AV, average vulnerability.
Sorted from the lowest to the highest incidence of the total vulnerable
group.
Source: See Table 3.1

TABLE 3.3
Poverty Categories by Province, 1999 (%)

No.	Province	Poor			High Vulnerability Group			TVG	AV
		TP	CP	Total	LLC	HVC	Total		
1.	Jakarta	2.9	0.1	3.0	0.3	0.6	0.9	3.7	6.2
2.	Riau	6.1	3.3	9.4	5.1	0.7	5.7	11.6	9.9
3.	West Sumatra	8.0	1.4	9.4	3.8	1.5	5.3	12.9	12.1
4.	Aceh	12.4	1.2	13.6	1.8	1.3	3.1	15.1	14.0
5.	Bali	10.7	3.2	13.9	5.0	2.1	7.1	16.7	15.0
6.	North Sumatra	12.9	2.2	15.1	3.1	1.4	4.5	16.8	16.3
7.	Jambi	12.6	4.5	17.1	6.8	1.5	8.3	20.1	16.3
8.	Bengkulu	13.4	7.2	20.6	8.0	1.7	9.7	22.2	16.4
9.	Central Kalimantan	7.3	5.0	12.2	14.2	1.6	15.8	22.9	21.8
10.	South Kalimantan	12.8	7.3	20.0	10.2	1.7	11.9	23.9	19.7
11.	East Kalimantan	11.6	10.2	21.8	12.5	4.8	17.2	26.4	21.1
12.	South Sulawesi	17.7	5.4	23.0	7.6	3.6	11.2	27.1	22.4
13.	North Sulawesi	9.9	14.1	24.0	19.0	0.8	19.8	29.3	23.4
14.	South Sumatra	17.5	6.0	23.5	11.5	4.3	15.8	31.4	23.4
15.	West Java	19.7	7.2	26.8	10.8	5.4	16.2	33.1	26.8
16.	Yogyakarta	16.6	10.3	26.9	14.8	5.2	20.0	33.6	26.7
17.	West Kalimantan	14.6	14.7	29.4	19.6	3.9	23.5	36.0	29.5
18.	Central Java	23.0	9.9	32.9	14.4	6.8	21.2	40.6	31.9
19.	East Java	23.3	10.3	33.6	14.6	7.3	21.9	41.0	32.3
20.	Central Sulawesi	11.9	16.1	28.0	29.1	2.3	31.4	42.6	36.6
21.	Southeast Sulawesi	16.7	19.9	36.6	23.9	6.9	30.9	43.3	34.0
22.	Lampung	20.8	17.2	38.1	24.0	7.8	31.8	48.1	35.6
23.	West Nusa Tenggara	21.5	20.1	41.6	27.4	9.1	36.6	52.7	39.7
24.	Maluku	11.4	36.8	48.2	47.5	0.5	48.0	59.2	48.6
25.	Papua	3.5	54.5	58.0	57.8	0.6	58.4	62.0	57.4
26.	East Nusa Tenggara	10.6	51.4	62.0	63.0	3.7	66.7	75.4	60.4

Note: See note to Table 3.2.
Source: See Table 3.1

TABLE 3.4
Changes in Poverty Categories by Province, 1996–99
(Percentage Point Change)

No.	Province	Poor			High Vulnerability Group			TVG	AV
		TP	CP	Total	LLC	HVC	Total		
1.	Jakarta	2.0	0.1	2.2	0.3	0.6	0.9	2.8	4.4
2.	Papua	−3.4	14.3	10.9	7.4	−3.2	4.3	3.1	8.1
3.	North Sulawesi	−4.3	8.9	4.6	11.4	−4.8	6.7	5.3	3.1
4.	Riau	1.9	2.5	4.4	4.0	0.1	4.1	6.2	2.8
5.	West Nusa Tenggara	−1.5	6.6	5.2	7.2	2.4	9.6	6.8	6.1
6.	East Nusa Tenggara	−2.8	11.6	8.8	10.4	−2.0	8.4	6.8	7.5
7.	Aceh	5.5	0.7	6.2	1.1	0.8	1.9	7.5	6.3
8.	Bali	3.7	1.8	5.5	3.5	0.9	4.3	7.6	5.5
9.	North Sumatra	4.8	1.9	6.7	2.7	0.7	3.4	8.0	6.3
10.	Bengkulu	4.9	5.2	10.1	4.9	0.5	5.3	9.9	3.9
11.	Southeast Sulawesi	0.6	9.0	9.6	9.5	1.6	11.1	10.0	7.5
12.	West Sumatra	5.2	1.4	6.7	3.8	1.4	5.1	10.0	8.7
13.	West Kalimantan	−1.8	9.7	7.8	12.5	−0.1	12.4	10.7	10.5
14.	South Sulawesi	6.3	2.4	8.6	3.6	1.8	5.4	10.8	7.3
15.	Jambi	5.6	3.6	9.3	5.7	1.0	6.7	11.5	3.6
16.	South Kalimantan	5.6	6.9	12.5	8.6	0.5	9.0	14.1	10.8
17.	Maluku	−0.4	14.2	13.8	16.6	−3.2	13.4	14.7	12.0
18.	Yogyakarta	2.3	8.5	10.8	12.1	2.9	15.0	15.3	11.2
19.	Central Java	4.5	7.5	12.0	10.4	3.3	13.7	16.7	10.0
20.	Central Kalimantan	3.6	4.9	8.5	14.2	1.4	15.6	19.0	17.1
21.	East Kalimantan	7.8	8.6	16.4	9.8	3.2	13.0	19.1	13.5
22.	South Sumatra	9.4	5.0	14.3	8.5	3.4	11.9	19.6	10.6
23.	East Java	6.9	7.9	14.8	11.0	4.6	15.6	19.9	13.2
24.	West Java	8.8	6.2	14.9	9.2	4.2	13.4	20.0	14.1
25.	Central Sulawesi	−1.0	12.6	11.6	23.3	0.9	24.3	23.0	19.3
26.	Lampung	5.6	15.1	20.8	20.5	6.0	26.5	28.1	17.5

Note: See note to Table 3.2.
Source: See Table 3.1

The proportion of the total vulnerable group in this province increased from 0.8 per cent in 1996 to 3.7 per cent in 1999. But since vulnerability levels in Jakarta were very low in 1996, this amounted to a proportional increase of more than 340 per cent. In fact, this is the second highest proportional change after Central Kalimantan, which had an increase of 465 per cent.

Despite regional variations, most provinces still exhibit a similar pattern to the changes in poverty categories at the national level. First, the increase in the total vulnerable group was due to increases in both the proportion of the poor and the proportion of the high vulnerability group in the population. Increases in both categories occurred in every province. Second, the increase in poverty was mostly driven by the increase in chronic poverty. All provinces experienced a much higher proportional increase in the incidence of chronic poverty than in transient poverty.

Due to this significant increase in the incidence of chronic poverty during the crisis, there were seven provinces with higher proportions of chronic poverty than transient poverty in 1999. Before the crisis, only three provinces were in this situation. All provinces in Java and Sumatra, however, still had significantly lower incidences of chronic poverty than transient poverty. A higher incidence of chronic poverty rather than transient poverty mostly occurred in provinces in the eastern part of Indonesia, plus some provinces in Nusa Tenggara and Kalimantan.

4.3 The Poor and the Vulnerable across Urban and Rural Areas

Despite the fact that the crisis hit urban areas relatively harder than rural areas (Sumarto et al. 1998), the incidence of poverty in rural areas remained higher than in urban areas (Pradhan et al. 2001). Table 3.5 shows the distribution of population by poverty categories as differentiated by urban and rural areas in 1996 and 1999. The table confirms that, throughout the entire period, the

TABLE 3.5
Poverty Categories by Urban and Rural Areas,
1996 and 1999 (%)

Area	Poor			High Vulnerability Group			TVG	AV
	TP	CP	Total	LLC	HVC	Total		
1996:								
Rural	15.8	4.6	20.4	6.8	2.9	9.7	24.0	21.1
Urban	6.4	0.7	7.1	1.2	0.9	2.1	8.1	8.4
1999:								
Rural	21.3	13.2	34.5	18.3	6.5	24.8	42.5	33.6
Urban	12.9	3.9	16.8	6.1	2.7	8.8	20.4	17.4
Change (% points):								
Rural	5.5	8.6	14.1	11.5	3.6	15.0	18.5	12.5
Urban	6.5	3.2	9.7	4.9	1.8	6.8	12.3	9.0

Note: AV, average vulnerability; CP, chronic poor; HVC, high variability of
  consumption; LLC, low level of consumption; TP, transient poor; TVG,
  total vulnerable group.
Source: See Table 3.1

proportions of the population who were poor and vulnerable to
poverty were always much higher in rural than in urban areas.

In 1996 the total vulnerable group made up 24 per cent of the
rural population and only 8.1 per cent of the urban population.
By 1999, however, the proportion had risen to 42.5 per cent in
rural areas and 20.4 per cent in urban areas. This means that the
increase was proportionally much higher in urban areas than in
rural areas. The increase in the proportion of the total vulnerable
group of 12.3 per cent in urban areas was an increase of more
than 150 per cent over the pre-crisis rate, while the increase of
18.5 per cent in rural areas was equal to a proportional increase
of 77 per cent. This means that the growth of the total vulnerable
group in urban areas was more than double the growth in rural
areas.

In both urban and rural areas the increase in the total vulnerable group was due to increases in both the proportion of the population who were poor and the proportion of the population with high vulnerability to poverty. The headcount poverty rate increased from 20.4 per cent in 1996 to 34.5 per cent in 1999 for rural areas and from 7.1 per cent to 16.8 per cent for urban areas. Proportionally, the poverty rate in urban areas rose by 137 per cent, while the increase in rural areas, at 69 per cent, was much lower. Meanwhile, the proportion of the high vulnerability group increased from 9.7 per cent to 24.8 per cent for rural areas and from 2.1 per cent to 8.8 per cent for urban areas. This means that the proportion of the high vulnerability group in urban areas increased more than fourfold, while the increase in rural areas was much lower at 155 per cent. This clearly confirms the fact that the crisis hit urban areas relatively more severely than rural areas.

The increase in the poor population in rural areas, however, occurred mostly in the category of chronic poverty. For every two additional transient poor people in rural areas, there were three additional people in the chronic poor category. As a result, the ratio of chronic to transient poverty in rural areas more than doubled from approximately 29 per cent before the crisis to 62 per cent in 1999. Meanwhile, in urban areas, although the proportional increase in chronic poverty was also much higher than the increase in transient poverty, the transient poor still made up the absolute majority of the post-crisis poor in urban areas. Nevertheless, the ratio of chronic to transient poverty in urban areas jumped from a pre-crisis figure of 11 per cent to 30 per cent after the crisis.

4.4 The Poor and the Vulnerable across Sectors

The incidence of poverty in Indonesia varies widely across sectors. Table 3.6 shows the distribution of population across poverty categories by the occupation of household heads. It is

TABLE 3.6
Poverty Categories by Occupational Sector of Household Heads,
1996 and 1999 (%)

Occupational Sector	Poor			High Vulnerability Group			TVG	AV
	TP	CP	Total	LLC	HVC	Total		
1996								
Agriculture	19.1	7.1	26.1	10.3	4.4	14.7	31.2	26.8
Industry	10.0	1.3	11.4	2.2	1.5	3.7	11.9	12.0
Trade	7.7	0.4	7.9	0.7	0.6	1.2	8.5	9.7
Services	7.5	0.4	8.0	0.7	0.4	1.1	8.4	8.2
Receiving transfers	6.1	0.7	6.8	1.0	1.2	2.2	7.5	8.7
1999								
Agriculture	21.7	18.7	40.4	25.8	7.8	33.6	51.0	39.3
Industry	17.2	6.8	24.1	9.2	4.1	13.3	28.4	23.4
Trade	15.8	2.1	18.0	3.5	3.1	6.6	20.9	18.8
Services	15.1	3.4	18.5	5.4	3.0	8.3	22.0	18.7
Receiving transfers	12.9	3.7	16.6	6.3	2.9	9.2	20.7	17.9
Change								
Agriculture	2.6	11.6	14.3	15.5	3.4	18.9	19.8	12.5
Industry	7.2	5.5	12.7	7.0	2.6	9.6	16.5	11.4
Trade	8.2	1.8	10.0	2.8	2.5	5.4	12.4	9.1
Services	7.6	2.9	10.5	4.6	2.6	7.2	13.6	10.5
Receiving transfers	7.7	3.0	9.8	5.3	1.7	7.0	13.2	9.2

Note: AV, average vulnerability; CP, chronic poor; HVC, high variability of
consumption; LLC, low level of consumption; TP, transient poor; TVG, total
vulnerable group.
Source: See Table 3.1

a well-known fact that the bulk of the poor in Indonesia are
in the agricultural sector. Both before and after the crisis, the
poverty rate and the proportion of the total vulnerable group in

the agricultural sector were much higher than in other sectors. Furthermore, as Table 3.6 shows, not only was the poverty rate in the agricultural sector much higher than the rate in other sectors but also the agricultural sector had a much higher proportion of the chronic poor than other sectors.

Before the crisis the agricultural sector had much higher proportions of both transient and chronic poor than other sectors of the economy. As a result of the crisis, the chronic poor in the agricultural sector jumped from 7.1 per cent in 1996 to 18.7 per cent in 1999, representing an increase of 11.6 percentage points or almost a 163 per cent proportional increase from the original rate. Interestingly, the crisis increased the proportion of transient poor in this sector by less than 3 percentage points, from 19.1 per cent in 1996 to 21.7 per cent in 1999. As a result, the proportion of the transient poor in the agricultural sector after the crisis was only slightly higher than in other sectors.

In all sectors the transient poor made up the majority of those in the poor category. This was true even though proportionally the increase among the chronic poor was much higher than among the transient poor. This is because the incidence of chronic poverty in most sectors prior to the crisis was very small. In the industrial sector, for example, although the chronic poor jumped more than fivefold from 1.3 per cent in 1996 to 6.8 per cent in 1999, the transient poor still made up the majority of the poor, even though they only increased by 72 per cent (from 10 per cent in 1996 to 17.2 per cent in 1999).

Similarly, the proportion in the high vulnerability group increased significantly across all sectors. As a result, the total vulnerable group as a proportion of the entire population also rose significantly across all sectors. The agricultural sector continued to have the highest proportion of the vulnerable population during the whole period. After the crisis, the total vulnerable group in the agricultural sector constituted more than half of the population in this sector. This is a much higher rate than in any other sector. The second highest rate was found in the industrial sector, where less than 30 per cent of the population was considered vulnerable to poverty. Meanwhile, the trade and services sectors and those receiving transfers had a much lower rate at approximately 20 per cent.

4.5 The Poor and the Vulnerable across Educational Levels

Education is a determinant of poverty because people with a higher level of educational attainment have a greater chance of obtaining better jobs with higher wages. Furthermore, if people acquire skills through education, a higher level of educational attainment is associated with higher marginal productivity of labour. Hence, it is expected that education is negatively correlated with poverty (that is, the higher the level of education, the lower the poverty rate).[7] Table 3.7 shows the distribution of population by poverty categories across the educational levels of household heads before and after the crisis.

Table 3.7 indicates that, for those households whose head was educated at the tertiary level, the crisis seems to have had no impact on their poverty incidence. The headcount poverty rate for this group of the population was constant at less than 2 per cent. This by no means implies that the crisis had no negative effect on their welfare. It is likely that the crisis reduced their welfare levels, as it had for most of the population, but their reduced welfare levels were still above the poverty line, so they recorded no apparent changes in their headcount poverty rate. In addition, both before and after the crisis, the poor among this group were mostly the transient poor and only a very small proportion among them was in the chronically poor category.

The crisis, however, had a very pronounced impact on the poverty rates of those households headed by individuals with less than a tertiary education. Even among those with an upper

TABLE 3.7
Poverty Categories by Educational Level of Household Heads,
1996 and 1999 (%)

Educational level	Poor			High Vulnerability Group			TVG	AV
	TP	CP	Total	LLC	HVC	Total		
1996								
Primary incomplete	18.4	6.3	24.7	9.5	4.5	13.9	30.1	26.0
Primary	13.1	1.9	15.1	2.8	1.2	4.0	16.6	15.8
Lower secondary	6.4	1.0	7.3	1.1	0.5	1.6	7.7	7.5
Upper secondary	2.6	0.3	2.9	0.5	0.1	0.6	2.2	3.8
Tertiary	1.8	0.1	1.9	0.2	0.1	0.3	2.0	2.7
1999								
Primary incomplete	21.7	19.0	40.6	26.3	8.4	34.8	52.2	40.1
Primary	22.5	7.6	30.1	10.9	5.6	16.4	35.8	29.4
Lower secondary	14.0	2.8	16.8	4.2	1.4	5.6	18.9	17.2
Upper secondary	8.0	0.6	8.6	1.2	0.4	1.6	9.4	9.0
Tertiary	1.7	0.2	1.9	0.8	0.1	0.9	2.6	3.2
Change								
Primary incomplete	3.3	12.6	15.9	16.9	4.0	20.9	22.0	14.0
Primary	9.4	5.7	15.0	8.0	4.4	12.4	19.3	13.6
Lower secondary	7.6	1.8	9.5	3.1	0.9	4.0	11.2	9.7
Upper secondary	5.4	0.2	5.7	0.7	0.3	1.0	6.2	5.2
Tertiary	0.1	0.1	0.0	0.6	0.0	0.6	0.6	0.4

Note: AV, average vulnerability; CP, chronic poor; HVC, high variability of consumption; LLC, low level of consumption; TP, transient poor; TVG, total vulnerable group.
Source: See Table 3.1

secondary education, the headcount poverty incidence jumped almost threefold from 2.9 per cent in 1996 to 8.6 per cent in 1999. Among the least educated, that is, those who had not completed primary education, the poverty rate increased very significantly from 24.7 per cent to 40.6 per cent over the same period.

Furthermore, among this least-educated group the increase in poverty incidence occurred mostly among the chronically poor, jumping more than threefold from 6.3 per cent to 19 per cent during the period, while the incidence of transient poverty increased only slightly from 18.4 per cent to 21.7 per cent. As a result, while before the crisis the extent of chronic poverty was only one-quarter of the total poor, after the crisis the chronically poor made up almost half of the poor in this group. At other levels of education, the incidence of chronic poverty also increased very significantly. Nevertheless, the proportion of the transient poor was still much higher than that of the chronic poor.

4.6 The Poor and the Vulnerable across Gender

In qualitative and participatory poverty assessments, female-headed households are often identified as the poorest of the poor (Dreze and Srinivasan 1997). Table 3.8 shows the distribution of population by poverty categories as differentiated by the gender of the head of the household. It reveals that the poverty rate among those households headed by females did not differ widely from the poverty rate among male-headed households. In fact, the poverty rate of male-headed households tended to be slightly higher than that of female-headed households, particularly after the crisis.

Furthermore, while the proportions of transient poor were almost equal between male-headed and female-headed households, the proportion of chronic poor was slightly higher for male-headed households. Similarly, male-headed households tended to have a slightly higher proportion of the high vulnerability group than female-headed households. As a result, the total vulnerable group among male-headed households also tended to be slightly higher than among female-headed households. Hence the results of the present study do not support the view that female-headed households are the poorest of the poor.[8]

TABLE 3.8
Poverty Categories by Gender of Household Heads,
1996 and 1999 (%)

Gender	Poor			High Vulnerability Group			TVG	AV
	TP	CP	Total	LLC	HVC	Total		
1996								
Male	12.4	3.3	15.7	4.9	2.2	7.1	18.4	16.6
Female	12.4	2.6	15.1	3.8	2.1	5.9	17.1	15.8
1999								
Male	17.9	9.6	27.6	13.6	5.0	18.6	33.9	27.3
Female	17.6	8.2	25.8	11.9	4.9	16.7	31.9	25.7
Change								
Male	5.5	6.3	11.9	8.7	2.8	11.5	15.4	10.7
Female	5.2	5.6	10.7	8.1	2.8	10.9	14.7	9.9

Note: TP = Transient Poor, CP = Chronic Poor, LLC = Low Level of Consumption,
HVC = High Variability of Consumption, TVG = Total Vulnerable Group,
AV = Average Vulnerability
Source: See Table 3.1

5 CONCLUSION

It is well known that the Indonesian economic crisis caused the country's poverty rate to increase very significantly. The findings of the present study indicate that not only did the poverty rate increase significantly but much of this was due to the increase in the chronic poor category (that is, the poor whose expected consumption is below the poverty line and who will most likely stay poor in the near future). As a result, the chronic poor, who made up only 20 per cent of the total poor before the crisis, constituted 35 per cent of the total poor in 1999.

The present study also finds that vulnerability to poverty among Indonesian households after the crisis unambiguously increased from the pre-crisis level. The average vulnerability to poverty (the probability that a person will be poor in the near future) increased very significantly from 16.6 per cent in 1996 to 27.2 per cent in 1999. Similarly, the proportion of the high vulnerability group (those with a >50 per cent vulnerability to poverty) jumped from 7 per cent before the crisis to 18.4 per cent after the crisis. As a result, the proportion of the total vulnerable group (the currently poor and the highly vulnerable non-poor) in the population almost doubled from 18 per cent before the crisis to 34 per cent after the crisis.

Currently, the quantitative method for estimating vulnerability to poverty is still in its infancy. Nevertheless, most of the early studies in this field, including the present study, agree that the vulnerable population is a significantly greater number than the currently poor. For example, nine-year panel research of households in South Indian villages indicated that 20 per cent of households were poor all the time and 12 per cent were never poor, while the vast majority moved in and out of poverty over time (Gaiha and Deolalikar 1993). Six-year panel research on households in rural China showed that only 6.2 per cent of households were always poor and that a cross section in any given year would find <20 per cent poverty, while 54 per cent of the sample experienced at least one episode of poverty (Jalan and Ravallion 2000). A summary of research using panel data finds that the fraction of households that have experienced an episode of poverty is, at times, much larger than either those who were never poor or those who were persistently poor (Baulch and Hoddinott 2000).

In the context of Indonesia, Pritchett et al. (2000) estimate that post-crisis vulnerability to poverty ranges relatively widely from 30 per cent to 50 per cent of the population. It is important to note that they use different methods and data types (panel versus cross-section) from those used in the present study. Nevertheless, it can be noted that the estimate of the present study is closer to the lower bound of their range.

Notes

Reprinted from Asep Suryahadi and Sudarno Sumarto, "Poverty and Vulnerability in Indonesia Before and After the Economic Crisis", *Asian Economic Journal* 17, no. 1 (2003): 45–64, with permission from Wiley-Blackwell.

1. Pritchett et al. (2000) argue that this midway cutting point has three attractive features. First, this is the point where the expected consumption coincides with the poverty line. Second, it seems intuitive to say that a household is vulnerable if it faces as least 50 per cent probability of falling into poverty. Third, if a household is just at the poverty line and faces a mean zero shock, then this household has one period ahead vulnerability of 0.5. This implies that, in the limit, as the time horizon goes to zero, then being "in current poverty" and being "currently vulnerable to poverty" coincide.

2. Since vulnerability to poverty is a measure of the probability of being poor, the current poor are obviously a part of the vulnerable group. As argued by Glewwe and Hall (1998) and Cunningham and Maloney (2000), what is necessary to categorize a household as vulnerable is some combination of both the probability of bad outcomes as well as some measure of their "badness" as given by a social welfare function.

3. For details of SUSENAS, see note 5 in Chapter 2

4. For details of PODES, see note 6 in Chapter 2.

5. These headcount poverty rates differ slightly from those reported in Pradhan et al. (2000), that is, 15.7 per cent in 1996 and 27.1 per cent in 1999. The differences arise because some observations were lost in the merging of the SUSENAS and PODES datasets.

6. Using two panel datasets, Pritchett et al. (2000) estimate that the proportion of households that were vulnerable to poverty in Indonesia in 1997–1999 was between 30 and 50 per cent. However, they use a different approach in defining vulnerable households. They define a household as vulnerable if it has 50 per cent or higher probability of at least one fall below the poverty line from three annual shocks.

7. In a society where education is not freely available, however, the poverty status of parents may determine an individual's educational attainment.

8. Similarly, Dreze and Srinivasan (1997) find that in India there is no evidence that female-headed households are poorer than male-headed households, while Glewwe and Hall (1998) find that in Peru female-headed households are no more vulnerable than male-headed households.

Chapter 4

SHORT-TERM POVERTY DYNAMICS IN RURAL INDONESIA DURING THE ECONOMIC CRISIS

Asep Suryahadi, Wenefrida Widyanti,
and Sudarno Sumarto

1 INTRODUCTION

During the economic crisis in Indonesia, the headcount rate on poverty changed relatively quickly over short periods of time. Poverty increased rapidly when the crisis worsened and, likewise, decreased rapidly when the economy stabilized. This implies that large numbers of households were moving in and out of poverty relatively frequently. It also implies that a significant number of households experienced relatively short periods of poverty, that is, just a fraction of a year.

Generally, the movement of households in and out of poverty is assessed on a yearly basis (for example, Bane and Ellwood 1983; Baulch and Hoddinott 2000; Jalan and Ravallion 1999a, 2000). These studies utilize panel data of households with a year as the basic time unit. According to these data, a household deemed not poor in two consecutive surveys will be considered as having never been poor during the whole period between the two surveys. In reality, however, the household could have experienced a period of poverty in between the two surveys. Such a situation could occur, for example, if each year the survey was conducted in the harvest season, a period when rural households are generally better off.

To understand the short-term dynamics of poverty, it is necessary to have panel data that rely upon a time unit that is less than a year. Muller (1997), for example, uses quarterly panel data in a one-year period between 1982 and 1983 to estimate the transient seasonal and chronic poverty of peasants in rural Rwanda. He finds that the worst poverty occurs after the dry season at the end of the year. Severe poverty is generally the result of a seasonal, transient component of annual poverty, where the seasonal component of the incidence of poverty is much smaller. Hence he concludes that the actual differences in the severity of poverty, either between developing and developed countries or between rural and urban areas in developing countries, may be much worse than shown by the usual chronic annual poverty measures or by measures of the seasonal incidence of poverty.

Similarly, Dercon and Krishnan (2000) use a panel data set of households in rural Ethiopia that were visited three times over an eighteen-month period. Their results show that, although on average year-to-year poverty is quite stable, there is high variability between consumption and poverty when measured across the seasons and year by year. They also found that consumption is affected by idiosyncratic and common shocks, including variability in rainfall and household-specific crop failure. In addition, households respond to seasonal incentives related to changing labour demand and prices. They conclude that greater numbers of households are vulnerable to shocks than proposed by standard poverty statistics. Some of the non-poor included in these statistics are otherwise poor households temporarily boosting their rates of consumption as an optimal response to changing seasonal incentives.

A similar data set from Indonesia is used in the present study. A panel of 10,640 households in rural areas was interviewed four times during a fourteen-month period from August 1998 to October 1999. The details of the data are discussed in the next section, which also explains how the poverty lines used in this study were estimated. Section 3 discusses the dynamics of poverty among households in the sample, while Section 4 provides conclusions.

2 DATA AND CONSTRUCTION OF THE POVERTY LINE

2.1 Data

The data used in the present study are derived from the 100 Village Survey.[1] This survey was originally meant to identify village-level variables that were closely correlated with characteristics of the poor, so that it could be used as a tool to test whether the much larger National Socio-Economic Survey (SUSENAS)[2] was appropriate as a basis for calculating the poverty rate in Indonesia.

During the first year of the economic crisis, there was a lack of data on its social impact. In order to overcome this problem, four rounds of the 100 Village Survey were implemented in the course of fourteen months, respectively in August 1998, December 1999, May 1999, and October 1999.[3] It was intended that the sample households would remain the same for all four rounds of the survey, but some replacements were made due to various unavoidable factors. In the end 10,640 households were visited in all four rounds of the survey and a complete panel data set was made.

While the 100 Village Survey sample was relatively large, it was not designed as a statistical representation of the country overall. The survey areas, however, had been chosen in 1994, based on a sampling approach that aimed to include a range of villages that were "representative" of various parts of the rural economy. Hence, there is no reason to suspect that these samples were influenced by the crisis. Furthermore, as the intention of this survey was to focus on rural and relatively poor areas, it is not representative of all social strata within the country. This necessarily means that the conclusions from this study can be applied only to this sample.

2.2 Construction of the Poverty Line

To obtain a consistent picture of household welfare during the four rounds of the survey, it was necessary to estimate poverty lines that would be comparable across regions as well as through time. These poverty lines, however, cannot be directly estimated from the 100 Village Survey data, which contain only information on the values of household consumption and not the quantities and prices of the household consumption items.[4] The poverty line estimates therefore have to be based on information from other sources.

This poverty-line estimation procedure is illustrated in Table 4.A1 in the Appendix. The second column of the table shows the February 1999 provincial poverty rates, which were estimated by Pradhan et al. (2001). These rates were calculated based on a single, national food poverty basket and hence represent welfare levels comparable across regions. The poverty lines calculated by Pradhan et al. (2001), however, cannot be applied directly in this study because they were calculated using the SUSENAS Consumption Module data, while the 100 Village Survey questionnaire was based on the SUSENAS Core questionnaire. Hence, in the third column the provincial poverty lines that correspond to the poverty rates in the second column have been estimated using the February 1999 SUSENAS Core data.

Using deflators based on the re-weighted provincial Consumer Price Index (CPI), the fourth to seventh columns in Table 4.A1 calculate the provincial poverty lines for each period during the four rounds of the survey. The proportion of food in the CPI basket is only 40 per cent. This is much lower than actual consumption and certainly understates the importance of food for the poor. Hence, in the deflators used in the present study, the food share of consumption is adjusted to reflect the food share of the poverty line, which is 80 per cent.[5]

3 INCOME, CONSUMPTION, AND POVERTY DYNAMICS

3.1 Macroeconomic Background

The following provides a brief, general picture of the developments that took place in the Indonesian economy during the survey period from August 1998 to October 1999. Figure 4.A1 in the Appendix illustrates the trends in the nominal exchange rate (defined as the price of the U.S. dollar to the rupiah), Consumer Price Index (CPI), real Gross Domestic Product (GDP), real manufacturing wage, and national poverty rate during the period. The values of all these indicators in August 1998 are normalized to a 100-point scale.

The macroeconomic indicators give some signs of stabilization during the period, particularly if contrasted with the very significant economic deterioration that occurred between mid-1997 and the second half of 1998. The exchange rate still showed relatively large fluctuations, but there was a clear tendency for the rupiah to appreciate during this period. The value of the rupiah in August 1998 was around Rp 11,000 per U.S. dollar, strengthening to around Rp 6,900 per U.S. dollar by October 1999. This should be contrasted with the large depreciation in the value of the rupiah in the previous period, when its value dropped sharply from around Rp 2,500 per U.S. dollar in June 1997 to around Rp 15,000 per U.S. dollar in June 1998. Similarly, domestic prices stabilized as indicated by the relatively flat CPI graphics, with an inflation rate of only around five per cent between August 1998 and October 1999. In contrast, inflation was approximately 78 per cent between August 1997 and August 1998.

This stabilization, however, had yet to result in the return of economic growth. The graphics of real GDP during the third quarter of 1998 right through until the third quarter of 1999 remained very flat, reflecting near zero economic growth. These results, however, are much improved compared to the more than 13 per cent economic contraction in the previous one-year period (Cameron 1999). Similarly, real wages had yet to recover from a one-third drop between August 1997 and August 1998 (Feridhanusetyawan 1999; Manning 2000). The figure shows, however, that during 1999 real wages had started to grow again. In line with this, starting in early 1999, the national poverty rate showed a declining trend again.

During the crisis the poverty rate increased fast. An estimate indicates that the national poverty rate rose from 15.7 per cent in February 1996 to 27.1 per cent in February 1999 (Pradhan et al. 2001). During this period the number of urban poor doubled, while the rural poor increased by 75 per cent. Another study that tracks down the poverty rate over the course of the crisis shows that the poverty rate increased by 164 per cent from the onset of the crisis in mid-1997 to the peak of the crisis around the second half of 1998 (Suryahadi et al. 2000).

3.2 Changes in Income, Consumption and Poverty

In line with improving macroeconomic stability during this period, there were also indications to suggest that the economic conditions of the households in the sample had improved. There were, however, also apparent fluctuations in welfare indicators during the period. Table 4.1 shows the changes in real per capita income, real per capita consumption, and the headcount poverty rate of the sample in the four rounds of the survey.

TABLE 4.1
Income, Consumption, and Poverty

	August 1998	*December 1998*	*May 1999*	*October 1999*
Real per capita income				
• Mean (Rp/month)	100,457	118,846	117,581	127,421
• Change over the previous period (%)	...	18.3	–1.1	8.4
Real per capita consumption				
• Mean (Rp/month)	85,003	88,074	89,463	93,082
• Change over the previous period (%)	...	3.6	1.2	4.0
Poverty				
• Headcount index (%)	43.0	36.2	36.5	31.0
• Percentage point change over the previous period	...	–6.8	0.3	–5.5

Source: 100 Village Survey

Table 4.1 indicates that there was a clear pattern, suggesting that most of the improvements took place in the period between August and December 1998, where average real per capita income increased by 18.3 per cent, average real per capita consumption grew by 3.6 per cent, and the headcount index of poverty fell by 6.8 percentage points. Between December 1998 and May 1999, however, there was stagnation in the average economic conditions of the sample. None of the three indicators changed significantly during this period. There were, however, some signs that the economic conditions of the sample improved again during the period between May and October 1999. During this period, average real per capita income grew by 8.4 per cent, average real per capita consumption increased by 4.0 per cent, and the headcount index of poverty fell by 5.5 percentage points.

TABLE 4.2
Income and Consumption Quintile Transition Matrices
(Row Percentages)

Per Capita Real Consumption							Per Capita Real Income					
		December 1998							December 1998			
		1	2	3	4	5			1	2	3	4	5
August 1998	1	49.67	26.53	14.34	6.80	2.67	August 1998	1	43.63	27.94	15.17	8.13	5.12
	2	28.97	30.45	23.11	12.37	5.10		2	27.80	28.56	22.09	15.20	6.34
	3	14.04	23.86	28.14	23.84	10.12		3	17.01	23.36	28.20	21.02	10.41
	4	6.59	14.51	23.27	32.36	23.27		4	7.07	14.52	22.59	31.59	24.24
	5	2.16	5.53	11.24	23.90	57.16		5	5.45	6.43	12.15	23.46	52.51

		May 1999							May 1999			
		1	2	3	4	5			1	2	3	4	5
December 1998	1	53.18	27.29	12.62	5.45	1.46	December 1998	1	49.23	27.32	12.96	7.05	3.45
	2	25.69	32.34	23.39	14.27	4.31		2	27.30	31.90	22.65	12.74	5.40
	3	13.79	24.77	30.96	23.11	7.38		3	13.59	22.19	30.26	24.49	9.47
	4	6.10	11.58	23.86	34.16	24.30		4	7.83	13.36	22.61	33.03	23.17
	5	2.47	4.94	9.42	22.40	60.78		5	3.04	6.01	11.64	22.08	57.23

		October 1999							October 1999			
		1	2	3	4	5			1	2	3	4	5
May 1999	1	57.84	23.97	9.73	6.16	2.31	May 1999	1	53.87	25.62	12.08	6.29	2.14
	2	24.28	35.08	24.46	12.30	3.88		2	25.84	32.95	24.84	12.08	4.29
	3	11.74	24.14	32.92	22.76	8.45		3	12.54	23.78	31.10	23.39	9.19
	4	5.20	12.56	23.58	35.14	23.51		4	5.97	12.29	23.14	35.99	22.61
	5	2.28	5.05	9.80	22.97	59.90		5	2.79	6.21	9.00	21.82	60.18

Note: The shaded diagonal cells represent the percentage of the sample households in each quintile in the initial period that did not experience a change in their respective quintile positions in the successive period.

Source: See Table 4.1

The changes that occurred at the household level turned out to be greater than what the aggregate figures indicate. Table 4.2 shows the transition matrices of the position of households in the quintiles of real per capita income and real per capita consumption between two consecutive survey periods.[6] In the matrices, the cells in the diagonal positions are shaded. These diagonal cells represent the percentage of the sample in each quintile during the initial period that did not experience a change in their respective quintile positions in the successive period.

As expected, all the transition matrices indicate that the income and consumption quintile positions of a large majority of households did change across survey rounds, particularly those in the second, third, and fourth quintiles. On the other hand, the majority of households in both the poorest and the richest quintiles in general did not experience a change in their quintile positions. This implies that most of the fluctuations in the relative position of households in regard to both income and consumption distributions took place among households in the middle of the distributions.

The poorest quintile consisted mostly of landless agricultural labourers and petty traders. In general, they were negatively impacted by the crisis, so it is not surprising that a majority of them remained in this bottom quintile. The richest quintile, that is, the best-off segment of the society, was also badly hurt by the crisis. It seems, however, that although most of these households suffered a setback in their welfare level, most of them were still relatively better off than most of the people. The middle quintiles, meanwhile, were made up of two distinct groups. The first group, which comprises those who were hurt by the crisis, consisted mostly of fixed-income public and private wage employees and the self-employed in the industrial and services sectors. The second group, on the other hand, consisted of those households that benefited from the crisis. These households were mostly producers of food (mainly rice) and cash crops for export, whose prices in rupiah increased after the large devaluation. This explains why churning occurred predominantly in the middle quintiles.[7]

3.3 The Pattern of Change in Poverty Status

The changes in real income and consumption of households were reflected in the changes in their poverty status across survey rounds, shown in Table 4.3. The table indicates that those who were always poor throughout the whole period make up only 18 per cent of the total sample. Meanwhile, those who were never poor during the whole fourteen-month period make up 42 per cent of the sample. The remaining 40 per cent of the sample experienced a mix of times when they were not poor and other times when they were poor. Throughout the four periods in which they were interviewed, 16 per cent were found to be poor once, 12 per cent were poor twice, and 12 per cent were poor three times.

Of the 16 per cent that experienced poverty once, around half were poor during the first period and then non-poor afterwards. In fact, approximately 85 per cent of this sample group was categorized as non-poor in the last period. Of the 12 per cent who were poor twice, approximately two-thirds were categorized as non-poor in the last period. Meanwhile, among those who were poor three times, approximately one-third had been poor throughout the first three periods but were found to be non-poor in the last period. This is the group of households that experienced improvements in welfare during the period. Meanwhile, around 4 per cent of the sample experienced continuing changes in status between poor and non-poor during the whole period. It is this bracket of the population whose welfare is the most volatile.

Table 4.4 provides a summary of the changes in poverty status of households in the sample. It calculates the proportion of households that experienced a change in poverty status from the previous period, that is, they either fell into poverty or moved out of poverty. The table indicates that there is a negative correlation between the two opposing poverty movements. As can be seen from the table, when the proportion of households that fell into poverty increased in a period, the proportion of households that moved out of poverty in the same period decreased and vice versa.

TABLE 4.3
The Pattern of Changes in Household Poverty Status

Pattern	Poverty Status				Frequency (%)
	August 1998	December 1998	May 1999	October 1999	
Always poor	Poor	Poor	Poor	Poor	17.5
Three times poor (12.0%)	Poor	Poor	Poor	Non-poor	4.6
	Poor	Poor	Non-poor	Poor	2.0
	Poor	Non-poor	Poor	Poor	2.9
	Non-poor	Poor	Poor	Poor	2.5
Twice poor (12.4%)	Poor	Poor	Non-poor	Non-poor	3.7
	Poor	Non-poor	Poor	Non-poor	3.0
	Poor	Non-poor	Non-poor	Poor	1.4
	Non-poor	Poor	Poor	Non-poor	1.7
	Non-poor	Poor	Non-poor	Poor	1.0
	Non-poor	Non-poor	Poor	Poor	1.6
Once poor (15.9%)	Poor	Non-poor	Non-poor	Non-poor	7.9
	Non-poor	Poor	Non-poor	Non-poor	3.2
	Non-poor	Non-poor	Poor	Non-poor	2.7
	Non-poor	Non-poor	Non-poor	Poor	2.1
Never poor	Non-poor	Non-poor	Non-poor	Non-poor	42.2

Source: See Table 4.1

TABLE 4.4
Poverty Movements (%)

Period	Fall into Poverty	Move out of Poverty	Total Change in Status	Net Change in Poverty	Poverty Rate
August 1998	–	...	...	...	43.0
December 1998	9.0	14.3	23.3	–6.8	36.2
May 1999	10.7	9.5	20.2	0.3	36.5
October 1999	6.7	11.6	18.3	–5.5	31.0

Source: See Table 4.1

Table 4.4 also shows that the total number of households that experienced a change in poverty status was always substantial. Throughout each period, between 18 and 23 per cent of households either fell in status from non-poor to poor or escaped their status as poor to become non-poor. The total proportion of households that experienced a change in poverty status was much larger than implied by the changes in the poverty rate. The change in poverty rate constitutes the difference between the proportion of households that fall into poverty and those that move out of poverty. For example, between December 1998 and May 1999 the poverty rate changed only very slightly from 36.2 to 36.5 per cent, implying a relatively stable poverty rate, but in fact 20 per cent of households either fell into poverty or moved out of poverty during this period. Hence, looking at the changes in total poverty rates alone could result in a misleading impression of actual household poverty dynamics.

Table 4.3 above indicates that 18 per cent of individuals in the sample were always poor during the whole period and 42 per cent were never poor, while the remaining 40 per cent experienced some change in their poverty status. Jalan and Ravallion (2000) classify those who were always poor as the "persistently poor", while those who were sometimes poor are classified into two categories. The first category is the "chronically poor", that is, those who were sometimes poor and whose mean real per capita consumption over the whole period was below the poverty line. The second category is the "transiently poor", that is, those who were sometimes poor but whose mean real per capita consumption over time was higher than the poverty line. Using these concepts, Table 4.5 shows the distribution of the household sample across these poverty categories. It also shows the mean and standard deviation of the ratio of their mean real per capita consumption to the poverty line.

Table 4.5 reveals that, in addition to the 18 per cent persistently poor and the 42 per cent never poor, the sample had 16 per cent chronically poor households and 25 per cent transiently poor households. This means that around one-third of the sample households had mean real per capita consumption below the poverty line.[8] The table also shows that, on average, the persistently poor have mean real per capita consumption rates over time of approximately 30 per cent below the poverty line, while for the chronically poor the rate is around 10 per cent below the poverty line. Meanwhile, the transiently poor

TABLE 4.5
Poverty Categories

Poverty Category	Incidence (%)	Ratio of Mean Real per Capita Consumption to Poverty Line	
		Mean	Std. dev.
Persistently poor	17.5	0.7	0.1
Chronically poor	15.5	0.9	0.1
Transiently poor	24.8	1.2	0.2
Never poor	42.2	1.9	0.7

Source: See Table 4.1

have mean real per capita consumption that is actually not very close to the poverty line — around 20 per cent above the poverty line. Finally, those who were never poor have mean per capita consumption that is around 90 per cent higher than the poverty line. This indicates that to be invulnerable to poverty, households need to have mean real per capita consumption over time that is substantially higher than the poverty line.

4 CONCLUSIONS

During the economic crisis, the headcount poverty rate in Indonesia changed relatively quickly in short periods of time, increasing rapidly when the crisis worsened and decreasing quickly when the economy stabilized. This implies that a large number of households moved in and out of poverty relatively frequently and hence a large number of households experienced relatively short periods of poverty.

The present study has utilized a panel data set of 10,640 rural households that were visited four times in a fourteen-month period from August 1998 to October 1999. During this period the Indonesian macroeconomic indicators had stabilized after a period of turbulence during the peak of the crisis. In line with the improving macroeconomic stability during the period, there were also indications to suggest that the economic conditions of the households in the sample on average had improved.

The study finds, however, that the changes that took place at the household level were actually greater than indicated by the aggregate figures. The changes in the real incomes and consumption of households were translated into changes in their poverty status. Around 40 per cent of the sample experienced a combination of being non-poor and poor during the period of study. In the four rounds of the survey, 16 per cent of the sample were found to be poor once, 12 per cent were poor twice, and 12 per cent were poor three times. Meanwhile, 42 per cent of the sample households were never poor and 18 per cent were always poor during the whole fourteen-month period.

During a certain period, the proportion of households that fell into poverty was negatively correlated with the proportion of households that moved out of poverty. The total number of households that experienced a change in their poverty status, however, was always found to be substantial and much larger than the implied changes in the poverty rate. Hence, looking at the changes in the total poverty rate alone could give a misleading impression of the actual poverty dynamics of households. The analysis also shows that in order to be invulnerable to poverty, households need to have mean real per capita consumption over time that is substantially higher than the poverty line.

APPENDIX FIGURE 4.A1

Selected Macroeconomic Indicators, August 1998 – November 1999

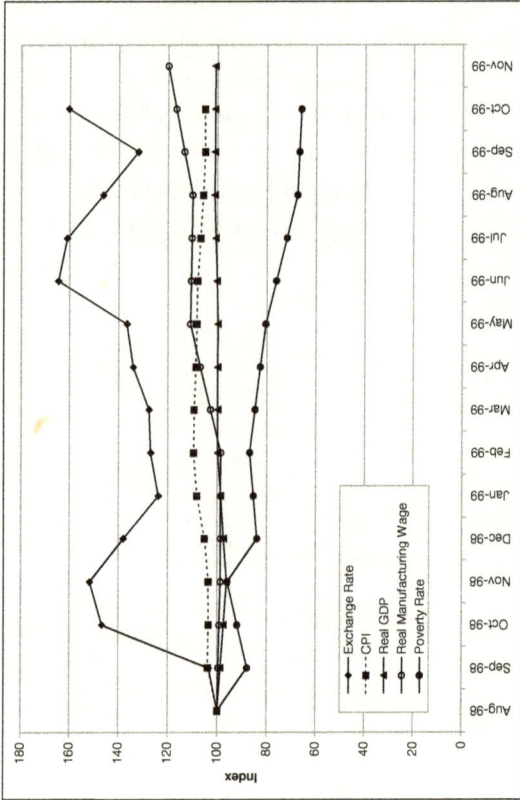

Source: Statistics Indonesia (BPS)

APPENDIX TABLE 4.A1
Poverty Lines for Selected Provinces

Province	February 1999		Poverty Line for the Sample (Rp/month)[C]			
	Poverty Rate (%)[A]	Poverty Line[B]	Aug. 1998	Dec. 1998	May 1999	Oct. 1999
Riau	9.21	73,515	64,741	68,977	72,002	68,372
Lampung	36.80	74,425	63,018	66,155	71,003	63,874
West Java	26.60	82,025	73,924	78,312	78,987	73,586
Central Java	32.78	72,508	62,517	67,655	69,083	62,517
Bali	13.62	86,357	72,686	79,688	84,690	74,687
East Nusa Tenggara	61.18	73,402	56,386	68,064	75,738	73,736
East Kalimantan	21.67	85,717	76,273	79,905	81,358	76,273
Southeast Sulawesi	36.61	71,218	59,212	67,944	72,310	66,580

Notes:
A is from Pradhan et al. (2001).
B is estimated using SUSENAS Core based on A.
C is deflated from B using re-weighted CPI.
Source: susenas 1999, Pradhan et al. (2001)

Notes

Reprinted from Sudarno Sumartio, Asep Suryahadi and Wenefrida Widyanti, "Short-term Poverty Dynamics in Rural Indonesia during the Economic Crisis", *Journal of International Development*, Vol. 15, no. 2 (2003): 133–144, with permission from The Blackwell Publishing House.

1 For details of the 100 Village Survey, see Chapter 2.
2 For details of SUSENAS, see Chapter 2.
3 A study of the social impact of the crisis was done by Skoufias et al. (2000) based on the results of the May 1997 and August 1998 rounds.
4 In Indonesia the poverty line is constructed based on food consumption that produces 2,100 calories per capita per day plus non-food consumption that is deemed essential. This requires information on the quantities consumed. The price information, meanwhile, is required to put values to the poverty basket calculated.
5 For a more detailed discussion of this point, see Chapter 2.
6 The quintiles are calculated at the district level.
7 For discussions of who were hurt and who benefited, see Frankenberg et al. (1999), Skoufias et al. (2000), and Wetterberg et al. (1999).
8 This is the sum of the persistently poor and the chronically poor.

Chapter 5

THE EVOLUTION OF POVERTY DURING THE CRISIS IN INDONESIA

Asep Suryahadi, Sudarno Sumarto, and Lant Pritchett

1 INTRODUCTION

The present study is an attempt to piece together a consistent series of data from various sources on the headcount measure of absolute consumption expenditure poverty during the crisis.[1] There are many broad issues in defining poverty, which is intrinsically a complex social construct. Even within a narrow definition of poverty based on a deficit of consumption expenditures, there are numerous thorny technical issues in setting an appropriate poverty line (Pradhan et al. 2001; Ravallion 1994; Sen 1981). This study avoids those issues and is limited to examining how poverty, defined on a consistent, welfare-comparable basis, changed in Indonesia over the course of the series of crises after the middle of 1997. We use a variety of data sets as well as various studies to put together a consistent series of the evolution of poverty over a six-year period from February 1996 to February 2002.

As the issues surrounding poverty measurements are complex, we begin with two basic issues. The first is the deflation of nominal to real expenditures to maintain comparability in welfare levels, while the second is the responsiveness of poverty rates to changes in real expenditures. With these basics in hand, we can estimate changes in headcount poverty rates over time, using a range of price deflators. Based on the outlined methods, we create a consistent set of estimates of poverty over the course of the crisis based on various data sets and studies that are available.

2 DEFINING REAL EXPENDITURES

The deflation of nominal to real expenditures is central to a "welfare-comparable" basis for comparisons of poverty over time. For any given distribution of expenditures across households, the determinant of the poverty rate is the poverty line. The poverty line is expressed in rupiah terms and is simply the amount of expenditure above which households are considered not poor and below which households are in (varying degrees of) poverty.

A fruitful way of thinking about deflation of the poverty line in nominal rupiah, so that it represents "the same" amount of "real" rupiah in another period, is to use the standard microeconomic theory of consumer choice with individual welfare maximization. The consumer choice problem is to choose a consumption basket for a given expenditure budget and prices so as to maximize their utility (Varian 1992, Chapter 7). This of course assumes for simplicity's sake that consumers do not save.

For any given preference mapping, the solution to that problem is the "indirect utility function", which gives the maximum level of utility achievable for given prices and expenditures. The "dual" of this maximization problem for the consumer is to choose a consumption basket that minimizes the expenditures necessary to achieve any given level of utility. The outcome of this problem is the "expenditure function", that is, the minimum level of expenditures necessary to achieve any fixed standard of living (level of utility):

$$e(p, U^0) = \min_x p'x, \text{ subject to } U(x) = U^0 \tag{5.1}$$

where p and x are N by 1 vectors of prices and quantities of commodities, e = expenditures and U = utility.

One way to conceptualize the poverty line is to choose a level of welfare below which a household is considered poor, $U^{poverty}$, and then define the poverty line as the money expenditures necessary to attain that level of welfare:

$$PL = e(p, U^{poverty}) \tag{5.2}$$

where PL is the poverty line.

The use of expenditure functions allows us to draw on a large body of consumer welfare economics in thinking about comparing poverty lines over time. Suppose that prices change from the ($N \times 1$ vector of) prices in base time t_0, p^0, to the ($N \times 1$ vector of) prices in one period ahead t_1, p^1. This shift in prices could involve changes in the level and changes in relative prices. The "exact" index of inflation in the poverty line is the amount of expenditures necessary at the new price level (p^1) to achieve the level of welfare that defined poverty at the old prices (p^0):

$$PL^1 = e(p^1, U^{poverty}) = (1 + \Pi_{PL}^{0.1})*e(p^0, U^{poverty}) = (1 + \Pi_{PL}^{0.1})*PL^0 \tag{5.3}$$

where $\Pi_{PL}^{0.1}$ is the poverty line's inflation rate between t_0 and t_1.

This "exact" inflation index is difficult to implement in practice, as the appropriate weights on the N individual prices in such an index would depend upon the underlying preferences, or empirically on the entire matrix of own- and cross-price elasticities.

Nevertheless, this approach provides a solid conceptual basis for inter-temporal comparisons: What are the money expenditures necessary to achieve the same utility level at the new prices as at the old prices?

The deflation of nominal expenditures in Indonesia over the crisis period is highly problematic because of the huge change in relative prices. If all prices had changed uniformly, then deflation would not be a serious problem as the price of any commodity (or any bundle of commodities) could be used. However, in Indonesia over this period, the relative price of food rose tremendously. Inflation in the price of food from February 1996 to February 1999 was 160 per cent, while the increase in the non-food components of the consumer price index (CPI) was much lower at 81 per cent. This means that when we deflate nominal expenditures into real expenditures, we have to be very careful in defining how "real" is calculated (Suryahadi and Sumarto 1999).

Table 5.1 illustrates this problem. Median nominal consumption expenditures increased by 110 per cent from February 1996 to February 1999. By how much did median real expenditures rise? If one made the mistake of defining real expenditures as purchasing power over non-food items only, then median real expenditures actually rose by 16.2 per cent. If, in contrast, a price deflator was defined only as purchasing power over rice, then real expenditures fell by 26 per cent. But this "rice-only" deflator is just as unrealistic as a "non-food only" deflator because all households actually consume a mix of goods.[2]

If the standard approach is used and nominal expenditures are deflated by the CPI, the implication is that real expenditures were only 1.3 per cent lower in February 1999 than in February 1996. But the share of food in the CPI basket, which is approximately 40 per cent, is much lower than in actual consumption expenditures as recorded in the SUSENAS and certainly understates the importance of food for the poor.[3]

TABLE 5.1

Sensitivity of Change in "Real" Expenditures between February 1996 and February 1999 to Deflator Used to Deflate Nominal Expenditures

Deflator	Food Share	Percentage Increase in Prices	Percentage Change in Median Real Expenditures
All non–food	0	81	16.2
CPI	0.40	113	–1.3
Mean food share of SUSENAS	0.55	124	–6.1
Household–specific deflator based on Engel's Law	0.63	131	–9.0
Food share based on actual consumption of the bottom 30 per cent of the population	0.70	136	–10.9
Fixed weights using poverty basket in 1996	0.80	144	–13.8
All food	1	160	–19.1
Rice price only	...	184	–26.0

Notes:
This table uses median expenditures, whose nominal value rose by 110 per cent (from Rp 52,123 to Rp 109,587). Mean nominal expenditures rose by less, only 96 per cent (from Rp 69,972 to Rp 137,284).

The percentage change in real expenditures (RE) does not fall one for one with a rise in inflation ($\%\Delta P = \Pi$) for a given percentage change in nominal expenditures (E). Since $\%\Delta RE = (\%\Delta E - \Pi)/(\Pi + 1)$ then:

$$\frac{\partial(\%\Delta RE)}{\partial \Pi} = \frac{(1 - \%\Delta RE)}{(\Pi + 1)^2}$$

Source: SUSENAS Consumption Module

If a price index is constructed using the CPI price series but with weights for prices based on the actual consumption basket of the poorest 30 per cent of households, then inflation in that consumption basket was 136 per cent and median real expenditures fell 10.9 per cent. This sensitivity of the measurement of real expenditure changes to deflation in the presence of large changes in relative prices particularly complicates the calculation of the poverty index because the poor have a higher share of food in the consumption basket than do the non-poor.[4]

3 SENSITIVITY OF THE POVERTY RATE TO THE POVERTY LINE

The second basic issue is how much poverty rates are "expected" to change from a given distributionally neutral change in real expenditures. Starting from a general class of decomposable poverty measures proposed by Foster et al. (1984), the formula for a poverty measure P with poverty line z, expenditures y, and poverty aversion parameter α is:

$$P(\alpha, z) = \int_0^z (z-y)/z^\alpha f(y)dy \qquad (5.4)$$

The estimate of the headcount poverty rate $P(0)$, when $\alpha = 0$, is simply the count of the number of households with expenditures below the poverty line divided by the total population. In terms of continuous distribution, this is simply the integral of the probability density function (pdf) up to the poverty line. But this integral is the cumulative distribution function (cdf), denoted $F(.)$, of expenditures:

$$P(\alpha = 0, z) = \int_0^z f(y)dy = F(z) \qquad (5.5)$$

This means that the sensitivity of the headcount poverty rate to changes in the poverty line at any given point is simply the slope of the cumulative density function, which is the value of the probability density function. This has two implications. First, this sensitivity is at a maximum at the mode of the probability density function. Second, generally the poverty rate will be more sensitive to changes in the poverty line around the mode when inequality is low, as this implies that more of the pdf is concentrated around that point and hence the steeper the slope of $F(z)$ at that point.[5] In the case of Indonesia, inequality is relatively low and the poverty line is relatively near the mode, so the sensitivity of the headcount poverty rate to the poverty line is quite high.

For a given percentage rise in the poverty line, how many percentage points does poverty change? Table 5.2 gives an illustration of the answer. Using both the 1996 and 1999 SUSENAS Consumption Module data, a poverty line is chosen that produces a 10 per cent poverty rate. We then increase these poverty lines by 5, 10, 15, 20, and 25 per cent, and calculate the respective poverty rates. Based on this, we estimate the (semi-)elasticity of the poverty rate as the percentage-point changes in the poverty rate with respect to percentage changes in the poverty line. The results are approximately 0.4, which suggests that for every one per cent fall in real expenditures, the poverty rate rises by 0.4 percentage point if the poverty rate is approximately 5 per cent. However, the sensitivity to poverty increases with the poverty line. At 25 per cent above the poverty line, a one per cent change in expenditures produces approximately 0.5–0.6 percentage-point change in poverty, as one moves into a range with higher values of the pdf (steeper cdf).

The combination of the sensitivity of measured price inflation to the changed food share, the change in real expenditures to changed inflation estimates, and the sensitivity of poverty rates to expenditure changes can give us some rough rules of thumb as

TABLE 5.2
Sensitivity of Headcount Poverty to the Poverty Line

Percentage Increase in Poverty Line Over Lowest Level	Using 1996 SUSENAS Data			Using 1999 SUSENAS Data		
	If Poverty Line is (Rp/Person/Month)	Then Headcount Poverty is (%)	Elasticity (Percentage Change in Poverty/Percentage Change in Expenditures)	If Poverty Line is (Rp/Person/Month)	Then Headcount Poverty is (%)	Elasticity (Percentage Change in Poverty/Percentage Change in Expenditures)
0	28,516	10.0[a]	...	62,877	10.0[a]	...
5	29,942	12.0	0.40	66,021	12.1	0.42
10	31,368	14.4	0.48	69,165	14.6	0.50
15	32,793	16.9	0.50	72,309	17.4	0.56
20	34,219	19.5	0.52	75,452	20.2	0.56
25	35,645	22.1	0.52	78,596	23.0	0.56

Note: [a]The starting poverty rate of 10 percent in each year is for illustrative purposes only.
Source: SUSENAS 1996, 1999

to what to expect from various food shares (ω) in price deflation embedded in the poverty calculations. The formula is:

$$\Delta Poverty(\omega) - \Delta Poverty(\omega') = (\omega - \omega')^*(\Pi_{food} - \Pi_{non\text{-}food})^*\left(\frac{\partial RE}{\partial \Pi}\right)$$
$$^*\left(\frac{\partial Poverty}{\partial RE}\Big|_{dist}\right) \qquad (5.6)$$

where RE = real expenditures.

Stated in words, the difference in the estimate of poverty between two periods from using two different weights given to food in a price deflator is the difference in the food share, times the difference in food and non-food inflation (which determines the change in measured inflation), times the extent of change in real expenditures due to a change in inflation, times the extent of change in the poverty rate for a distributionally neutral change in real expenditures.

4 METHODS FOR ESTIMATING THE CHANGE IN HEADCOUNT POVERTY

Even though we are just estimating changes in poverty, to understand the deflation of the poverty line we need to explain what the food share of the poverty basket is and how it is arrived at. In other words, we need to explain how our poverty line is set. Simply, the poverty line is set as a food poverty line (FPL) plus a non-food allowance (NFA):

$$PL = FPL + NFA \qquad (5.7)$$

The food poverty line (FPL) is defined as the level of expenditures necessary to reach a defined minimum calorie intake requirement of 8786.4 J (joules) at the consumption pattern (quantities [q] of the K commodities in the poverty basket) and prices (p over the same K commodities) of a reference group. The reference group is defined on the basis of real expenditures (e):

$$\sum_{k=1}^{K} p_k(e)^* q_k(e)^* \theta(e) \qquad (5.8)$$

where the constant θ is the ratio of 8786.4 to the actual daily calorie total of the food basket represented by q times the calorie intake per unit (J). This constant serves to scale up the quantities in the consumption basket so that caloric intake is 8786.4 J per person per day to fulfill the defined minimum calorie intake requirement:

$$\theta(e) = \frac{2,100}{\sum_{k=1}^{K} q_k(e)^* c_k} \qquad (5.9)$$

Therefore, FPL is the expenditures of those households that can just afford to attain 8786.4 J at the consumption patterns of the reference group if all their expenditures are spent on food.[6]

The non-food allowance (NFA) is set as the actual non-food expenditures of those households with total expenditures equal to the food poverty line. These non-food expenditures are derived from an Engel curve estimated using food share (ω) with natural log of ratio of expenditures to the food poverty line (FPL). Using this specification, the estimated constant of the regression is the predicted food share of those at the FPL:[7]

$$\omega_i = \varpi + \beta^* \ln\left(\frac{e_i}{FPL}\right) + \varepsilon_i \qquad (5.10)$$

Now let us assume that we have a poverty line PL^0 at the time t_0 and see how the poverty line changes between t_0 and t_1. The poverty line at t_1 is:

$$PL^1 = (1 + \Pi_{PL})*PL^0 \tag{5.11}$$

where Π_{PL} is the poverty line inflation rate. As described above, the ideal or exact inflation (Π_{PL}) rate should be chosen so that the money expenditures of the poverty line in t_1 (PL^1) at the level and pattern of prices in t_1 provide the same level of welfare as the poverty line in t_0 (PL^0). While this is impossible to implement because of the large changes in relative prices, the key issue is the weight given to food (w_F) in the poverty line's deflator:

$$\Pi_{PL} = w_F*\Pi_F + (1 - w_F)*\Pi_{NF} \tag{5.12}$$

where II F = food inflation rate and II NF = non-food inflation rate.

Using three different methods of choosing weights for food versus non-food process, we now explore possible poverty-line deflators. We are building an overall price index out of two sub-indices, one for food and one for non-food. For food prices, there are currently two choices, as a food price index can be constructed either from the underlying CPI price series or from the unit prices (values divided by quantities) reported in the SUSENAS database (for a given reference group). Either of these detailed food price series can be used to construct an inflation rate for food using expenditure shares for items within the food basket based on a sample of poor consumers.[8] For non-food prices, however, only CPI prices exist as there is no SUSENAS equivalent.

We begin by using two Laspeyres indices, with the only issue being the weight on food and non-food inflation (both from the CPI).[9] The first deflator (Method I) uses the actual expenditures of each household. This would be the natural deflator in defining household real expenditures, as it uses their actual food and non-food consumption shares. In order to do this we estimate an Engel curve:

$$\omega_i = \varpi + \beta^* \ln (e_i) + \varepsilon_i \qquad (5.13)$$

Based on the predicted values of the food share from this regression, we create a deflator for each household:

$$\Pi_i = \hat{\omega}_i^* \Pi_F + (1 - \hat{\omega}_i)^* \Pi_{NF} \qquad (5.14)$$

Using this Method I deflator for updating the poverty line, Table 5.3 shows that, if the poverty rate is set at 10 per cent in February 1996, then by February 1999 the poverty rate had increased by 53 per cent using the CPI for food and non-food inflation rates and by 69 per cent when using SUSENAS unit prices for the food inflation and the CPI for non-food inflation.[10] Obviously, this difference in the magnitude of poverty increase arises because of the differences in food price inflation in the CPI versus SUSENAS unit prices. Table 5.4 shows that in aggregate the SUSENAS food price inflation is eight percentage points higher than the CPI food price inflation. When Method I and CPI prices are used, the inflation rate is 137 per cent, whereas when the same method is used with SUSENAS prices, the inflation rate is 142 per cent, that is, a difference of five percentage points.[11]

The second method (Method II) uses the share of food in the poverty basket in base time as the weight for food in the estimate of inflation. Given the methodology used, where the non-food allowance (NFA) is the non-food expenditures of those at the food poverty line (FPL), it might be thought that the share of food in the poverty basket (FPL/PL) would be the actual food share of those at the food poverty line, or perhaps the actual share of food of those at the poverty line (PL). The share of food in the poverty basket, however, is substantially higher than both of

TABLE 5.3

Changes in Poverty Rates Using Various Food Shares and Prices (%)

Method: Share of Food in Inflation	Base Case[a]	Using Consumer Price Index		Using SUSENAS Unit Prices for Food	
	1996	1999	% Change	1999	% Change
Method I: Predicted share of food in each household's consumption expenditures	10	15.3	53	16.9	69
Method II: Using the share of food in the poverty basket	10	16.3	63	17.9	79
Method III: Using new food poverty line and recalculating non-food share[b]	10	20.3	103	22.4	124

Notes:

[a]The base case of a 10 per cent poverty rate in 1996 is for illustrative purposes only.

[b]This procedure is methodologically consistent but not welfare-consistent. "Methodologically consistent" means that the poverty basket is calculated using the same procedure each year, while "welfare-consistent" means that the individual is at the same level of utility (the same material standard of living) in the two periods. "Methodologically consistent" is not necessarily "welfare-consistent" and vice versa.

Source: SUSENAS, CPI

TABLE 5.4
Differences in Inflation Rates between the Consumer Price Index
(CPI) and SUSENAS Unit Prices (%)

	Food share	Inflation Rate (%)	
		Using Consumer Price Index	Using SUSENAS Unit Prices for Food[a]
Food		160	168
Non-food		81	81
Total:			
CPI	0.4	113	116
Method I	Actual	137	142
Method II	0.8	144	151
Method III	1.0	160	168

Note:
[a]The Statistics Indonesia food poverty basket has fifty-two commodities. The weights of each of the fifty-two commodities in the SUSENAS Unit Prices are based on their shares in the 1996 poverty line.
Sources: SUSENAS, CPI

these. Since FPL is lower than PL, those at the food poverty line are (much) poorer than those at the poverty line. As shown in Figure 5.1, the reason for this is simply that the Engel curve is non-linear. This non-linearity implies that when an NFA is added to the FPL to reach the PL, the marginal propensity to spend on food is lower than the average propensity to spend. This implies that in moving from the FPL to PL, total expenditures increase by NFA but food expenditures increase less proportionally.

Figure 5.1 shows that the food share at the food poverty line (FPL) is:

$$\omega(e = FPL) = \frac{FPL - NFA}{FPL} \tag{5.15}$$

so the non-food allowance (NFA) can be calculated as:

$$NFA = 1 - [\omega(e = FPL)]*FPL \tag{5.16}$$

FIGURE 5.1
The Engel Curve and Poverty Line

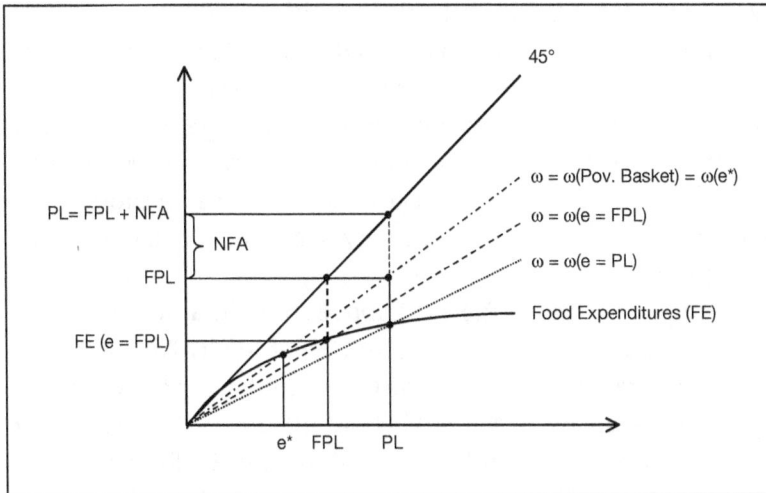

Source: Compilation by the authors

From this we can calculate that the resulting share of food expenditures in the poverty line (FPL/PL) is not the food share of those at the FPL, but equal to:

$$\frac{FPL}{PL} = \frac{FPL}{FPL + NFA} = \frac{FPL}{FPL + [1 - \omega(e=FPL)]*FPL}$$

$$= \frac{2}{2 - \omega(e=FPL)} = \omega(PB) \qquad (5.17)$$

where PB = the poverty basket.

As shown in Figure 5.1, this "food share" of the poverty line is in fact higher than the actual food share of those households at either the FPL or PL. Therefore, the fixed weights price deflator of Method II is:

$$\Pi_{PL}^{\omega(PB)} = \omega(PB)*\Pi_F + (1 - \omega(PB))*\Pi_{NF} \qquad (5.18)$$

where $\omega(PB)$ is the food share of the poverty basket or poverty line. Because rays from the origin in Figure 5.1 represent constant food shares, it can be seen that there is an expenditure level (e^*) at which the food share chosen equals the food share in the poverty basket. As $\omega(e^*)>\omega(e=FPL)>\omega(e=PL)$, this implies $e^*<FPL<PL$. This suggests that the price index using the food share of the poverty basket represents the welfare change of a very poor group. This price index will overstate the real expenditure loss of those above that level and hence will moderately overstate the change in the poverty rate.

Using this deflator, Table 5.3 above shows that if the poverty rate is set at 10 per cent in February 1996, then by February 1999 the poverty rate had increased by 63 per cent using the CPI series and 79 per cent using the SUSENAS unit prices. The reason for this difference, as shown in Table 5.4, is that the SUSENAS unit prices total inflation rate is seven percentage points higher than the CPI inflation rate.

The third possible procedure (Method III) is to inflate the food poverty line (FPL) from t_0 to t_1 by a food price index and then compute the non-food allowance (NFA) again in t_1 using the same Engel curve methodology as for t_0. This is a procedure that is methodologically consistent but not welfare-consistent as it produces, implicitly, a weight on the share of food in the inflation rate that is extremely high, that is, almost 1. The impact of this procedure, when considered as an inflation in the poverty line, is:

$$PL^1 = PL^0 * (1 + \Pi_F) * \left(\frac{2 - \omega^1_{e=FPL^1}}{2 - \omega^0_{e=FPL^0}} \right) \qquad (5.19)$$

In this method, the FPL in both periods is calculated as a proportion of the PL. If the food share is unchanged between t_0 and t_1, then the final term in the bracket is equal to 1. This will make the inflation in the poverty line the same as the food price inflation, implying that the weight of food in the deflator is 100 per cent ($\omega=1$). In fact, when the FPL in February 1996 was inflated to an FPL in February 1999 and the food share of the PL was recalculated in 1999, the food share was very nearly the same (79.42 per cent versus 80.21 per cent).[12] Therefore, this method produces a much higher inflation rate than any reasonable price deflator, as the poverty line is raised by essentially the full amount of food price inflation. Hence, Table 5.3 shows that, if this deflator is used, the poverty rate climbs by approximately 103 per cent using CPI inflation and approximately 124 per cent using SUSENAS unit prices inflation. This is an important point as it shows that the methodologically consistent procedure for fixing the non-food basket does not produce a welfare-consistent ranking.

We know from basic consumer theory that Method I, using a Laspeyres index of food and non-food inflation rates based on the actual consumption shares of each household, should overstate the welfare impact, as it does not allow for consumer response to changing relative prices by changing their consumption patterns. As is well known, the Laspeyres index will exceed the "exact" inflation rate from an expenditures function, as the increase in the amount of money expenditures needed to reach the same level of utility is lower when allowance is made for substitution across commodities (for example, buying relatively less of items whose prices have increased).

Method II, using the poverty basket food share, also overstates poverty increases, not only because it does not allow substitution (as in Method I) but also because it does not use the actual consumption bundle of each household. This method is perhaps defensible, however, as the food weight in the price index represents the actual consumption pattern of some group in poverty (although a group considerably below the poverty line).

On the other hand, Method III, which expands the 1996 inflation line to 1999 by more than the amount of Method II, creates a poverty line at which the welfare of those at the poverty line in 1999 is higher, perhaps substantially higher, than those at the poverty line in 1996. The repetition of the same method on different data sets does not guarantee a result such that the material standard of living represented by the resulting poverty lines is equivalent. Why this is so is something of a puzzle. Apparently, the Engel curve relationship shifted over time. Therefore, for consistent welfare measures over time, Method III should not be used.

5 A CONSISTENT SET OF POVERTY ESTIMATES DURING THE CRISIS

Over the course of the crisis there have been a number of estimates of poverty rates using various large-scale but not necessarily nationally representative household surveys. Unfortunately, each used a different and non-comparable base for the "pre-crisis" poverty rate and a different method of deflation for changes in the poverty line, which means that these estimates of the headcount poverty rate are not comparable either in terms of levels or changes. In this section we create a consistent series of poverty rates using our own estimates from the various data sets to which we have access and by adjusting the estimates from various sources in cases where we do not have the raw data.

All of the estimates must start from a consistent base. First, we must take into account the fact that the economy was growing from February 1996 at least through to the middle of 1997, just before the crisis started.[13] It is likely that this additional income would have reduced poverty, so the poverty rate just before the crisis is not simply the level of poverty in February 1996, but the level reached after accounting for poverty reduction from February 1996 to the beginning of the crisis. Second, the estimates must use a common method of computing changes over time, particularly with regard to how the poverty line is inflated.

The household survey databases to which we have access and from which we calculate our own estimates are (a) the SUSENAS Consumption Module (with a sample of 65,000 households): February 1996, February 1999, and February 2002; (b) the Mini SUSENAS (with a sample of 10,000 households): December 1998 and August 1999; (c) the SUSENAS Core (with a sample of 200,000 households) in February 1999, February 2000, and February 2001; and (d) the 100 Village Survey (with a sample of 12,000 households): May 1997, August 1998, December 1998, May 1999, and October 1999.

These databases were all collected by Statistics Indonesia (BPS). Two types of questionnaires on household consumption were used: (i) the detailed consumption questionnaire that contains 339 goods, used in the SUSENAS Consumption Module and the Mini SUSENAS, and (ii) the aggregated consumption questionnaire that contains only 23 goods, used in the SUSENAS Core and 100 Village Survey. Since the former produces a significantly higher level of household consumption than the latter (Sumarto et al. 2002), this difference in the types of questionnaires that were used has to be taken into account in calculating poverty lines.

Table 5.5 illustrates how we calculate poverty rates over time using these primary data. We start with the poverty rate for February 1999 of 27.1 per cent as estimated by Pradhan et al. (2001) as the basis. We then use Methods I and II for calculating changes in poverty lines during the period. As the regional representation of the databases varies, we use a single, national-level poverty line and the national-level CPI prices to calculate poverty rates.

Using the SUSENAS Consumption Module for February 1999, we calculate a national-level poverty line that produces a national poverty rate of 27.1 per cent as the first step. Then, using both Method I and Method II, we inflate the poverty line backwards

TABLE 5.5
Estimates of Poverty Rates Calculated from Primary Data

Data Source	Period	Method I (%)	Method II (%)
SUSENAS Consumption Module	February 1999	27.1	27.1
	February 1996	23.0	18.7
	February 2002	14.2	13.1
Mini SUSENAS	December 1998	23.3	22.9
	August 1999	19.9	18.7
SUSENAS Core	February1999	27.1	27.1
	February 2000	14.9	14.2
	February 2001	11.2	10.3
100 Village Survey	December 1998	23.3	22.9
	May 1997	18.0	15.4
	August 1998	28.7	28.0
	May 1999	22.5	22.3
	October 1999	18.8	18.1

Source: SUSENAS, 100 Village Survey

and forwards to February 1996, December 1998, August 1999, and February 2002. We then apply the estimated poverty lines to the corresponding SUSENAS Consumption Module and Mini SUSENAS databases to obtain the estimates of poverty rates for the respective periods.

A similar procedure is then carried out for the SUSENAS Core databases. First, using the SUSENAS Core for February 1999, we calculate a national-level poverty line that produces a national poverty rate of 27.1 per cent for this database. Then, using both Method I and Method II, we inflate the poverty line forward to February 2000 and February 2001. We then apply the estimated poverty lines to the corresponding SUSENAS Core databases to obtain the estimates of poverty rates for those periods.

The 100 Village Survey data need to be treated differently for two reasons. First, this survey was not a nationally representative sample. Second, its sample areas and households were purposely selected to represent the poor. So in this case we calibrate the 100 Village Survey poverty rate to match those of the other surveys at one point in time. As a first step, therefore, for each method we calibrate the poverty line for the 100 Village Survey December 1998 database so that it produces the same poverty rate as that calculated from the Mini SUSENAS December 1998. In the final step we then update the resulting poverty line backwards to May 1997 and August 1998 and forwards to May and October 1999, and then calculate the poverty rates in the respective periods.

Confirming expectations, the Method II deflator results in greater changes in poverty rates during the period by comparison with the Method I deflator. In general, however, the differences in the poverty rates produced by both methods are not large.

In addition to these data, we use three studies that estimate poverty rates for at least two points in time during the crisis: (a) Gardiner (1999), which used the SUSENAS Core to create poverty estimates for February 1996, February 1997, and February 1998; (b) Strauss et al. (2002), which used the Indonesia Family Life Survey (IFLS) to produce poverty estimates for August–November 1997 (IFLS2) and June–October 2000 (IFLS3); and (c) Frankenberg et al. (1999), which also used the IFLS to produce poverty estimates for August–November 1997 (IFLS2) and September-December 1998 (IFLS2+).[14]

Table 5.6 shows the original poverty estimates from these studies and the adjusted estimates that make them consistent with the threshold of a 27.1 per cent poverty rate in February 1999 and with changes in poverty according to Method II.[15] For Gardiner (1999), in the first step, the poverty estimate for February 1996 of 11.5 per cent was changed to 18.7 per cent to make it consistent with the estimate for the period in Table 5.5. In the second step, the estimates for February 1997 and 1998 were then changed proportionally. Because the deflator used in this study has a food share of 0.7, which is quite close to the 0.8 food share in our Method II, there was little need to adjust the deflator.

TABLE 5.6
Estimates of Poverty Rates Calculated from Secondary Data

Study and Data Source	Period	Original Rate (%)	Adjusted to Method II (%)
Gardiner (1999) using SUSENAS Core	February 1996	11.5	18.7
	February 1997	9.4	15.3
	February 1998	14.8	24.1
Strauss et al. (2002) using IFLS2 and IFLS3	August–November 1997	17.4	17.4
	June–October 2000	15.5	15.5
Frankenberg et al. (1999) using IFLS2 and IFLS2+	August–November 1997	11.0	17.4
	September–December 1998	19.9	33.2

Source: Gardiner (1999), Strauss et al. (2002), Frankenberg et al. (1999)

Strauss et al. (2002) calculate all poverty estimates following Pradhan et al. (2001), making their estimates already consistent with the threshold of the 27.1 per cent poverty rate in February 1999 and changes in poverty according to Method II. Following this, the estimate of Frankenberg et al. (1999) for August–November 1997 is adjusted from 11 per cent to 17.4 per cent. The estimate for September–December 1998 is then adjusted proportionally plus an amount to take into account the fact that the deflator has a food share of only 0.55. During the period, the increase in the Method II deflator is 31 percentage points higher than CPI inflation.[16]

The reconciliation of all the above estimates using Method II in Tables 5.5 and 5.6 is presented in Figure 5.2. The December 1998 estimate point is not connected because the temporary drop in poverty during this period is difficult to explain. Overall, this series of poverty estimates paints a very reasonable picture, around which the data show a striking consensus, as it neatly tracks known events (devaluation, inflation, rice prices, riots, stabilization, and economic growth).

FIGURE 5.2
Consistent Estimates of Poverty Rates,
February 1996–February 2002

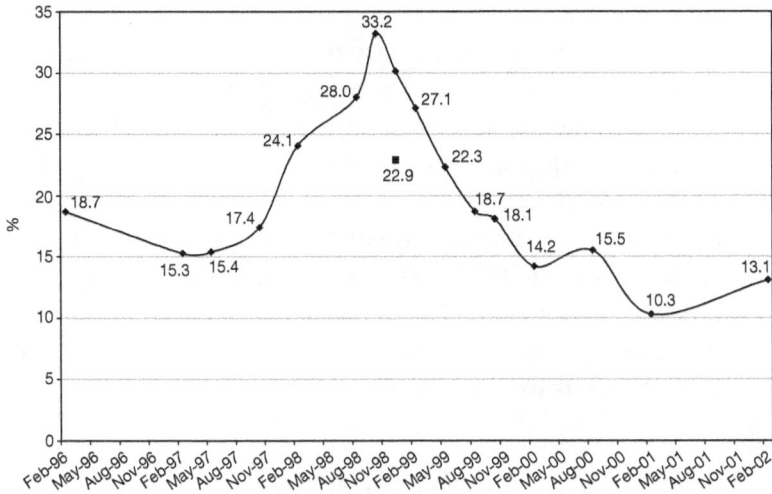

Source: Based on Tables 5.5 and 5.6

Five points emerge from Figure 5.2:

- The estimates confirm that from February 1996 to around
  the middle of 1997 the poverty rate fell. This adjustment
  is important, as the assumption that the poverty rate
  immediately before the crisis was the same as the February
  1996 rate would not give a true picture of the impact on
  poverty of the crisis.
- The maximum increase in the poverty rate, from the lowest
  point of approximately 15 per cent just before the crisis to
  the highest point of around 33 per cent at the peak of the
  crisis, is approximately 18 percentage points. This implies
  that some 36 million additional people were pushed into
  absolute poverty due to the crisis. In relative terms, this was
  an increase of 120 per cent from the pre-crisis rate.

- The poverty rate appears to have peaked at some time around the end of 1998, following the large surge in the price of rice and before the beginning of the stabilization of general inflation in 1999.
- After the peak point, the poverty rate started to decline again. It reached the pre-crisis level of around 15 per cent at the end of 1999. Therefore, according to this series, the lost time in poverty reduction due to the crisis was approximately two and a half years.
- The poverty rate after this point appears to have fluctuated. During the first half of 2000, it worsened again slightly, then decreased again during the second half of the year until early 2001. During 2001 until early 2002, however, the poverty situation seems to have worsened again.

6 CONCLUSIONS

In 1997 and 1998 Indonesia was hit severely by the effects of a combined currency, financial, natural, economic, and political crisis that caused the economy to contract substantially. This was made worse by skyrocketing domestic prices, particularly for food. The impact of the crisis on social welfare was substantial and is still continuing years after the crisis began.

Given the large change in the relative price of food during the crisis, the comparison of poverty rates over time depends critically on the choice of price deflation and, within that, the choice of the weight (explicitly or implicitly) put on the food price inflation rate. These choices greatly affect the resulting poverty level. On the other hand, computation of the poverty line in a way that adopts the same method in each period may not produce consistent comparisons of welfare. Likewise, such a method may not produce poverty lines that represent the same material standard of living in the two periods.

Reconciliation of various estimates from primary and secondary data provides a very reasonable picture of poverty evolution in Indonesia during the crisis and neatly tracks events. The poverty rate increased from the lowest point of approximately 15 per cent at the onset of the crisis in the middle of 1997 to the highest point of approximately 33 per cent near the end of 1998. The maximum increase in poverty during the crisis of 18 percentage points implies that approximately 36 million additional people were pushed into absolute poverty due to the crisis, albeit temporarily.

The poverty rate peaked some time around the end of 1998, following the large surge in the price of rice and before general inflation began to be stabilized in 1999. After the peak point, the poverty rate started to decline again and reached the pre-crisis level of approximately 15 per cent at the end of 1999. This implies that the lost time in poverty reduction due to the crisis was approximately 2.5 years. After this point, however, the poverty rate appears to have fluctuated. During the first half of 2000 it increased again slightly, but then decreased again during the second half of the year until early 2001. During 2001 and until early 2002, however, poverty appears again to have worsened.

Notes

Reprinted from Asep Suryahadi, Sudarno Sumarto and Lant Pritchett, "Evolution of Poverty during the Crisis in Indonesia", *Asian Economic Journal* 17, no. 3 (2003): 221–241, with permission from Wiley-Blackwell.

1. In July 1998 there was considerable debate on the impact of the crisis on poverty as estimates of the increase in headcount poverty rates ranged from as high as 30 to as low as 3 percentage points. These attempts at "real time" estimates suffered from a variety of methodological problems (Poppele et al. 1999).

2. Rice is indeed a very important component of household consumption in Indonesia. In 1999, average expenditures on rice made up 20 per cent of total household expenditures and 30 per cent of food expenditures. The analysis in this study, however, does not separate rice as a specific component in the price deflator. Rather, it focuses on the weight of food versus non-food in the deflator as the main issue is the fact that the share of food as a whole in the Consumer Price Index (CPI) is too low.

3. For details of SUSENAS, see Chapter 2 above and also Imawan and Ahnaf (1997).

4. This relationship is known as Engel's Law.

5. Imagine the special case in which everyone has exactly the same expenditures. Then either everyone is in poverty or no one is, and the cumulative distribution function (cdf) is discontinuous (that is, it has essentially an infinite slope) at that point.

6. But this is not the only way as there are cheaper as well as more expensive ways to attain a calorie intake of 2,100 calories.

7. This uses the fact that $\ln(1)=0$, so that when actual expenditures are equal to the food poverty line (e = FPL), the predicted value of the food share is just the constant since the $\beta*\ln(.)$ term of the prediction disappears.

8. The expenditure shares were taken from the consumers in the 100 Village Survey, whose food share was near that of the bottom 30 per cent of consumers from the SUSENAS.

9. It is well known from consumer theory that a fixed weights (Laspeyres) price index overestimates the change in welfare from a given change in prices because the fixed weights do not allow for substitution effects from the relative price changes.

10. The food and non-food price inflation of the consumer price index used is the provincial level. Meanwhile, the food price inflation of SUSENAS unit prices is varied not only across provinces but also across urban-rural areas within provinces.

11. The aggregate inflation rates are obtained as the weighted averages of inflation rates faced by households in the sample.

12. Hence, in Method II and hereafter, the food share at the poverty line is fixed at 0.8.

13. February 1996 is the last SUSENAS Consumption Module available before the crisis.
14. The IFLS2 and IFLS2+ were carried out jointly by RAND and the Demography Institute of the University of Indonesia (LDUI), while the IFLS3 was carried out jointly by RAND and Gadjah Mada University. The extended periods for each round are due to the tracking of individuals in the panel survey.
15. Adjustments following Method I cannot be implemented because they require access to the primary data to calculate the predicted household-specific food share.
16. The increase in the poverty rate due to this factor is approximated as $[(0.8-0.55)/(0.8-0.4)]*0.31*$(the percentage-point increase in original poverty rates).

Part Two

POVERTY ALLEVIATION POLICIES AND PROGRAMS

Chapter 6

DESIGNS AND IMPLEMENTATION OF THE INDONESIAN SOCIAL SAFETY NET PROGRAMS

Sudarno Sumarto, Asep Suryahadi, and Wenefrida Widyanti

1 INTRODUCTION

At the onset of the Indonesian economic crisis, an important concern was raised over whether the achievements that had been made in the social sectors and poverty reduction over the previous decades could be sustained. Furthermore, there were some warnings about the looming social impacts of the crisis. This prompted the Indonesian Government to react rapidly and to institute a number of interventions aimed at safeguarding real incomes as well as access to social services for the poor.

To mitigate the social impact of the economic crisis, the Indonesian Government established a series of new and expanded programs known as the JPS (*Jaring Pengaman Sosial*, or Social Safety Net) programs. They were launched in early 1998, although many did not start until the second half of the year. It was hoped that through the implementation of these programs, the worst impacts of the crisis, such as widespread hunger, malnutrition, poverty, unemployment, and children dropping out of school, could be prevented or at least reduced.[1]

This paper is an evaluation of how effective the various social safety net programs have been in reaching their intended target, namely, the traditionally poor and those newly poor due to the crisis.[2] This is done by assessing the coverage of the programs among the poor as well as the way in which the benefits of the programs have been distributed between the poor and the non-poor.

2 THE SOCIAL SAFETY NET PROGRAMS

2.1   Indonesia's Social Safety Net Prior to the Crisis

The Indonesian people had never relied heavily on government-run safety net programs. The country has had neither the economic apparatus nor the political mechanisms necessary to deliver large-scale and widespread transfer programs. Instead, government social spending was largely focused towards "social services" such as health and education, while the family and communities provided "social insurance" in times of difficulty. There was some subsidized health care and a workers' social security program, made compulsory for all formal sector employees by the 1992 law on Workers' Social Security (McLeod 1993), but Indonesia did not have a social safety net system like the JPS. Establishing the social safety net programs in 1998 was, therefore, more like casting a new net rather than merely expanding an existing one.

2.2   Social Safety Net Programs as a Response to the Crisis

The JPS programs were launched as a response to the crisis. They were intended to help protect the traditional poor as well as the new, crisis-created poor through four strategies: (a) ensuring the availability of food at affordable prices, (b) supplementing purchasing power among poor households through employment creation, (c) preserving access to critical social services, particularly health and education, and (d) sustaining local economic activity through regional block grant programs and the extension of small-scale credit. Table 6.1 recapitulates the areas and major programs of the social safety net.

TABLE 6.1
Areas and Major Programs of the Indonesian Social Safety Net

Safety Net Area	Program
Food security	OPK program: sale of subsidized rice to targeted households
Employment creation	*Padat Karya*: a loose, uncoordinated collection of several "labour-intensive" programs in a variety of government departments
	PDM-DKE: a "community fund" program providing block grants directly to villages for either public works or revolving credit funds
Education	Scholarships and block grants: a program providing • Scholarships directly to elementary (SD), lower secondary (SMP), and upper secondary (SMA) students • Block grants to selected schools
Health	JPS-BK: a program providing subsidies for • Medical services • Operational support for health centres • Medicine and imported medical equipment • Family planning services • Nutrition (supplemental food) • Midwife services

Source: Compilation by authors

The programs launched were designed by the central government and were intended to have the following characteristics: quick disbursement, direct financing to beneficiaries, transparency, accountability, and participation of society in monitoring program implementation, though these intended characteristics were not always achieved (Tim Dampak Krisis SMERU 2000). A brief description is now given of each specific major program.[3] This is followed by a discussion of the targeting methods of the programs.

(a) *The Sale of Subsidized Rice*

This program has been the main component of the government's effort to maintain food security, particularly for the traditional poor and the crisis-induced, new poor who have suffered from both falling real income and food price escalation. It is popularly called the OPK program (*Operasi Pasar Khusus*, or Special Market Operation). Under this program, each eligible household is allowed to purchase ten kilograms of rice per month at the highly subsidized price of Rp 1,000 per kg.[4] By comparison, the average market price for medium quality rice in the second half of 1998 was around Rp 3,000 per kg. Originally, only households classified in the lowest official category of poverty were eligible to participate in the program.[5] But coverage was expanded during the course of the year to include the second-lowest category. The target of this program was around 7.4 million households or around 15 per cent of all households in the country.

Since this program has tried to ensure that the poor can afford to buy rice, the staple food of most Indonesians, it is probably the most critical component of the JPS programs. One impact of the crisis was the sudden rise in prices, particularly of food, that put basic necessities practically out of reach of the poor, at least in the initial short run before their nominal incomes could expand to keep pace. These provisions of cheap rice for the poor, therefore, were deemed essential for avoiding widespread hunger, which might exacerbate the already chaotic political and economic situation of the country at that time.[6]

(b) *Employment Creation*

This program is popularly known as the *padat karya* (labour-intensive) program. It is actually not a single program but a large set of activities under the category of employment creation. These programs were created as a response to the threat of burgeoning unemployment because of economic contraction, which had forced many firms to either lay off workers or shut down completely (SMERU 1999*a*). In accordance with the urban nature of the crisis, the initial geographical targets for the first round of *padat karya* "crash programs" in fiscal year 1997/98 were mainly urban areas, but some rural areas that had experienced harvest failures were also included.[7]

In the wake of these "crash programs", in fiscal year 1998/99 there was a proliferation of *padat karya* programs, with sixteen different programs that fell into the "employment creation" category.[8] These programs can be classified into four types. First, ongoing investment and infrastructure projects were redesigned into more labour-intensive type programs and modes of contract. Second, there were programs that gave block grants to local communities, such as the Kecamatan Development Program (PPK), the Program for Underdeveloped Villages (IDT), and the Regional Empowerment Program to Overcome the Impact of the Economic Crisis (PDM-DKE). These funds were directed to poorer areas and had "menus" for the utilization of the funds that included the possibility of public works that had an employment-creating effect. The third set was special, labour-intensive undertakings carried out by sectoral ministries (for example, forestry, rural-urban, and retraining of laid-off workers by the Ministry of Manpower). In addition, there was a fourth type of program made up of "food for work" activities, typically launched by international donors and NGOs in drought-stricken areas.

(c)   *Scholarships and Block Grants to Schools*

Early in the crisis there was a worry that parents would be forced to withdraw their children from school in response to falling incomes and rising costs, hence triggering a large increase in school drop-out rates. This rightly alarmed the government, which established an education funding support program. The program was started in the 1998/99 academic year and there was a plan to end it in 2003. It had two components: scholarships for students from poor families to enable them to stay in school, and block grants (DBO) to schools to help them continue operating. The scholarships provided cash in the amounts of Rp 10,000, Rp 20,000, and Rp 30,000 per month for primary, lower secondary, and upper secondary school students respectively. These amounts generally covered the cost of school fees and could be used for that or other expenses.

This program was intended to reach at most 6 per cent of primary school students, 17 per cent of lower secondary school students, and 10 per cent of upper secondary school students nationwide, including students from religious schools. Since the program was targeted, the expectation was for coverage to be higher in some districts and lower in others. Meanwhile, 60 per cent of schools in each district were targeted to receive block grants. The schools selected were those located in the poorest communities within each district.

(d)   *Health*

There was also concern early in the crisis that falling real incomes and the increasing costs of medical services due to the crisis might force poor and newly poor households to abandon modern medical services, even when family members fell sick and urgently needed medical treatment. This would cause general health conditions to deteriorate, reversing improvements in this sector accumulated during the previous decades.

To forestall this, the government established social safety net programs in the health sector, known collectively as the JPS-BK (*JPS Bidang Kesehatan*, or Health Sector JPS) programs. It was hoped that through these programs the poor would not be forced to stop using modern medical services because they could not afford them anymore. Various programs were specifically established that provided subsidies for medicines and imported medical equipment, operational support funds for community health centres, free medical and family planning services, and supplemental food for pregnant women and children under three years old.

2.3 Method of Targeting

In general, the targeting for the Indonesian social safety net programs was based on a combination of geographic and household targeting. Table 6.2 summarizes the targeting of the major social safety net programs. The targeting for some programs used a household classification created by the National Family Planning Coordinating Board (*Badan Koordinasi Keluarga Berencana Nasional*, or BKKBN). In this classification households are grouped into four socioeconomic categories: "pre-prosperous households" (*keluarga pra-sejahtera*, or KPS),[9] "prosperous I households" (*keluarga sejahtera* I, or KS I), KS II, and KS III.[10] Originally, eligible recipients for some programs were KPS card-holders only, but for some programs eligibility was extended to include KS I households (for example, the OPK rice program). The sale of subsidized rice and the health (JPS-BK) programs explicitly used this BKKBN household classification for their targeting methods. The selection of recipients in the scholarship programs was also supposed to take into account the BKKBN status of the household.[11]

TABLE 6.2
Targeting Mechanisms in the Social Safety Net Programs

Program	Targeting	Fiscal Year 1998/99	Fiscal Year 1999/2000
OPK	Geographic	None	None
	Household	BKKBN list	BKKBN list with flexibility
PDM-DKE	Geographic	Pre-crisis (1997) data on poverty rate by district	Updated with BAPPENAS* regional data
	Household	Local decision-making	Local decision-making
Padat Karya	Geographic	None, various ministries (e.g., manpower, forestry, public works)	Urban areas, based on unemployment rate
	Household	Weak self-selection (arbitrary wage rate)	Self-selection (wage rate set below minimum wage)
Scholarships and block grants to schools	Geographic	Data on enrolment in 1997	Poverty data updated to 1998
	Household	School committees following criteria	School committees following criteria
JPS-BK	Geographic	BKKBN pre-prosperous rates	Updated pre-prosperous estimates to 1999
	Household	BKKBN list	BKKBN list with flexibility

Note: *Badan Perencanaan Pembangunan Nasional (National Development Planning Agency)
Source: See Table 6.1

The *padat karya* programs, meanwhile, consisted of quite diverse programs and, although specific programs were targeted at certain areas (for example, drought-affected areas), the lack of coordination meant that there was little or no systematic geographic targeting of this set of programs overall. Within programs there was a variety of disagreements about the desired characteristics of intended participants, but typically the beneficiaries were not chosen according to any fixed administrative criteria. Hence, to the extent that there was targeting, it was primarily through self-selection. Only those who were willing to work should have been able to receive the benefits. This self-selection mechanism had the advantage of allowing individuals to choose to participate or not and created the possibility of being more flexible than administrative criteria with regard to unobserved household shocks.

Although there was a variety of *padat karya* programs, all were established in the hope that the wages would be paid as a benefit to the poor and those newly unemployed due to mass lay-offs and declining economic activities during the crisis. While these programs were supposed to be available only for those who were already unemployed and willing to accept the lower wages, it is well known that the level of the wage is critical for achieving good targeting outcomes in employment programs. If the target is achieved, most if not all of the jobs will go to the poor.[12]

In the scholarship program, funds were first allocated to schools in such a way that schools in poorer areas received proportionally more scholarships. In each school the scholarships were then allocated to individual students by a school committee that consisted of the principal, a teacher representative, a student representative, the head of the parents' association as the representative of the community, and the village head. The scholarship recipients were selected based on a combination of administrative criteria (including such factors as household data from school records, the family's BKKBN status, the size of the family, and the likelihood of the student dropping out) and the committee's decision.[13]

School students in all but the lowest three grades of primary school were officially eligible for the scholarships. In principle, the students selected to receive the scholarships were supposed to be from the poorest backgrounds. As a guideline, scholarships were to be allocated first to children from households in the two lowest BKKBN rankings. If the number of eligible students was too large for all poor students to receive a scholarship, additional indicators were used to identify the neediest. These additional indicators included distance of the student's home from the school, the existence of a physical handicap, and a background consisting of large or single-parent families. Furthermore, a minimum of 50 per cent of scholarships was to be allocated if possible to girls.

In the health programs, meanwhile, the free medical and family planning services program was implemented by giving "health cards" to eligible households. Eligibility for this program was also based on the household's official "welfare" status. A health card given to a household could be used by all members of the household to obtain free services from designated hospitals, clinics, and health care centres for medical and family planning purposes, including pregnancy check-ups and childbirth.

3 METHODS AND DATA

3.1 Methods: Coverage and Targeting Effectiveness

In a program using targeted intervention, the success and failure of the program in meeting its objective is determined very much by the accuracy of the targeting that actually occurs in practice. A simple measure of targeting outcomes is illustrated in Table 6.3. This shows that for a program providing benefits targeted at a certain group in the population, there are two possible successful

TABLE 6.3
Evaluating Targeting Outcomes

Participation in Program	Population		Total
	Target	Non-target	
Participants	Success (A)	Type II (inclusion) error (B)	(E) = (A) + (B)
Non-participants	Type I (exclusion) error (C)	Success (D)	(F) = (C) + (D)
Total	(G) = (A) + (C)	(H) = (B) + (D)	(I) = (A) + (B) + (C) + (D)

Source: Compilation by authors

outcomes and two possible negative outcomes. The successful outcomes are when the target population participates in the program and when the non-target population does not participate in the program. Conversely, the negative outcomes arise when the target population does not participate (an exclusion error) and when the non-target population participates in the program (an inclusion error).

The framework of analysis illustrated in Table 6.3 can be used as the basis for calculating various program performance indicators such as the implementation ratio, the targeting expenditure ratio, the leakage ratio, and the coverage ratio. The implementation ratio (IR) is the ratio of the actual total coverage of the target population. In the example in Table 6.3, a program has a target population that is (G), but actual total coverage is (E). Then IR = (E)/(G) = [(A) + (B)]/[(A) + (C)]. The targeting expenditure ratio (TER) is the fraction of beneficiaries who are the target population. In Table 6.3, TER = (A)/(E) = (A)/[(A) + (B)]. The leakage ratio (LR), on the other hand, refers to the fraction of program beneficiaries who are the non-target population. Hence, $LR = 1 - TER = (B)/(E)$ $= (B)/[(A) + (B)]$. Meanwhile, the coverage ratio (CR) is the fraction of the target population that is actually covered by a program. In Table 6.3, $CR = (A)/(G) = (A)/[(A) + (C)]$. It can be established that $CR = IR \times TER$ since $(A)/(G) = (E)/(G) \times (A)/(E)$.

The focus of this study is the coverage and targeting effectiveness of seven major Indonesian social safety net programs in reaching the poor. Instead of using the absolute poverty measure based on the absolute poverty line, the analysis is based on a relative poverty measure using a quintile approach. The reason for this is that estimates of the absolute poverty line in Indonesia are available only at the provincial level, differentiated by urban and rural areas.[14] In the current analysis, the samples in each district are grouped into quintiles of per capita expenditure. The first quintile (Q1) is classified as the poor, while the second to fifth quintiles (Q2-Q5) are the non-poor. This is equivalent to using a relative poverty line of the twentieth percentile of per capita expenditure in each district.[15]

Grouping households by quintiles of nominal per capita expenditure in each district has two advantages. First, it makes the results of this study on program participation consistent with the large and growing literature on benefit incidence, which typically uses income or consumption expenditure quintiles (Baker 2000; Grosh 1994; Ravallion 1992). Second, this study does not attempt to capture differences in poverty across districts in the sample. Instead, the focus is only on the targeting within a district, that is, whether the households that are relatively poor within the district (that is, the bottom 20 per cent) receive the benefits in that district.

3.2 Data: The JPS Module of SUSENAS

The data analysed in this study were collected in a special social safety net module of the February 1999 SUSENAS by Statistics

Indonesia (*Badan Pusat Statistik*, or BPS).[16] To carry out the method of analysis outlined above, the data on program participation from the social safety net module SUSENAS need to be combined with data on household consumption expenditures from the Core SUSENAS. The household consumption expenditure data in the February 1999 Core SUSENAS, however, contain a problem that originates in the way the data were collected. This is due to the fact that the Core SUSENAS sample actually consists of two different groups of samples: those that are and those that are not included in the Consumption Module SUSENAS sample.

Out of a total of around 200,000 households randomly selected to be included as a sample in the Core SUSENAS, a subset of around 65,000 households is further randomly selected to be included as a sample in the Consumption Module SUSENAS. Although both surveys ask about household consumption expenditures, the Consumption Module SUSENAS uses a detailed questionnaire that contains 339 goods with a recall period of one week for food and one month or one year for non-food, while the Core SUSENAS uses an aggregated questionnaire of consumption expenditure that contains only 23 goods with the same recall periods as the detailed questionnaire.

Theoretically, all households sampled in the Core SUSENAS should be asked to fill out the same questionnaire. However, a test shown in Appendix Table 6.A1 clearly points out that for those households sampled in the Core SUSENAS that were also sampled in the Consumption Module SUSENAS, the answers in the aggregated consumption expenditure questionnaire were copied from the detailed consumption expenditure questionnaire. This caused an instrument bias due to the fact that there are two groups of households in the sample that were asked to respond to different consumption expenditure questionnaires.

The first three columns in Appendix Table 6.A1 take information from households that were sampled in both the Core SUSENAS and the Consumption Module SUSENAS. The first column presents the average household expenditures in the Core SUSENAS data by area and education level, while the second column presents the same information but obtained from the Consumption Module SUSENAS data. The third column, showing the difference between the two, indicates that the levels of expenditures in both Core SUSENAS and Consumption Module SUSENAS for this sample are practically the same. This indicates that the expenditure data in the aggregated questionnaire were copied from the detailed questionnaire.

The last three columns in Appendix Table 6.A1 compare the level of expenditures between the two groups of households in the sample of the Core SUSENAS data. The comparison clearly shows that the level of expenditures of households that were sampled in the Core SUSENAS only is substantially lower than that of households that were sampled in both the Core SUSENAS and the Consumption Module SUSENAS. The difference is 14 per cent in rural areas and 18 per cent in urban areas. This difference in expenditure levels does not reflect the actual difference in living standards between the two groups of households, but it is merely due to the difference in the instruments used for data collection. The detailed consumption module questionnaire produces higher levels of expenditure than the aggregated core questionnaire.

This creates a problem in grouping households into quintiles of expenditures if all households in the Core SUSENAS sample are treated as one sample. Households that were sampled in the Core SUSENAS only will tend to be grouped in lower quintiles of per capita expenditure, while households that were sampled in both the Core SUSENAS and the Consumption Module SUSENAS will tend to be grouped in the higher quintiles of per capita expenditure.

To overcome this problem, the households in both sets have been grouped separately into quintiles of expenditure. Households that were sampled in the Core SUSENAS only are grouped into five quintiles of per capita expenditure. Likewise, households that were sampled in both the Core SUSENAS and the Consumption Module SUSENAS are grouped into five quintiles of per capita expenditure. Since the households in the two groups of samples were randomly selected, the same quintile of per capita expenditure of both groups may be treated as a single group of households with similar living standards.

4 PROGRAM COVERAGE AND TARGETING

The results of our analysis of the coverage and targeting effectiveness of seven major social safety net programs implemented in fiscal year 1998/99 are now presented. The methods and data outlined above are used in the analysis of the following programs: the sale of subsidized rice (OPK), employment creation (*padat karya*), primary, lower secondary, and upper secondary school scholarships, free medical services, and nutrition (supplemental food). The period evaluated is the six months before the February 1999 SUSENAS survey, except for the medical services program, for which it is the three-month period before the survey. The results of the analysis are shown in Appendix Table 6.A2.

4.1 Program Coverage

Based on the results from Appendix Table 6.A2, Figure 6.1 shows the coverage for the total population, the poor, and the non-poor of the social safety net programs analysed in this study. The sale of subsidized rice stands out as the program with the highest level of coverage — 40 per cent of all households. More than half of all poor (Q1) households in Indonesia reported receiving the benefits of this program, while more than a third of non-poor (Q2-Q5) households also reported receiving the benefits. The second highest coverage is found in the nutrition program. Around 16 per cent of both poor and non-poor households reported receiving the benefits of this program.

FIGURE 6.1
Coverage of Various Social Safety Net Programs

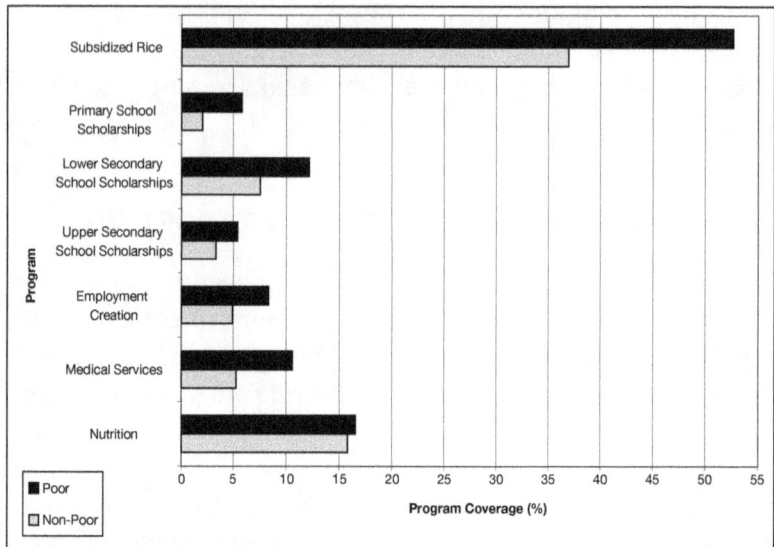

Source: Appendix Table 6.A2

Meanwhile, the two programs with the lowest coverage are the primary and upper secondary school scholarship programs. In both programs only around 5 per cent of poor students reported receiving the scholarships. The coverage among the poor for the other programs ranges between 8 and 12 per cent, far below the coverage of the subsidized rice program. Overall, these results indicate a large degree of undercoverage in the social safety net programs, that is, there were large numbers of poor households that were not covered by the programs.

Furthermore, the coverage of the sale of subsidized rice program indicates that 40 per cent of over fifty million households all over the country are estimated to have received the benefits of this program during the six-month evaluation period. The implied number of households that reported having received the benefits of this program is around 20.2 million households. This is double the number of the officially reported beneficiaries, which was around 10.4 million households in February 1999.

This discrepancy indicates two things. First, while the official report indicates the number of beneficiaries in a certain month, the SUSENAS data indicate the total number of households that received the program benefits during the six-month evaluation period. The data show that almost half of the recipients reported that they bought rice only once or twice under the program, indicating irregular delivery of benefits in most areas. Second, and more importantly, while the official report tends to reflect the number of eligible households, the SUSENAS data reflect the actual number of beneficiaries. The implication of this is that, while the rice allocated to an area was based on the number of eligible households, it had to be allocated to a much larger number of households, implying a lower amount of rice for each recipient than stipulated in the program guidelines.[17]

In the employment creation programs, the data indicate that 5.6 per cent of households have at least one member who participated in a *padat karya* program. Program coverage among poor households is 8.3 per cent compared to 4.9 per cent among non-poor households. On average, each participating household claimed to have spent 27 man-days in *padat karya* programs during the six-month evaluation period, or an average of 4.5 man-days per month. The type of activity done was mostly repairing roads, with 64 per cent of program participants reporting that they had been involved in this activity. Other activities included repairing irrigation systems, done by 35 per cent of participants, cultivating idle land by 14 per cent of participants, repairing floodplains by 12 per cent of participants, and other activities by 16 per cent of participants. Many participants were involved in more than one activity.

The significant participation of non-poor households in *padat karya* programs probably has to do with the level of wages offered by these programs. The average daily wage received by participants of *padat karya* programs was Rp 6,073. This is comparable to daily wages in the food crop sector which averaged Rp 6,350, according to the 1999 National Labour Force Survey (SAKERNAS). The level of wages received and the average working day of participating households imply that each program participant on average received benefits of around Rp 27,500 per month from this program.

For the scholarship program, as mentioned above, the targeted coverage was 6 per cent for primary level, 17 per cent for lower secondary, and 10 per cent for upper secondary. If the 6 per cent coverage target at the primary level had been achieved and all the scholarship recipients were students from poor households, we would expect a 30 per cent program coverage among the poor and zero coverage among the non-poor. The data indicate that 4 per cent of all primary school students in the country received the scholarships.[18] This means that only 67 per cent of the 6 per cent target was achieved. Furthermore, the figure shows that program coverage among poor students was only 5.8 per cent, which is far less than the 30 per cent result expected with perfect targeting. This is compared to 3.6 per cent coverage among non-poor students.

For the lower secondary school scholarship program, if the 17 per cent target of this program had been achieved and all recipients were students from poor households, we would expect an 85 per cent program coverage among poor students, while no non-poor students would receive a scholarship. The data show that in reality the national coverage of this scholarship program was 8.4 per cent, which is only about half of the 17 per cent target. The actual program coverage among poor students was only 12.2 per cent, far below the 85 per cent result expected with perfect targeting. The coverage among non-poor students, meanwhile, was 7.5 per cent.

For the upper secondary school scholarship program, if the 10 per cent target of this program had been achieved with perfect targeting, we would expect a 50 per cent program coverage among poor students and none among non-poor students. The data show that the national coverage of this scholarship program was only 3.7 per cent, which is much less than the 10 per cent target. Meanwhile, the program coverage among poor students was only 5.4 per cent or around only a tenth of the 50 per cent result expected with perfect targeting. The coverage among non-poor students for this program was 3.3 per cent.

In terms of the amount disbursed with each scholarship, the data indicate that 78 per cent of the primary school recipients reported receiving the exact amount of Rp 10,000 per month as stipulated. Six per cent of the recipients claimed to have received less than Rp 10,000 per month, which may indicate that the schools had already deducted school fees from the scholarships of these students. However, 16 per cent of recipients reported receiving more than Rp 10,000 per month. This could indicate two things. First, schools gave the scholarships to a smaller number of students than the scholarship allocation, so that each student received a higher amount than stipulated. Second, some of these students received scholarships from more than one source. Unfortunately, this cannot be verified from the data.

As with the primary school scholarship program, 77 per cent of lower secondary school scholarship recipients reported receiving the exact amount of money stipulated, that is, Rp 20,000 per month. Those who claimed to have received less formed 11 per cent, while 12 per cent claimed to have received more. By contrast with the primary and lower secondary scholarships, 85 per cent of the upper secondary scholarship recipients claimed to have received less than the stipulated amount of Rp 30,000 per month. Only 6 per cent reported receiving the exact amount, while the remaining 9 per cent claimed to have received higher amounts.

The medical services program, as explained above, was implemented through the distribution of health cards to eligible households. The card could be used by all members of an eligible household to obtain free services from designated public hospitals, community health centres or village clinics for medical or family planning purposes, including pregnancy check-ups and childbirth. Households that possessed health cards, however, did not always use the cards when a household member visited a designated provider. The data show that of the 11 per cent of the population that were given health cards, 31 per cent experienced an illness in the three months prior to the survey, but in this group only 50 per cent sought medical care.[19] Of those who went to public hospitals, only 60 per cent used their health cards, while for community health centres the proportion was 52 per cent, for village midwives 12 per cent, and for other health facilities 31 per cent.

One possible reason for the non-use of health cards was to obtain better service from the providers. Among those who had health cards and sought medical services in public hospitals, the average out-of-pocket expense paid by those who used the health cards was around Rp 41,312 per person per sickness incident, while those who chose not to use their health cards on average spent around Rp3 million per person per sickness incident. This indicates a very large potential saving from the use of a health card. Hence, there must be a strong reason why those who possessed health cards did not use them. Seeking better service (for example, because of the seriousness of the illness) is a plausible reason as the cost for those who chose not to use their health cards was even higher than the cost for those who did not have health cards and who sought medical services in public hospitals — around Rp 2.6 million per person per sickness incident.[20]

Due to the prevalence of non-use of health cards, the calculation of coverage of this program is applied only to individuals who had illnesses, visited a provider for treatment, and used their health card in the past three months.[21] The data indicate that 6.3 per cent of all the people who underwent medical treatment used health cards to obtain free services. Among poor people only, the proportion of those who used health cards was 10.6 per cent, while among non-poor people 5.3 per cent used health cards to get the benefits of this program.

Meanwhile, the coverage of the supplemental food program for pregnant women and children under three years of age was 15.9 per cent. There were 16.5 per cent of poor pregnant women and children under three who received the benefits of this program, while the coverage among the non-poor was only slightly lower at 15.8 per cent.[22] Of those who received supplemental food, 55 per cent reported receiving both food and vitamins, 31 per cent reported receiving food only, and the remaining 14 per cent claimed to have received only vitamins.

4.2 Program Targeting

In terms of targeting, Figure 6.2 shows the coverage of the social safety net programs across quintiles of per capita expenditure relative to the level of coverage at the poorest quintile. A steeper curve indicates sharper targeting across per capita expenditure. It turns out that the best and worst targeting was to be found in the health programs. The medical services program had the sharpest targeting, while the nutrition program had the least accurate targeting. In the medical services program coverage dropped sharply in the second quintile and then fell gradually from the third to the richest quintile. Actually, the coverage of the employment creation program at the richest quintile was almost as low as that in the medical services program, but the drops in program coverage across quintiles were more gradual. Meanwhile, there was also a notable drop in the coverage of the upper secondary school scholarship program from the second to the third quintile.

In the subsidized rice program, coverage at the highest quintile was still quite high, as almost a quarter of households in the richest group still received the program benefits — almost half

FIGURE 6.2

Coverage of Various Social Safety Net Programs by Quintiles of per Capita Expenditure Relative to Q1

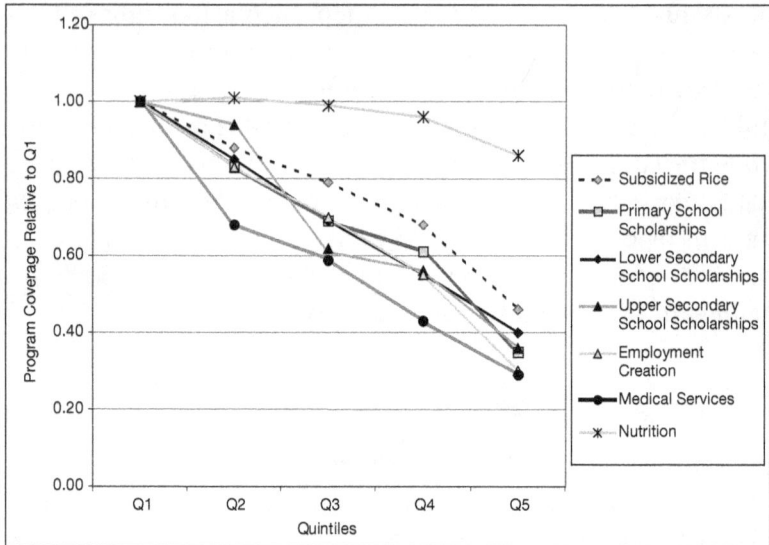

Source: See Figure 6.1

of the level of coverage at the poorest quintile.[23] Meanwhile, the proportion of households at the richest quintile who participated in an employment creation program was 30 per cent of the participation at the poorest quintile. For other programs, coverage at the highest quintile relative to that at the lowest quintile was 35 per cent for primary school scholarships, 40 per cent for lower secondary school scholarships, 37 per cent for upper secondary school scholarships, 29 per cent for medical services, and 86 per cent for the nutrition program.

4.3 Overall Program Performance

Based on the results shown in Appendix Table 6.A2, Table 6.4 calculates the implementation ratio (IR), targeting expenditure

TABLE 6.4
Calculation of the Implementation Ratio, Targeting Expenditure Ratio, and Coverage Ratio of the Social Safety Net Programs (%)

| Programs | Program Beneficiaries (% of total population) | | | % of Population Targeted | Implementation Ratio (IR) | Targeting Expenditure Ratio (TER) | Coverage Ratio (CR) |
| | Poor | Non-poor | Total | | | | |
	(a)	(b)	(c)= (a) + (b)	(d)	(e) = (c)/(d)	(f)=(a)/(c)	(g) = (e) × (f)
Subsidized rice	10.53	29.52	40.09	15	267.27	26.26	70.19
Employment creation	1.66	3.95	5.61	15	37.40	29.63	11.08
Primary school scholarships	1.16	2.88	4.03	6	67.17	28.78	19.33
Lower secondary school scholarships	2.43	6.02	8.42	17	49.53	28.86	14.29
Upper secondary school scholarships	1.08	2.66	3.71	10	37.10	29.11	10.80
Medical services	2.12	4.22	6.33	15	42.20	33.49	14.13
Nutrition	3.31	12.63	15.94	15	106.27	20.75	22.05

Note: In the above table numbers have been rounded.
Source: Appendix Table 6.A2

ratio (TER), and coverage ratio (CR) of the social safety net programs. Columns (a) to (c) in Table 6.4 show the number of program beneficiaries as a proportion of the total population. For example, in the subsidized rice program, program coverage among the poor was 52.64 per cent; the poor make up 20 per cent of the population. This means that the program beneficiaries who were poor made up $52.64 \times 0.2 = 10.53$ per cent of total population. The fraction of the population targeted by this program, as noted above in section 2.2, was 15 per cent, that is, 7.4 million households in the "pre-prosperous" category out of the total 50 million. The figures for the scholarship program are also obtained from section 2.2. The rest of the programs, however, did not have explicit numerical targets. Hence, for these programs the fraction of the population targeted is set as 15 per cent, that is, the same as the target population of the subsidized rice program, which was based on the number of "pre-prosperous" households.

The IR, TER, and CR indicators are then calculated using the method explained above in section 3.1. Figure 6.3 depicts the coverage ratio obtained from Table 6.4. The figure shows that, apart from the subsidized rice program, most of the Indonesian social safety net programs had relatively low coverage ratios. The subsidized rice program had a CR of 70 per cent[24] but the CRs of the other programs ranged from only 11 per cent to 22 per cent. Furthermore, Table 6.4 shows that the reason for this low coverage ratio is that all programs had a low targeting expenditure ratio that ranged from 20 per cent to 33 per cent. In addition, some programs also had a low implementation ratio. In particular, the employment creation, upper secondary school scholarships, and medical services programs had IRs of less than 50 per cent.

FIGURE 6.3
Coverage Ratio (CR) of Various Social Safety Net Programs

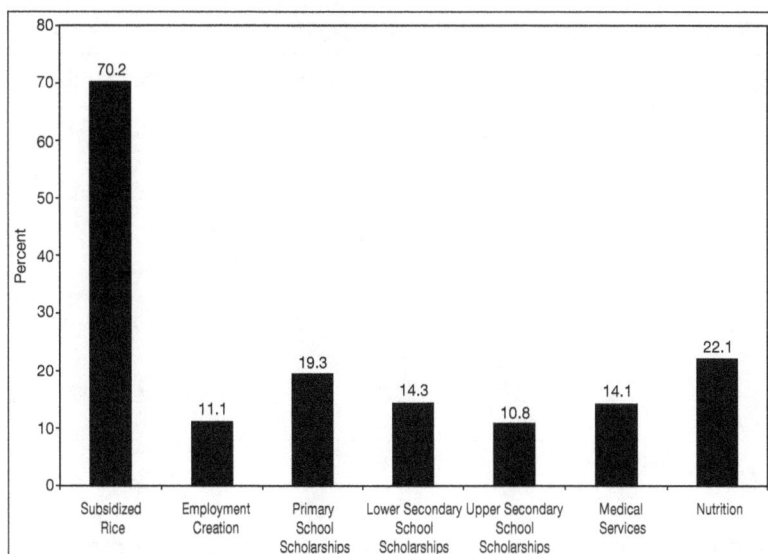

Source: See Table 6.4

4.4 Multiple Coverage

As there were many social safety net programs in place at the same time, the multiple participation of households in different programs needs to be assessed. Table 6.5 shows the distribution of households by the number of social safety net programs in which they participated.[25] The table shows that, even though many social safety net programs have been established by the government, they still entirely left out 32 per cent of households in the poorest quintile. On the other hand, the programs have given some benefits to 21 per cent of households in the richest quintile.

Among households that participated in the social safety net programs, the large majority participated in only one program.

TABLE 6.5
Distribution of Households by Participation in JPS Programs and Quintile of Per Capita Expenditure

Number of Programs	QI	QII	QIII	QIV	QV	Total
0	32.1	42.4	51.6	62.5	78.7	53.5
1	47.2	43.8	38.7	32.1	19.3	36.2
2	16.9	11.8	8.7	5.0	1.9	8.8
3	3.4	1.8	0.9	0.4	0.1	1.3
4	0.4	0.2	0.1	0.0	0.0	0.1
5	0.0	0.0	0.0	...	...	0.0
6	0.0	0.0	...	...	...	0.0
7	...	...	...	...	...	...

Source: See Table 6.4

Very few households participated in more than three programs and none participated in all seven programs. Among the poorest 20 per cent of households, 17 per cent received benefits from two programs and 3.4 per cent from three programs. Meanwhile, among households in the richest quintile, those that received benefits from the social safety net programs mostly participated in one program, and less than 2 per cent participated in more than one program. Among households in the second richest quintile, however, a substantial proportion, that is, more than 5 per cent, received benefits from more than one program.

4.5 Regional Heterogeneity

Over the last thirty years Indonesia has been administered through a heavily centralized form of government. As a result, all of the key social safety net programs have also been designed by the central government. Even when the programs allowed for local decision-making, the structure and scope of those local decisions were carefully specified in centrally drafted program guidelines. Despite this, there were huge variations across regions in how widely and how well the programs have been implemented.[26]

The estimates of district-level coverage of two social safety net programs among the poor and the non-poor are now contrasted. Figure 6.4 presents the coverage of the subsidized rice program, that is, the program that has the highest coverage, while Figure 6.5 shows the coverage of the medical services program, that is, the program that has the sharpest targeting. Each dot in Figures 6.4 and 6.5 represents a district, of which there are more than 350 throughout Indonesia.

From Figure 6.4, two conclusions immediately emerge about the district-level coverage of the subsidized rice program. First,

FIGURE 6.4
Coverage of the Subsidized Rice Program at District Level

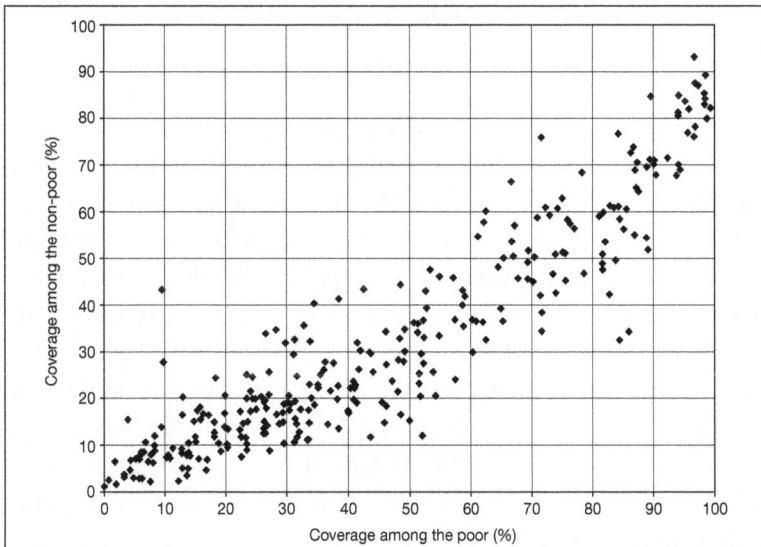

Note: Each dot represents a single district.
Source: See Table 6.4

FIGURE 6.5
Coverage of the Medical Services Program at District Level

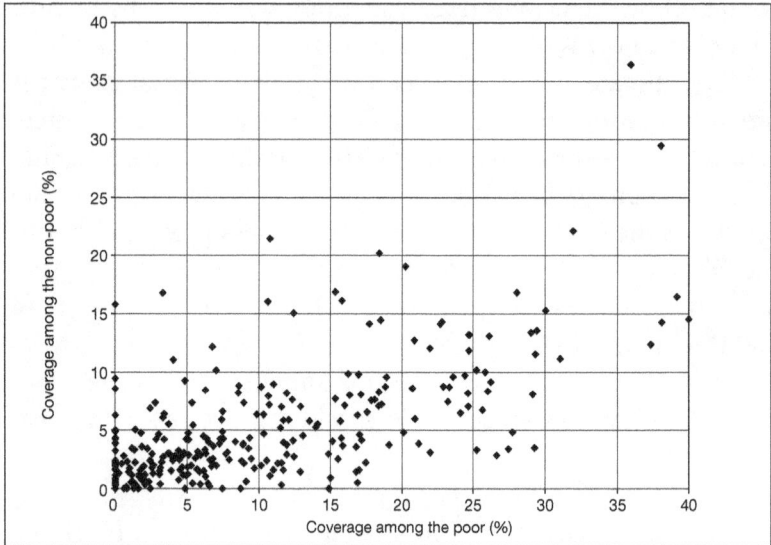

Note: Each dot represents a single district.
Source: See Table 6.4

coverage among the non-poor was highly positively correlated with coverage among the poor (the correlation is 0.92). Districts that had low coverage among the poor also had low coverage among the non-poor, and vice versa. Very few districts specifically favoured the poor in the distribution of OPK rice. This means that no conspicuous differences among regions were observed, probably due to the low targeting expenditure ratio. Second, the range in the level of coverage across districts was very wide, running from near zero to almost 100 per cent coverage. This suggests that the resources distributed through this program varied widely across districts. Some districts received a lot of resources, while others received very little.

Meanwhile, Figure 6.5 indicates that the medical services program also faced difficulties in reaching out to the majority of the poor. Most districts achieved coverage among the poor of less than 10 per cent; very few districts had coverage among the poor of higher than 20 per cent. In this program, however, differences across regions were large. Furthermore, compared to the other programs, the program on the whole achieved better targeting. In most districts, coverage among the non-poor remained under 10 per cent, even in those districts where coverage among the poor reached up to 30 per cent.

4.6 Budget for the Social Safety Net Programs

Implementing the social safety net programs was a costly exercise, particularly for a country suffering from an economic crisis. On the one hand, the government faced shrinking revenues as the tax base was eroded by the crisis. On the other, it had to deal with the severe social impact of the crisis. But the government had no alternative as the social costs from doing nothing to lessen the impending social impact of the crisis were expected to outweigh the financial costs of the social safety net programs. Hence the government implemented the programs with a budget that was partly supported by foreign loans.

Table 6.6 shows the budget allocation of the social safety net programs during fiscal year 1998/99 to 2000. The budget continued to decline over time both in terms of the absolute amount as well as in terms of the proportion of the total government budget. This reflects three things. First, financing constraints continued to be a major problem in implementing these large-scale programs. Second, over the course of time it became apparent that the social impact of the crisis was not as catastrophic as earlier predicted, so the government could afford to downsize the overall program. Third, as lessons were learned, the government became more selective in choosing the programs it wanted to continue and dropped the ones that were considered non-essential or ineffective.

TABLE 6.6

Budget Allocation of the Social Safety Net Programs (Rp billion)

Programs	1998/1999	1999/2000	2000*
Sale of subsidized rice	5,450	6,235	2,232
Scholarships and school block grants	1,138	1,251	667
Employment creation	2,066	1,000	441
Health (JPS-BK)	1,043	1,030	867
Other programs	5,123	2,357	1,255
Total social safety net programs	14,820	11,873	5,462
Total government budget	263,888	212,699	183,069
Percentage of social safety net budget	5.62	5.58	2.98

Note: In the year 2000 the government changed its fiscal calendar from April-March to January-December. Hence the transitional fiscal year 2000 was only for a nine-month period from April to December.

Source: BAPPENAS

As indicated by the budget allowance, the sale of subsidized rice continued to be the program that was deemed to be the most essential by the government. When in fiscal year 1999/2000 the overall budget for the social safety net programs was reduced from Rp 14.8 to 11.9 trillion, the budget allocated to the subsidized rice program was in fact increased from Rp 5.5 to 6.2 trillion. Thus the proportion of budgeting allocated to this program increased from 37 to 53 per cent of the total budget for the social safety net programs. Similarly, the budget allocation also indicates that the government viewed the scholarship program and the health program as essential. On the other hand, the employment creation program, which received a relatively large budget in the first year, was downsized substantially in subsequent years.

5 CONCLUSION

In early 1998, in anticipation of the adverse social impact of the economic crisis, the Indonesian Government established social safety net programs. The programs were intended to protect both the traditional poor and the newly poor, as it was feared that these groups would not be able to cope with the impact of the crisis without outside help.

The findings of this study, unfortunately, point out that in many cases the target groups have been largely missed by the programs, in terms of both low coverage and loose targeting in practice. The programs have been plagued by problems in targeting the beneficiaries and delivering benefits to intended target groups. Except for the subsidized rice program, all programs have suffered from undercoverage, that is, there have been large numbers of the poor who have not been covered by the programs. At the same time, all of the programs have faced the problem of leakage, that is, a large proportion of program benefits has gone to the non-poor. The findings of this study indicate that the leakage is due to the fact that all programs suffer from bad targeting. In addition, some programs also suffer from inadequate implementation.

Nevertheless, it should be emphasized that the effectiveness of the programs varies across programs and regions. Some programs in some districts have high coverage among the poor and at the same time show a reasonable amount of targeting. Nationally, the subsidized rice program has the highest coverage, while the upper secondary school scholarship program has the lowest coverage. In terms of targeting, the medical services program has the sharpest targeting, while the nutrition program has the least targeting. It is also important to note that the findings of this study refer to a certain period of time. Program performance may change — either improve or worsen — across time.

One notable feature of the coverage and targeting of the various social safety net programs is the heterogeneity of performance across programs as well as across regions. Three factors presumably contribute to this heterogeneity in performance: program design, budget allocations across programs and regions, and regional capabilities in program implementation. In addition, other factors may also influence the performance of a certain program, such as active monitoring and supervision by communities, which may enhance the performance of a program in a particular region.

The findings of this study point to certain things that need to be done in the future. First, Indonesia needs to have a formal social safety net system in place as a buffer since, when the crisis occurred, the country was not prepared to deal with its social impact. The maintained system should be small in scale but capable of quick expansion whenever needs arise. The system should be well prepared for dealing not only with the impact of social, economic or political crises but also with the impact of natural disasters, which occur relatively frequently in Indonesia.

Secondly, sharper targeting and higher coverage of beneficiaries in the social safety net programs have been hampered by the unavailability of reliable, up-to-date data at both geographic and household levels. The use of the BKKBN classification of households as the basis for targeting has apparently been problematic. This is not to suggest, however, that the BKKBN data are at fault, since they were never meant for targeting in social safety net or poverty reduction programs in the first place. Instead, there is clearly a need for Indonesia to develop and maintain a database that is specifically designed for this purpose.

Thirdly, one of the main reasons for the large degree of leakage in the social safety net programs has been the pressure from communities to distribute program benefits more uniformly. This indicates that such programs need to have an effective public education component, so that the people can understand why the program benefits should be prioritized for the needy and the poor.

APPENDIX TABLE 6.A1

Comparison of Mean per Capita Expenditures in Core SUSENAS and Consumption Module SUSENAS (Rp/month)

Area/Educational Level	Sample in Both Core and Consumption Module			Expenditures of Two Groups of Sample in Core		
	Core Expenditure	Module Expenditure	Per cent Difference	Core Only	Core and Module	Per cent Difference
URBAN:						
Not completed primary school	139,120	139,991	0.63	121,906	139,120	14.12
	(82,509)	(82,936)		(70,258)	(82,059)	
Primary school	156,959	156,622	-0.21	130,601	156,959	20.18
	(109,019)	(102,299)		(79,911)	(109,019)	
Junior secondary	188,470	188,710	0.13	160,173	188,470	17.67
	(118,353)	(117,444)		(105,663)	(118,353)	
Senior secondary	237,082	236,921	-0.07	197,914	237,082	19.79
	(164,350)	(160,495)		(138,015)	(164,350)	
Tertiary	336,757	333,792	-0.88	276,825	336,757	21.65
	(279,675)	(248,442)		(284,280)	(279,675)	
Total	196,773	196,523	-0.13	166,942	196,773	17.87
	(157,344)	(149,370)		(140,155)	(157,344)	

APPENDIX TABLE 6.A1 (continued)
Comparison of Mean per Capita Expenditures in Core SUSENAS and Consumption Module SUSENAS (Rp/month)

Area/Educational Level	Sample in Both Core and Consumption Module			Expenditures of Two Groups of Sample in Core		
	Core Expenditure	Module Expenditure	Per cent Difference	Core Only	Core and Module	Per cent Difference
RURAL:						
Not completed primary school	106,163	106,789	0.59	95,998	106,163	10.59
	(51,324)	(52,465)		(50,602)	(51,324)	
Primary school	113,234	113,774	0.48	98,118	113,234	15.41
	(61,124)	(61,058)		(52,493)	(61,124)	
Junior secondary	133,027	134,394	1.03	110,944	133,027	19.91
	(77,077)	(99,958)		(63,386)	(77,077)	
Senior secondary	158,588	159,410	0.52	131,093	158,588	20.97
	(92,072)	(91,615)		(81,378)	(92,072)	
Tertiary	201,152	202,011	0.43	158,171	201,152	27.17
	(108,746)	(106,807)		(93,127)	(108,746)	
Total	116,294	116,955	0.57	101,575	116,294	14.49
	(65,651)	(68,472)		(57,195)	(65,651)	

Note: Numbers in parentheses are standard deviations.
Source: SUSENAS

APPENDIX TABLE 6.A2
Coverage of Various Social Safety Net Programs by Quintiles of per Capita Expenditures

Programs	Number of Eligible Recipients	Program Coverage (%)							
		Poor		Non-Poor				Total	Total
		Q_1	Q_2	Q_3	Q_4	Q_5	$Q_2 - Q_5$	$Q_1 - Q_5$
Subsidized rice	50,385,444	52.64	46.24	41.71	35.76	24.33	36.90	40.09
Employment creation	50,385,444	8.31	6.89	5.79	4.58	2.53	4.94	5.61
Primary school scholarships	29,745,369	5.80	4.84	4.02	3.52	2.04	3.60	4.03
Lower secondary school scholarships	10,394,621	12.15	10.31	8.34	6.73	4.85	7.53	8.42
Upper secondary school scholarships	6,430,146	5.40	5.06	3.32	3.04	1.96	3.32	3.71
Medical services	27,567,138	10.60	7.24	6.30	4.52	3.09	5.28	6.33
Nutrition	19,970,948	16.54	16.64	16.38	15.94	14.24	15.79	15.94

Note: The quintiles are calculated at the district level.
Source: Compilation by the authors

Notes

Reprinted from Sudarno Sumarto, Asep Suryahadi and Wenefrida Widyanti, "Designs and Implementation of the Indonesian Social Safety Net Programs" *Developing Economies* 40, no. 1 (2002): 3–31, with permission from Wiley-Blackwell.

1. Funding for the JPS programs came from the state budget as well as loans provided by the World Bank, the Asian Development Bank, and bilateral donors, either directly through project support or indirectly through program loans that provided budget support.
2. These two groups of poor people cannot be distinguished in the data used in this study. To be able to distinguish them requires the use of panel data that cover both the pre- and post-crisis periods. For an example of such an analysis in the context of the Indonesian social safety net programs, see Sumarto et al. (2000).
3. There were some changes in the social safety net programs across fiscal years.
4. The program was introduced in July 1998 in the Jakarta area and then expanded all over the country. The benefit was later increased to 20 kilograms in April 1999 and then changed again to between 10 and 20 kilograms in April 2000 (Olken et al. 2001).
5. The classification, created by the National Family Planning Coordinating Board (BKKBN), is outlined in Chapter 2.
6. Since the amount of subsidized rice was substantially below total consumption, in practice the program served as the equivalent of an income transfer. However, since the price was fixed in nominal terms, the magnitude of the income transfer was scaled to the need for food. In this sense the program can be seen as a combination of income transfer and food security.
7. These "crash programs" were launched in December 1997 and lasted until the end of the fiscal year in March 1998.
8. In fiscal year 1999/2000, however, *padat karya* programs were cut back to only two: the Public Works Sector *Padat Karya* Program and the Special Initiative for Unemployed Women Program.
9. See note 16 in Chapter 2 for a definition of "pre-prosperous".

10. Suryahadi et al. (1999) found a lack of correlation between this official classification and the consumption-based measure of poverty. While only 15 per cent of the "prosperous" households were "poor", 75 per cent of the "pre-prosperous" households were "non-poor". On the other hand, 46 per cent of the "non-poor" households were "pre-prosperous" and 38 per cent of the "poor" households were "prosperous".

11. The BKKBN classification of households was originally created for BKKBN's own family planning purposes. It was never meant to be used for targeting in social safety net or poverty reduction programs. It was selected for targeting purposes in the social safety net programs because it was the only database available that recorded almost all households in Indonesia.

12. Ferreira et al. (1999) argue that a relatively low wage rate ensures that only those in need apply and that as many people as possible can be employed. A low wage rate also protects the incentive to take up regular work when available.

13. The extensive monitoring that has been done on the program finds, however, that the parent representative played only a minor role in validating implementation of the criteria and the decision of the school officials.

14. See Pradhan et al. (2000) and Sutanto and Irawan (2000).

15. The official estimate of the poverty rate in February 1999 was 23.6 per cent (Sutanto and Irawan 2000). This implies that there was a large overlap between the first quintile and the absolute poor.

16. See note 5 in Chapter 2 for details of SUSENAS.

17. This is confirmed by the qualitative findings in Tim Dampak Krisis SMERU (2000).

18. The program guidelines stipulated that students in the lowest three grades of primary school were not eligible for the scholarships. The data on primary school recipients, however, show that the proportion of first to third graders who received the scholarships was only slightly less than the proportion of fourth to sixth grade recipients. Therefore, the analysis of the primary school scholarship program in this study is based on all students.

19. Even though the health card was meant only for the poor, only 35 per cent of all the health cards distributed were given to the poor (Saadah et al. 2000). This means that only around 19 per cent of poor households possessed health cards, while around 9 per cent of non-poor households also had health cards.

20. Saadah et al. (2000) hypothesize that another possible explanation of the large degree of non-use of health cards is that some health providers refused to honour the promise of free services for health card-holders. The reason is that the providers were not reimbursed based on the number of actual services performed, but instead received an advance lump sum payment based on a predicted demand for services.

21. Treatments include those for both in-patients and out-patients. The calculation of this program coverage, however, does not include the use of health cards for family planning and birth delivery services.

22. It seems that there is no relationship between receiving supplemental food and possession of a health card. Of those who received supplemental food, only 17 per cent reported having a health card.

23. This indicates strong pressures from communities for a more equal distribution of program benefits across all households (Sumarto et al. 2000).

24. It is important to note, however, that most beneficiaries of this program received benefits that were less than stipulated due to a distribution of benefits that was much broader than the targeted population.

25. The programs are limited to the seven programs evaluated in this study.

26. These regional variations in performance are certain to grow as the policy of expenditure decentralization, which began in January 2001, allows for greater autonomy at the district level.

Chapter 7

SAFETY NETS OR SAFETY ROPES? DYNAMIC BENEFIT INCIDENCE OF TWO CRISIS PROGRAMS IN INDONESIA

Sudarno Sumarto, Asep Suryahadi, and Lant Pritchett

1 INTRODUCTION

Mountain climbers scaling a sheer cliff face, understandably, want protection from falling. One method of protection is to place a safety net at the bottom of the cliff, to catch falling climbers just before they hit the ground. The alternative is a safety rope attached to a set of movable devices anchored at higher and higher levels as climbers ascend, so that falling climbers are caught after falling at most the length of the rope. The "safety net" guarantees against falls past an absolute level, while the "safety rope" guarantees against a fall more than a given distance, irrespective of the original height. For climbers near the bottom the safety net provides reassurance, but for climbers who have already made substantial progress scaling the cliff face, a safety net, which benefits them only after they have lost nearly all of their progress, is much less attractive than a safety rope.

The now ubiquitous metaphor of a "social safety net" conflates two distinct objectives in the design of transfer programs.

One possible objective is to minimize a measure of income or expenditure poverty.[1] An alternative objective is to mitigate risk, that is, reduce household vulnerability to the wide variety of potential adverse shocks that they could face (death, accident, fire, crop loss, job loss), whether or not the shocks push households below some absolute threshold. If program targeting is judged exclusively on static benefit (or poverty) incidence, then risk mitigation programs benefiting households that have suffered large shocks but are not "poor" may appear to have large "leakage" when in fact they are simply serving a different social objective — risk mitigation.

The undifferentiated metaphor of "safety net" also confuses thinking about the political economy of transfer programs.[2] Governments may choose to implement "safety net" and "safety rope" programs for completely different reasons.[3] While a "safety net" program might be more popular with the poor the more effectively it transfers wealth from richer to poorer households, a "safety rope" program will be more popular with middle-income groups if it serves an important insurance function in transferring resources from good times to bad times.

This paper uses household panel data with three periods: consumption expenditure data from before (May 1997) and after (August 1998) the severe crisis in Indonesia and data on participation in the crisis mitigation programs from December 1998 to document the very different patterns of static and dynamic benefit incidence of two crisis programs which used different targeting mechanisms.

2 DYNAMIC BENEFIT INCIDENCE

Examining dynamic benefit incidence across programs brings together three literatures: static benefit incidence, program design and targeting, and the dynamics of household income.

2.1 Static Incidence of Benefits from Public Expenditures

The incidence of taxes and expenditures — "who pays" and "who benefits" — is a long-standing concern in public finance[4] and the techniques for calculating static benefit incidence of public spending are well known (Musgrave & Musgrave 1989). The relationship between economic status and program participation can be estimated using data on household economic status (income, consumption expenditures, or wealth measures) and on household participation (e.g., attendance at school, use of public health facilities, reported receipt of program transfers, consumption of subsidized goods). To estimate the "benefits" from participation in publicly provided services requires either household reports on the magnitude of receipts (e.g., from transfer programs) or budget data.[5] Poverty incidence studies, which examine program participation or expenditure incidence for "poor" and "non-poor" (defined by income or expenditure), are a special case of standard benefit incidence techniques (van de Walle & Nead 1995).[6] The spread of multimodule household surveys has spawned a now enormous literature on "benefit incidence" (and poverty incidence) in developing countries that spans education, health, social insurance, price subsidies (food, housing, and fuel), credit and micro-credit, and poverty alleviation programs.[7]

The SUSENAS surveys have provided high-quality, publicly accessible, large sample, multimodule data on Indonesia and so there are numerous studies of static benefit incidence in Indonesia: van de Walle (1994) shows the differential incidence of primary versus tertiary health expenditures. Lanjouw et al. (2000) use the 1998 SUSENAS to examine the average and marginal static benefit incidence for education and health. Earlier studies have also calculated the benefit incidence of subsidies to specific commodities like rice and fuels (World Bank 1993b). There are more and more studies that examine the benefit incidence of the crisis programs (Pritchett et al. 2002).

2.2 Targeting and Program Design

There are two main classes of targeting that can be built into program design: administrative targeting or self-selection (Grosh 1994). Administrative targeting can be based on eligibility requirements using any number of criteria: fixed characteristics (e.g., all women are eligible), demographic characteristics (e.g., all children under five), current economic status (e.g., households below specific criteria), residence or location (e.g., all households in poor neighbourhoods), experience of some negative shock (e.g., those laid off), observable outcome (e.g., all children less than two standard deviations below a nutritional norm), or some combination of the above (e.g., a feeding program implemented only in poor areas for children under two who are underweight for age in households with less than two-thirds median income[8]). Administrative targeting also includes targeting not on fixed criteria that completely determine eligibility, but where the beneficiaries are chosen using a process that follows some broad criteria. For example, Galasso and Ravallion (2000) examine a program in Bangladesh that uses community-based targeting to choose recipient households. In Indonesia the children who received scholarships in the Scholarship and Block Grant program were chosen by local school committees using criteria that included input from local school officials, while the new generation of community projects (such as the Kecamatan Development Project) allows local flexibility in choosing how to use block grants.

The second broad type of targeting is self-selection targeting, in which the program is made universally available (at least within some broad geographic region) but in which the program design limits uptake by making the program unattractive to those not intended as beneficiaries. Self-selection targeting can subsidize only low-quality goods and services (e.g., staple foods or poor-quality health care), choose locations (e.g., only relatively poor neighbourhoods), make program benefits difficult to obtain (e.g., through waiting times) or impose some type of hurdle requirement (e.g., a requirement to work for wages in a public employment scheme).

Program targeting can be evaluated for either compliance or effectiveness. A compliance study examines only whether the program benefits were actually distributed, and, if distributed, whether the selection of beneficiaries followed the program design. It does not question whether compliance with the design led to desirable targeting outcomes.

Targeting effectiveness examines program performance along two dimensions: coverage — what fraction of the intended beneficiaries actually received program benefits[9] (and what fraction of the total program budget they received), and leakage — what fraction of program benefits did not go to the intended beneficiaries. Targeting effectiveness outcomes are determined by magnitude of budget, compliance with the targeting design, and the precision with which the targeting design identifies intended beneficiaries. For instance, if the program's intended beneficiaries are the consumption-expenditure poor but the only administratively usable proxy about households is their neighbourhood, then perfect compliance with an imperfect proxy will lead to targeting errors of both type I (undercoverage) and type II (leakage).

2.3 Dynamics of Household Income and Expenditures

While risk has always been a major topic in economics, there has been increasing attention to the volatility of household incomes and how this can cause people to move into and out of poverty (e.g., World Bank 2001a). The study of household income or expenditure dynamics in developing countries has been limited by data availability but the increasing number of panel surveys has expanded empirical investigations of expenditure and poverty dynamics. Many studies have examined income mobility and the "transition matrix" in the distribution of income — what is the likelihood that a household in the pth percentile in period t is in the $p+/-j$th percentile in period $t + n$. These papers have generally found that there are substantial amounts of mobility in the observed distribution of expenditures — although what fraction of that is income and what fraction measurement error is an unresolved problem (see Fields and Ok 1999 for a review). Using data on the same households for T periods allows the estimation of poverty dynamics — what fraction of households were poor in all T periods, what fraction were non-poor in all periods, and what fraction were poor and then non-poor, etc.

2.4 Defining Dynamic Benefit Incidence

We extend the definition of static benefit incidence to dynamics of household expenditures. Let e be household (natural log) real expenditures per person in period t:

$$e_t^h = \ln(HH\ expenditures/N_t^h * P_t^h) \tag{7.1}$$

Data for N households can be used to define ranks of the expenditure distribution

$$r_t(e_t^h) = \left[\sum_{n=1,n\neq h}^{N} I(e_t^n \leq e_t^h) \right] \tag{7.2}$$

Extension to dynamics is straightforward as we define the expenditure "shock" between periods t and t-n as the change in (natural log) real expenditures as defined above[10]

$$s^h_{t,t-n} = e^h_t - e^h_{t-n} \tag{7.3}$$

Ranking of households by their expenditures shock is defined as

$$r(s^h_{t,t-n}) = \left[\sum_{n=1, n\neq h}^{N} I(s^n_{t,t-n} \leq s^h_{t,t-n}) \right] \tag{7.4}$$

Since this is most relevant to our application below, let us focus on the incidence of program participation alone (that is, hold to one side the issue of the magnitude of benefits conditional on participation). The probability that household h will participate in program A, given its rank in the distribution of the level and shock of expenditures, is a function

$$\textit{Prob(household h participates in program A)} = p^A[r_t(e^h_t), r_t(s^h_{t,t-n})] \tag{7.5}$$

In this framework static benefit incidence of participation (SBIP) is the relationship between the probability of participating in program A and the rankings of households by their current expenditures, conditional on the shock:

$$\textit{SBIP: Prob(household h participates in program A)}$$
$$= p^A_S[r_t(e^h_t) | r_t(s^h_{t,t-n})] \tag{7.6}$$

Standard static benefit incidence is clearly just a special case which ignores dynamics altogether.[11]

The dynamic benefit incidence of participation (DBIP) in program A is defined as the relationship between the probability of participating in program A and the percentiles of households by their expenditure shock, conditional on the level of expenditures.[12]

DBIP: Prob(household h participates in program A)

$$= p_D^A[r_t(s_{t,t-n}^h)|r_t(e_t^h)] \tag{7.7}$$

Within these definitions, *coverage* for program A is higher than for program B at any combination of expenditure and shock iff:

Coverage: $\quad p^A[r_t(e_t^h), r_t(s_{t,t-n}^h)] > p^B[r_t(e_t^h), r_t(s_{t,t-n}^h)] \tag{7.8}$

Targeting can be defined as changes in the probability of participation with respect to level of either expenditures or shocks. Program A is more "targeted" with respect to expenditures than program B iff at a point:

Targeting w.r.t. expenditures:

$$\left\{ \frac{\partial p^A[r_t(e_t^h), r_t(s_{t,t-n}^h)]}{\partial r(e)} \right\} > \left\{ \frac{\partial p^B[r_t(e_t^h), r_t(s_{t,t-n}^h)]}{\partial r(e)} \right\} \tag{7.9}$$

Similarly, program A is more "targeted" with respect to shocks than program B iff:

Targeting w.r.t. shock:

$$\left\{ \frac{\partial p^A[r_t(e_t^h), r_t(s_{t,t-n}^h)]}{\partial r(s)} \right\} > \left\{ \frac{\partial p^B[r_t(e_t^h), r_t(s_{t,t-n}^h)]}{\partial r(s)} \right\} \tag{7.10}$$

Static benefit incidence is often visualized as a graph of the frequency of participation in the program (vertical axis) against the level of expenditures (horizontal axis). In this graph coverage is represented by the height and targeting by the slope (either at a point or over a range). When this is extended to include dynamics, the graph is now a surface in three-dimensional space and program participation is the vertical axis and the level of expenditures could be on one horizontal axis and changes in expenditures on another. Different programs can have different coverage and targeting performances with respect to expenditure levels and shocks, so one program's incidence graph could be steep w.r.t expenditures at all levels of shock, flat (non-targeted) w.r.t. shocks, or vice versa. A pure "safety rope" program could be sharply targeted w.r.t. shocks but flat in the expenditures dimension.

3 THE JPS PROGRAMS, TARGETING DESIGN, DATA, AND METHODS

As a result of the intertwined natural, financial, and political crises that began in August 1997, the Government of Indonesia launched several "crisis" programs. This set of programs, widely known as JPS (*Jaring Pengaman Sosial*, or the Social Safety Net), was intended to help protect the traditionally poor and those suffering from the crisis. The present paper examines the static and dynamic benefit incidence of two of the JPS programs, the OPK (*Operasi Pasar Khusus*, or Special Market Operation), which was a program of selling subsidized rice to targeted households, and the employment creation programs (which were a collection of many different programs operated by different ministries). We want to stress this narrow focus on targeting and the fact that this is not a comprehensive evaluation of all of the JPS programs or even of these two programs.

3.1 Targeting of the Two Programs

The two programs used different targeting methods. The basis for official household eligibility for the cheap rice program was the list prepared by the family planning agency BKKBN, which classified households into four levels of socioeconomic status: "pre-prosperous" and "prosperous" levels I, II and III.[13] The rice program began in August 1998 and was brought up to roughly full scale, covering households that were "pre-prosperous" and "prosperous level I", by December 1998 (Tabor, Dillon, and Sawit, 1999). During the period covered by the data (August–December

1998), each eligible household was entitled to purchase 10 kg at Rp 1,000/kg, while the market price for medium quality rice during October–November 1998 was around Rp 2,500 per kg.[14] So the value of the subsidy was approximately Rp 15,000 per household per month compared to the total household expenditures at the 20th percentile in this sample of Rp 232,000 per month.

There are four major criticisms of using a family planning list for targeting the rice program. First, because the list was based on relatively fixed assets (like not having a floor made of improved materials and owning changes of clothing), it did not capture transitory shocks to income. Second, the criteria included non-economic questions (e.g., is the family able to meet religious obligations?). Third, the list was compiled by relatively poorly trained workers at the village level so consistency across regions was not assured. Fourth, the list was susceptible to changes by local government officials.[15]

There is a great deal of evidence, however, that the targeting mechanism was not always implemented as specified in the rules.[16] Each village was allowed to purchase a quantity of rice, based on the total number of eligible households in the village, from the local depot of the logistics agency and transport it to the village (or neighbourhood in urban areas).[17] Once in the village the actual distribution of the rice to households was carried out by village-level officials. Local decision-makers felt pressure from communities to extend the distribution of rice beyond the "eligible" households to include other households.[18] A commonly heard argument was that, since the whole community was expected to contribute to community endeavours (such as *gotong royong*, or "self-help" undertakings), all should benefit equally from the "windfall" assistance from the central government (SMERU 1998). Thus in many cases the rice was divided up equally among all households, which meant that KPS and KS I households received less rice.[19]

The other "program" that we examine was not a single program but a large set of activities under the name of *padat karya*, meaning "labour intensive". The programs were often not classic "public works" programs or "employment guarantee" programs but activities aimed at expanding employment. This collection of employment programs was diverse and, although specific programs were geographically targeted (such as food for work in drought-affected areas), the lack of coordination meant that there was little or no systematic geographic targeting of the overall set of programs. Within programs there was a variety of disagreements about the desired characteristics of intended participants but typically the beneficiaries were not chosen according to any fixed administrative criteria. Hence, to the extent that there was targeting, it was primarily through self-selection. This self-selection mechanism had the potential advantage over administrative criteria of allowing individuals to choose to participate or not, and it created the possibility of being more flexible to unobserved household shocks than administrative criteria (Jalan and Ravallion 1999*a*, 1999*b*).

In practice, however, there were numerous problems with the targeting in the employment programs. First, the programs were not held rigorously to a minimum wage and in many cases would raise wages (or shorten daily hours worked for the same wage) to attract workers so that the money could be spent. In some regions the wage was set at a higher rate than the prevailing local wage rate, inducing some people already working to switch or add jobs. Second, some spot field investigations uncovered evidence of "ghost workers" who were present on the records as being paid for the day but were not present on the site. Third, reports from the field also indicated other shortcomings in the selection of beneficiaries, such as favouritism in giving jobs to the close family and friends of local officials.

Nevertheless, the design of the two programs offers a clear contrast: rice eligibility was based on the administrative criteria of the family planning agency's list, while participation in any of the employment programs was based on self-selection. In practice, both programs had a variety of deviations from this design and the actual targeting with respect to household expenditures and poverty status. Hence, the actual targeting is a matter for empirical inquiry.

3.2 Data: The 100 Village Survey

The 100 Village Survey (*Survei Seratus Desa*, or SSD) was carried out by the national statistics agency (BPS). The present study utilizes data from three rounds of the SSD[20] carried out in May 1997, August 1998, and December 1998. Although the sample size was 12,000 households in each round, not all households were "panel" households. Due to sample replacement, only 6,200 households could be identified as the same households interviewed in all three rounds.[21]

The December 1998 round of the SSD had a module on respondents' awareness of and participation in various JPS programs. The households were asked if they had "participated" in these programs in the period since 31 August 1998, so the recall period was roughly three months. There are three unfortunate aspects of the data. First, the questions do not allow identification of which of the many employment programs the household participated in. Second, the questionnaire inquires only about the receipt of *sembako* ("basic necessities") without specifically identifying the government-subsidized rice program, although other sources of *sembako* do exist (e.g., religious activities, private charities, NGOs). In all references we assume that the data on *sembako* reflect the OPK program and hence refer to "receiving rice" or "participating in the rice program" as we believe that OPK accounts for the vast proportion of *sembako*. The third limitation is that there is no indication of the extent of participation or the magnitude of benefits, the number of days of employment-program labour (or wages paid), or the amount of rice received (which, as noted above, varied widely depending on the distribution rule in the local community). Hence we limit attention to how "participation" in these programs varied across households' level of and change in expenditures.

3.3 Methods

Data on program participation from the December 1998 round were combined with the rankings of levels and shocks to expenditure for the same households from the May 1997 and August 1998 rounds. To enhance comparability with the existing literature on static benefit incidence we calculated program participation by quintiles of expenditures in both periods. We also computed program participation by quintiles of the expenditure shock experienced by the household between May 1997 and August 1998 and the combination of the two pre-crisis levels and shocks. In the analysis below we focus on May 1997 (which is the pre-crisis, observed level of expenditures and which best corresponds to information available for administrative targeting) and the subsequent shock.

Table 7.1 presents the cut-off points that define the quintiles of levels and shocks and the number of households in each of the twenty-five (five by five) cells, about which two points should be made. First, there is enormous variation in the observed shock to expenditures — the upper two quintiles reported increased expenditures and those in the upper quintile had expenditure increases of over 20 per cent. As we examine the fraction of households in the upper quintile by "shock" who participated in the crisis "safety net" programs, keep in mind that these are households that appear to have fared relatively well. Second, while substantial numbers of households fell into each of the cells, there was a tendency for those in the lowest expenditure categories in 1997 to have larger (proportionate) positive shocks and for those in higher expenditure groups to have larger (proportionate) negative shocks; this pattern is plausible because on average one would expect those with low expenditures to have

TABLE 7.1
Number of Households in 100 Village Data by Quintile of per Capita Household Expenditures in May 1997 and Quintile of per Capita Household Expenditure Changes between May 1997 and August 1998

| | | Totals by Shock Quintiles | Quintiles of Changes in (Natural Log) Real Expenditures from May 1997 to August 1998 | | | | |
			I: ≤−0.49	II: −0.49<s≤−0.23	III: −0.23<s≤−0.03	IV: −.03<s≤0.22	V: s>0.2228
			1,240	1,240	1,240	1,240	1,240
May 1997 Expenditure Quintiles	I: e<30,497	1,240	112	154	217	316	441
	II: 30,497<e<39,922	1,240	138	223	270	326	283
	III: 39,922<e<50,166	1,240	191	258	308	255	228
	IV: 50,166<e<65,296	1,240	289	324	266	191	170
	V: 65,296<e	1,240	510	281	179	152	118

Source: 100 Village Survey

suffered from a temporarily poor outcome. At the same time, this may also indicate a fair degree of pure measurement error in consumption expenditures, which is a problem we have worried about (ineffectually) but which should in general produce the usual attenuation biases and understate the degree of targeting.

We calculate the fraction of households in each cell that participated in either rice or employment programs. For example, for quintiles of expenditure and rice participation this is (where $I[\ ]$ is an indicator function that takes on the value 1 if the condition is "true" and LL and UL are the lower and upper limits)

Proportion in quintile Qe of expenditures participating in rice program

$$= \left\{ \frac{\sum_{i=1}^{N} I[i \in \text{``received rice''}] * I[r(LL_{Qe}) < r_i(e_t^i) < r(UL_{Qe})]}{N} \right\} \quad (7.11)$$

When we combine expenditures and shock, the formulas that create the proportion participating in each of the twenty-five (five by five) cells of participation are

Proportion in quintile Qe of expenditures and Qs of shock participating in rice program

$$= \left\{ \frac{\sum_{i=1}^{N} I[i \in \text{``received sembako''}] * I[r(LL_{Qe}) < r_i(e_t^i) < r(UL_{Qe})] \\ * I[r(LL_{Qs}) < r_i(e_t^i) < r(UL_{Qs})]}{N} \right\}$$

$$(7.12)$$

4 ESTIMATES OF STATIC AND DYNAMIC BENEFIT INCIDENCE

4.1 Static and Dynamic Incidence of the Two Programs

Table 7.2 shows the static incidence of participation (classified by the 1997 levels of expenditures) in the columns. According to these data, the program shows some targeting by level of expenditures. Column I shows that 59.8 per cent of the poorest quintile of households received some rice compared to 45.2 per cent of the second quintile, falling to only 20.6 per cent of the richest quintile. Households in the richest quintile were 34 per cent as likely to receive rice as the poorest households. The other columns show the targeting by initial level of households that experienced various shocks. For instance, of those receiving the worst shock, those that began in the richest quintile were only 40 per cent as likely to receive rice as those in the poorest quintile. Looking across the rows shows the dynamic incidence of participatio. On average, the program was not at all targeted by the shocks that households experienced — 33.9 per cent of households experiencing the worst shock received rice, as did roughly 40 per cent of all other quintiles. In fact, on average households that experienced the least shock (that is those with a substantial increase in real expenditures) were 18 per cent more likely to receive rice than the worst affected households.

The numbers in bold in the table show the ratio of participation in each cell relative to the participation of the "worst" households — those that began in the bottom quintile and had the worst quintile of shock. So, for example, of the households that were in the middle quintile in 1997 and experienced the worst shock, 42.4 per cent received some rice, which meant that they were only 75 per cent (42.4/56.2) as likely to receive some rice as households with the same shock that were in the poorest quintile in 1997.[22] The decline in numbers moving along rows shows

TABLE 7.2

Households in 100 Village Survey Data who Received Sembako (Rice) in the Three Months Prior to December 1998, by Quintile of per Capita Household Expenditures in May 1997 and Quintile of per Capita Household Expenditure Changes between May 1997 and August 1998

		Dynamic Benefit Incidence: Quintiles of "Shock" ((ln) Changes in Real Expenditures from May 1997 to August 1998)					
		I (worst shock)	II	III	IV	V (least shock)	Targeting by Shock (ratio QV to QI) by Expenditure Quintile
	Average: 39.3	33.9	41	40.8	40.8	39.9	1.18
Static Benefit Incidence (Quintiles of Expenditures May 1997)	I	59.8	1 (56.2)	0.92	0.98	1.13	1.12	1.12
	II	45.2	0.91	0.93	0.89	0.78	0.61	0.67
	III	40.1	0.75	0.86	0.79	0.66	0.48	0.64
	IV	31.1	0.55	0.66	0.58	0.46	0.41	0.75
	V	20.6	0.4	0.43	0.3	0.26	0.3	0.75
Targeting by expenditures (ratio QV to QI) by shock quintile		0.34	0.40	0.47	0.31	0.23	0.27	

Source: 100 Village Survey

the dynamic benefit incidence — the targeting with respect to changes in expenditures. This reconfirms that the rice program was not strongly targeted by a household's expenditure shocks. Of the households in the middle quintile in 1997, households that experienced the worst shock were 75 per cent as likely to receive rice as the worst households (QI–QI), but households with the best shock were 48 per cent as likely. This means that a household with the best shock outcomes was 64 per cent (0.48/0.75) as likely to receive rice as the worst affected. Figure 7.1 graphs the numbers in bold from Table 7.2. The slopes across the top of the bars from left to right (from worst quintile to best shock quintile) show dynamic incidence for households in each of the quintiles of expenditure in 1997, and slopes from back

FIGURE 7.1

Household Participation in Subsidized Rice Program by Quintiles of Level and Changes in per Capita Consumption

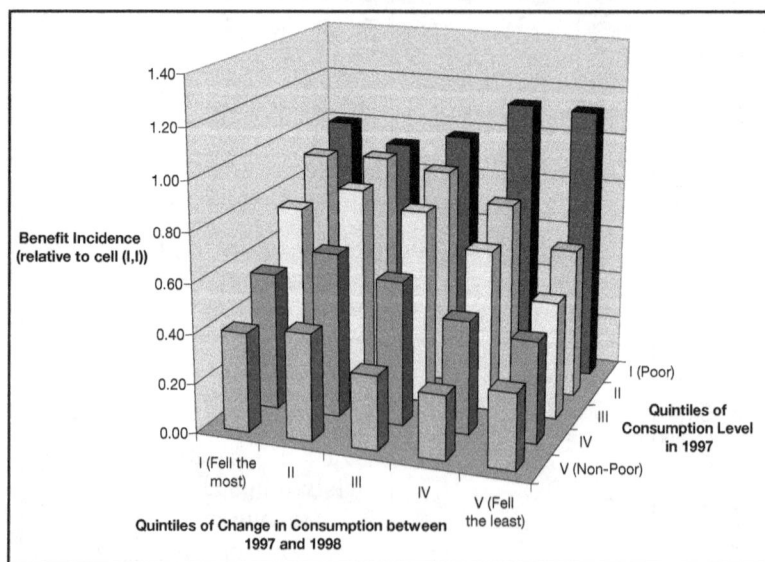

Source: Table 7.2

to front show static incidence for households in various shock categories based on their 1997 expenditures.

Table 7.3 reports comparable results for the employment programs. There was a much lower average participation in this program (12.3 per cent of households) than in the rice program (39.3 per cent), but the program was much more targeted than the rice program in both levels and changes in expenditures. Households from the lowest quintile in 1997 with the most favourable shock were only 38 per cent as likely to participate in public works programs as those with worse shocks.

Figure 7.2 shows the static and dynamic participation in employment programs. The targeting is much sharper in both directions. For each quintile of initial income, the likelihood of participation falls off sharply as households were less affected by the crisis (from left to right), so that, for instance, those in

FIGURE 7.2
Household Participation in Employment Creation Programs by Quintiles of Level and Changes in per Capita Consumption

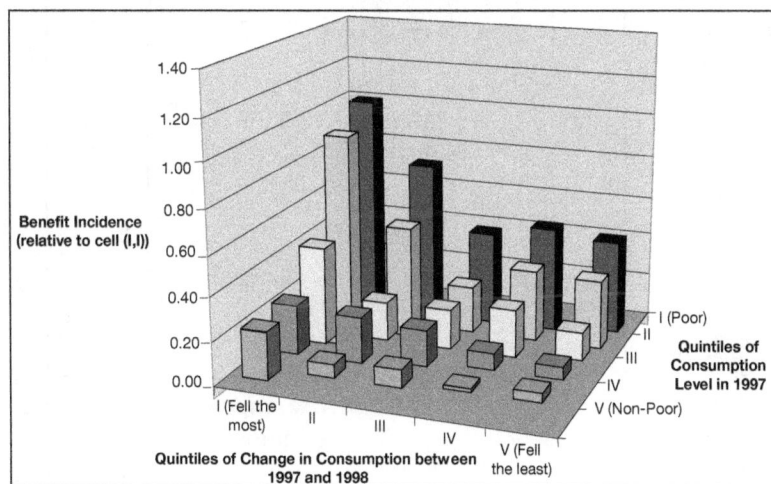

Source: Table 7.2

TABLE 7.3
Households in 100 Village Survey Data who Participated in Any *Padat Karya* (Employment Creation) Work in the Three Months Prior to December 1998, by Quintile of per Capita Household Expenditures in May 1997 and Quintile of per Capita Household Expenditure Changes between May 1997 and August 1998

		Dynamic Benefit Incidence: Quintiles of 'Shock' ((ln) Changes in Real Expenditures from May 1997 to August 1998)					
	Average: 12.3	I (worst shock)	II	III	IV	V (least shock)	Targeting by Shock (Ratio QV to QI) by Expenditure Quintile
Average:		17.7	12.6	8.9	11.3	10.8	
Static Benefit Incidence (Quintiles of Expenditures May 1997) — I	23.10	1.00 (47.3)	0.70	0.38	0.43	0.38	0.38
II	17.00	0.89	0.45	0.19	0.29	0.28	0.31
III	9.40	0.40	0.18	0.16	0.19	0.11	0.28
IV	6.90	0.20	0.18	0.14	0.09	0.05	0.25
V	5.00	0.19	0.05	0.07	0.01	0.04	0.21
Targeting by Expenditures (Ratio QV to QI) by Shock Quintile	0.22	0.19	0.07	0.18	0.02	0.11	

Source: 100 Village Survey

the middle quintile with the best shock were only 28 per cent as likely to have benefited from public works programs as those that experienced the worst shock.

4.2 Comparing the Two Programs

Table 7.4 compares the targeting of the two programs. We control for differing coverage by comparing the relative likelihood of benefiting from the two programs for a household in any given cell (combination of initial level and shock) compared to the worst quintile (worst level in 1997, worst shock). This table compares for each of the twenty-five cells (quintiles by level and changes in expenditures) the ratio of household participation in the rice program of households against participation of households in the worst cell, to the same ratio for participation in the employment programs. For example, of the 228 households that were in the middle quintile in 1997 and in the best [least severe] quintile of shock (their expenditures increased the most), 26.7 per cent received rice compared to 56.2 per cent of those in the worst cell, so their relative participation was 0.48 (Table 7.2). Meanwhile, only 5.3 per cent of those 228 households benefited from employment programs, compared to 47.3 per cent of the worst cell for a relative participation of 0.11 (Table 7.3). Therefore, the comparison in Table 7.4 shows that a family from the middle quintile with the best shock was 4.36 times (26.7/56.2)/(5.3/47.3) more likely to receive rice than to participate in the employment programs relative to the worst level, worst shock households.

Clearly, the employment programs were far more targeted to shocks for all initial income groups. The final column of Table 7.4 shows the ratio of program participation rate for the least affected to worst affected households for each quintile. No matter what level the households started from in 1997, the dynamic targeting ratio, that is, how much more likely those with positive shocks were to receive assistance than the worst affected households,

TABLE 7.4

Targeting of Sembako (Rice) Relative to Padat Karya (Employment Creation) Programs: Ratio of Proportion Receiving in Each Cell Relative to the Cells of Poorest Quintile, Worst Shock for the Two Programs

| | | Dynamic Benefit Incidence: Quintiles of 'Shock' ((ln) Changes in Real Expenditures from May 1997 to August 1998) | | | | | |
		I (worst shock)	II	III	IV	V (most positive shock)	Ratio of Best to Worst Quintile of Shock for Each Initial Quintile
Static Benefit Incidence (Quintiles of Expenditures May 1997)	I	1.00	1.31	2.58	2.63	2.95	2.95
	II	1.02	2.07	4.68	2.69	2.18	2.13
	III	1.88	4.78	4.94	3.47	4.36	2.33 (= 4.36/1.88)
	IV	2.75	3.67	4.14	5.11	8.20	2.98
	V	2.11	8.60	4.29	26.00	7.50	3.56
Ratio of Highest Initial Expenditures to Lowest, for Each Quintile of Shock		2.11	6.54	1.66 (= 4.29/2.58)	9.89	2.54	

Note: Rows show targeting by shock, columns show targeting by expenditures. Numbers larger than 1 indicate 'worse' targeting.

Source: 100 Village Survey

was roughly three times worse for rice. The labour programs were also more targeted by level of income.

Figures 7.3 and 7.4 show the relative participation rates in Table 7.4 graphically for two quintiles of initial expenditures in 1997. Figure 7.3 shows the relative likelihood of program participation (each program relative to worst level-worst shock) across the severity of the observed expenditures shock. The likelihood of receiving rice actually increases as households had better shocks (remember, the impact of the program is not included in measuring the shock), while the likelihood of benefiting from any of the employment programs substantially declined. The same is true in Figure 7.4 of those beginning in the middle quintile of expenditures in 1997; the fraction of households receiving rice actually increases with less severe shocks so that households with the middling shocks (expenditure reductions from 3 per

FIGURE 7.3
Probability of the Poorest Households in 1997 Receiving Subsidized Rice and Participating in Employment Creation Programs, by Quintile of Shock

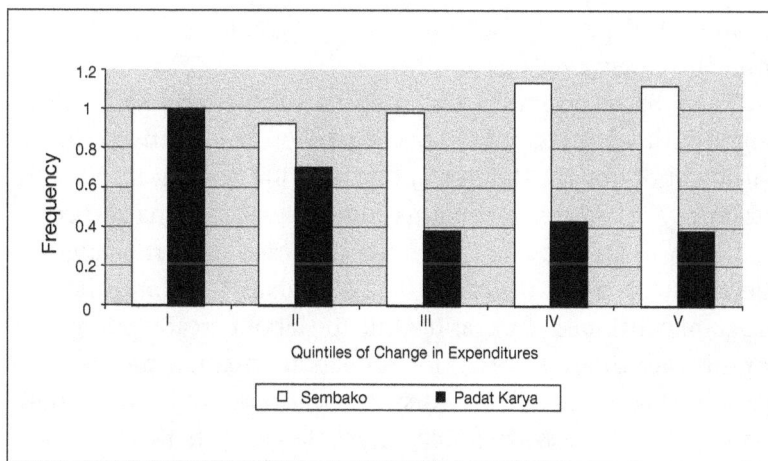

Source: Table 7.4

FIGURE 7.4

Probability of Middle-Quintile Households in 1997 Receiving Subsidized Rice and Participating in Employment Creation Programs by Quintile of Shock

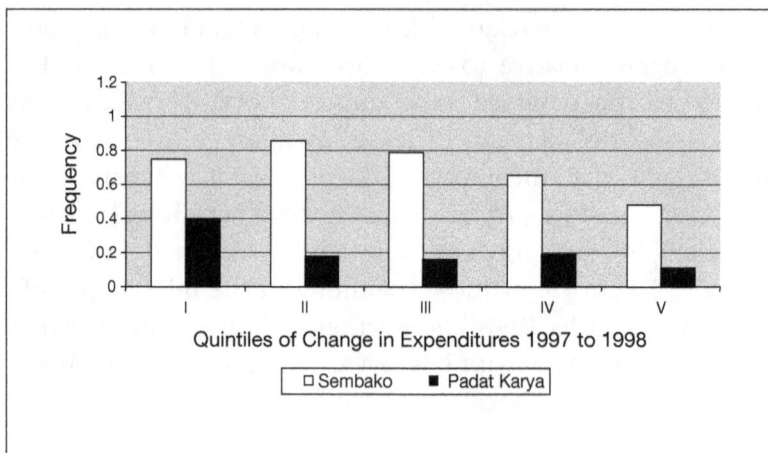

Source: Table 7.4

cent to 23 per cent) were more likely than those with the worst shock, whose expenditures fell by almost 50 per cent. In contrast, likelihood of participation in works programs declines sharply from the worst affected quintile.

Keep in mind, however, that the above comparisons of targeting (and the graphs) are focused on the relative odds of participation for the different programs. But as is clear in Tables 7.2 and 7.3, in absolute terms almost twice as many people in the "worst shock" quintile received rice as participated in the labour creation programs — 33.9 versus 17.9 (and the rice program continued to expand while the labour creating programs shrank over time). In order for the labour creation programs to have reached more of the "worst shock" households, they would have had to have been much, much larger. Whether that was administratively and politically feasible is an open question.

5 SAFETY NETS OR SAFETY ROPES: ARE PROGRAMS TRANSFER OR INSURANCE?

Insurance is a contingent contract, one that pays off different amounts depending on the realization of an outcome, and transfers income from good times to bad times. If an insured house does not burn down, fire insurance pay-out is zero, while if the house does burn down, the pay-out is (some fraction of) the value of the house. The transfers from a program can be contingent either on a level or on a shock, or both. How do the program pay-out patterns stack up as "safety ropes" or insurance against a negative shock? This section examines the question from a budgetary, utility, and political economy perspective.

5.1 Targeting and Budget Allocations

From the perspective of potential recipients, what is important is their (net) receipt from any program across the various states. From the government point of view, it is important to assess the targeting efficiency of a program by evaluating which groups actually receive most of the budget (Grosh 1994). The first step in either of these calculations would be to estimate how much of a given program budget is received by beneficiaries in various groups (cells). No information is available, however, on how large the benefits distributed by either program were, as we know neither the amount of rice received nor the number of days worked, nor do we have data on administrative costs and other program costs (e.g. materials for the employment schemes). Therefore, we calculate an elaborate hypothetical. We ask: if a total amount of benefits was to be distributed with equal amounts per person according to the targeting pattern of rice versus the targeting pattern of employment programs, what is the expected amount that would be received by each group, and how much of the budget would go to individuals in the various quintiles by initial income and shock?

Suppose there was a budget that could be distributed without cost to the 6,200 individuals in the sample and that it was adequate to provide each household with Rp 10,000 per month.[23] We compare three possible hypothetical allocations.[24] First, there is a uniform allocation so that every household receives exactly the same amount, irrespective of initial income and shock. Second, the budget is distributed according to the coverage and targeting pattern of rice, assuming every household that "participates" receives exactly the same amount. Third, the budget is distributed according to the coverage and targeting pattern of the employment programs, again with the assumption of equal distribution to each person with any reported "participation". It must be emphasized that these are hypothetical allocations, not evaluations of actual programs; we refer to these hypothetical pay-offs as uniform (or untargeted), rice, or employment.

Table 7.5 shows the "expected" amount that would be received by a household in each group in these hypothetical schemes. The uniform transfer is easy: total budget is Rp 62 million and there are 6,200 households, so each recipient receives Rp 10,000 and the expected amount is Rp 10,000. For the rice pattern of targeting, the number of participants is 2,440 of 6,200, so the transfer per recipient would be Rp 62 million/2,440 = Rp 25,410, which is assumed equal for all participants. The expected value for each household is that amount times the likelihood of participating in that cell. For example, in the worst cell (QI-QI) 63 of the 112 households participated, so therefore the expected value for households in that cell is the amount times the chance of participating, which is Rp 25,410*(63/112) = Rp 14,293. Since for the employment pattern the overall participation is lower, the amount per recipient is higher at Rp 81,579, while the participation in the first cell is 53 of 112 households. The expected value for households in the worst level-worst shock cell is therefore Rp 38,604.

TABLE 7.5
Receipts and Budget Shares

			Quintiles of 'Shock' to Expenditures			
		Average Over Shocks	I (Worst)	II	III	IV	V (Best)

Average Across All Levels of Expenditures

		Average Over Shocks	I (Worst)	II	III	IV	V (Best)
Uniform/untargeted	Amount	10,000	10,000	10,000	10,000	10,000	10,000
	Budget share	20	20	20	20	20	20
Rice	Amount	10,000	8,607	10,430	10,410	10,410	10,143
	Budget share	20.	17.2	20.9	20.8	20.8	20.3
Employment	Amount	10,000	14,474	10,263	7,237	9,211	8,816
	Budget share	20	28.9	20.5	14.5	18.4	17.6

Households Initially in Poorest Quintile in Expenditures

		Average Over Shocks	I (Worst)	II	III	IV	V (Best)
Uniform/untargeted	Amount	10,000	10,000	10,000	10,000	10,000	10,000
	Budget share	20	1.8	2.5	3.5	5.1	7.1
Rice	Amount	15,184	14,293	13,200	13,934	16,163	16,018
	Budget share	30.4	2.6	3.3	4.9	8.2	11.4
Employment	Amount	18,816	38,604	27,016	14,662	16,522	14,614
	Budget share	37.6	7	6.7	5.1	8.4	10.4

TABLE 7.5 (continued)
Receipts and Budget Shares

		Average Over Shocks	Quintiles of 'Shock' to Expenditures				
			I (Worst)	II	III	IV	V (Best)
Households Initially in Middle Quintile in Expenditures							
Uniform/untargeted	Amount	10,000	10,000	10,000	10,000	10,000	10,000
	Budget share	20	3.1	4.2	5	4.1	3.7
Rice	Amount	10,184	10,776	12,212	11,302	9,367	6,798
	Budget share	20.4	3.3	5.1	5.6	3.9	2.5
Employment	Amount	7,632	15,376	6,956	6,092	7,358	4,294
	Budget share	15.3	4.7	2.9	3	3	1.6
Households Initially in Highest Quintile in Expenditures							
Uniform/untargeted	Amount	10,000	10,000	10,000	10,000	10,000	10,000
	Budget share	20	8.2	4.5	2.9	2.5	1.9
Rice	Amount	5,225	5,730	6,149	4,259	3,678	4,307
	Budget share	10.5	4.7	2.8	1.2	0.9	0.8
Employment	Amount	4,079	7,358	2,032	2,734	537	1,383
	Budget share	8.2	6.1	0.9	0.8	0.1	0.3

Source: Compilation by the authors

Table 7.5 shows trade-offs from the perspective of a potential recipient. While the likelihood of receiving rice is higher for every group, this also means that the total amount must be spread over a larger group. Therefore, the more equal the distribution across the population, the smaller the amount available per person. As a result there is less difference in the expected receipts between rich and poor and between receipts when there were good and bad shocks to expenditures. So, for households in the bottom quintile the expected benefit from the rice targeting pattern is Rp 14,293 if they experience the worst shock, and higher if they experience the best shock (when presumably they have less need of a transfer). In contrast, the employment pattern pays out more in bad states than good states, so the expected benefit for the poorest quintile households with the worst shock is Rp 38,604 versus Rp 14,614 if they benefit from the best shock.[25]

Table 7.5 also indicates the proportion of the budget that goes to the various groups. This is a product of the targeting and distribution across groups. In the employment pattern, 29 per cent of the budget goes to those with the worst shock, 38 per cent goes to those in the bottom quintile, and 60 per cent goes to those in either the poorest or the worst shocked quintile. In the rice pattern of targeting, only 17 per cent goes to the worst shocked, while 30 per cent goes to those in the bottom quintile.

5.2 Household Aversion to Risk, Preferences

To address the welfare implications of these targeting patterns, we need to adopt a specific utility function. We adopt a very simple exponential utility function which represents constant relative risk aversion (CRRA):

$$U(y) = \frac{y^{1-\theta}}{1-\theta}, \text{ for } \theta \neq 1 \tag{7.12}$$
$$= \ln(y), \quad \text{for } \theta = 1$$

where U is utility, y is expenditures, and θ is the coefficient of relative risk aversion. This utility function exhibits declining marginal utility (and hence) risk aversion (if $\theta > 0$), but a household's attitude toward risk does not depend on its level of expenditures.

Suppose a household does know its quintile of expenditures but does not know future shocks, which pattern of pay-offs would the household prefer? There are two effects, a level of expenditures effect and a risk effect. Poor (quintile I) households will always prefer the employment pattern because they get more on average (Rp 18,816 versus Rp 15,184 versus Rp 10,000) and more with negative than positive shocks. For the poorest quintile the program is superior in both transfer and insurance.

Households in the top quintile of initial expenditures (in the absence of altruism) prefer the uniform distribution over either the rice or employment pattern of pay-outs because they receive more in every state with uniform transfer than with rice, and more with rice than employment, as the latter two redistribute from rich to poor. The superiority of the insurance function of employment never dominates the superior transfer of the rice function, because this quintile receives more in every state even though the proportions are higher.

For those households in the middle group of expenditures, the choice gets interesting. The employment program pay-off in the worst shock state is much higher than that of rice (Rp 15,376 versus Rp 10,776), but the average pay-out over all shock outcomes is much lower (Rp 7,632 versus Rp 10,184). Hence, which pattern of pay-offs the middle group prefers depends on the degree of risk aversion. If the household is risk neutral so that only average pay-offs matter, it would prefer the rice pattern over uniform transfers (barely, Rp 10,184 versus Rp 10,000). But if the household is sufficiently risk averse (and hence has a very large desire to reallocate resources from good to bad states), it would prefer the employment pattern, even though the pay-outs

TABLE 7.6
Choices Over Programs*

Risk Aversion (θ)	Maximizing Social Welfare Function	Rice vs. Uniform	Middle Quintile (median voter)		
			Employment vs. Uniform	Rice vs. Employment	Preferred by QIII
0 (risk neutral)	Indifferent	Rice	Uniform	Rice	Rice
1 (ln utility)	Employment	Rice	Uniform	Rice	Rice
2	Employment	Rice	Uniform	Rice	Rice
3	Employment	Rice	Employment	Rice	Rice
4	Employment	Rice	Employment	Employment	Employment

Notes:

*Based on the expected values received in Table 7.5 using a CRRA utility function on the levels and shocks in Table 7.1. The value of the risk aversion parameter at which the QIII switch from preferring uniform to employment pay-outs is 2.37 and the switching value for employment over rice is 3.5.

Source: Compilation by the authors

in the good states are very low because the employment pattern does a better job as insurance, moving expenditures from good times to bad times.

Using the utility function in equation (7.12), preferences over uniform, rice, and employment pay-offs are evaluated in Table 7.6 for various values of the risk-aversion parameter θ for the middle-quintile households. The choice depends on the level of risk aversion.

- *Low levels of risk aversion* ($\theta<2.37$). At low degrees of risk aversion, the middle-quintile household would choose the rice pattern as its preferred scheme, over both the uniform transfer and the employment pattern. The reason for this is that the rice pattern redistributes more from richer households to middle-quintile households, but does not give too much to the poor.
- *Moderate levels of risk aversion* ($2.37<\theta<3.5$). At higher levels of risk aversion the middle-quintile household prefers the employment pattern over the uniform transfer. The rice program continues, however, to be preferred to the employment pattern. Even though there is less of an "insurance" element, the average transfer to the middle quintile is still high enough to offset the advantage of the pattern targeting to changes in expenditures.
- *High levels of risk aversion* ($\theta>3.5$). At high levels of risk aversion the middle-quintile households prefer the employment pattern to either the uniform transfer or the rice pattern. As the "insurance" value of a given transfer rises with the degree of risk aversion at these levels of risk aversion, the insurance value of pay-offs that are more closely aligned with shocks overcomes the lower average pay-offs.

5.3 Social Welfare Maximizing Choice and Voting Outcomes

If we ignore taxation and focus only on benefits, what pattern of pay-offs would a welfare-maximizing policy-maker choose if the social welfare function was the simple sum of utility functions of this type (equation 7.13)?

$$SWF(y_1, \ldots y_N) = \sum_{i=1}^{N} \frac{y_i^{1-\theta}}{1-\theta}, \ \theta \neq 1 \tag{7.13}$$

With zero risk aversion, a social planner would be indifferent because all three schemes give equal expected utilities (because, by construction, the hypothetical expected money pay-outs are equal). But, at all positive values of the risk aversion parameter, a social planner would prefer the employment pattern to that of rice, and the rice pattern to a uniform transfer. This is because, with declining marginal utility of expenditures, the employment pattern is preferred as it gives more both to those who are poorer initially and to those who suffer negative shocks, that is, it is better both as a transfer and as insurance. Rice is less targeted in both dimensions, but is still preferred to a uniform transfer.

Targeting is, however, a political as well as a technocratic issue (Besley 1996; Sen 1995), and the differing preferences over program pay-offs between the social planner and the middle quintile is potentially a politically interesting comparison. Gelbach and Pritchett (1997, 1999) have explored the political economy of targeting, examining the difference in decisions between a "politically naïve" and a "politically sophisticated" policy maker. In that model the "naïve" policy maker simply maximizes a social welfare function taking budget support as given. Gelbach and Pritchett (1999) show, however, that if budget support for a transfer program is endogenous, the "naïve" technocratic solution actually sufficiently erodes political support, so that "more for the poor is less for the poor" and the welfare of the poor declines as their share of a smaller transfer means that they receive less in absolute terms.

While it is well known that one can construct theoretical examples, what is interesting is that the actual pattern of static and dynamic incidence from these two programs in Indonesia appears to present an example of this possible trade-off. For all values of the risk aversion parameter θ, the two poorest quintiles always prefer the employment pattern to the rice pattern and the rice pattern to the uniform transfer, because it is better targeted both as an income transfer and as insurance. On the other hand, the two richest quintiles (QV and QIV) always get their highest expected utilities from the uniform transfer (zero targeting). In the absence of altruism or spillover motives, in a simple, one person-one vote decision mechanism households in the middle quintile would be the median voter and their choice would be decisive.

These empirical patterns of program pay-outs point to the complex nature of the political economy of targeting. The "inequality-averse social planner" consistently prefers the "most targeted" program (represented by the employment pattern of pay-outs). In a direct vote, however, if middle-income voters have low levels of risk aversion, the employment program pay-outs would lose a vote to either a uniform transfer or to a "less targeted" program such as rice. When risk aversion is low, the political support of the middle group is only forthcoming with either substantial "leakage" (rice pay-outs), so that the redistribution is substantially from the higher quintiles to the middle group and is not sharply targeted to the poor (Gelbach and Pritchett 1999). Suppose the social planner could set the agenda for a binary choice. If the vote was presented between the employment pattern of pay-offs and either the rice pattern or uniform transfer, then the social planner's preferred program would lose in a simple (unweighted) majority vote. If the social planner controls the agenda, she should never propose a vote between the employment pattern and uniform transfer, as this would produce the least preferred outcome for the poorest quintile. Instead, a social planner controlling a voting agenda would propose a vote between the rice pattern (which is the second best alternative from a social welfare function point of view) and a uniform transfer, a race that the rice program could win.

When risk aversion of the middle-quintile group is sufficiently high, the desire for a "safety rope" dominates and the orderings shift. The welfare gain from the insurance-like aspects of the "safety rope" pay-offs dominates the fact that the pay-off is lower on average, and the middle quintile would therefore prefer the "safety rope". Even though the expected receipts are Rp 10,184 for the "safety net" and only Rp 7,632 for the "safety rope", the fact that the pay-offs are over three times higher in the worst versus the best shock states (Rp 15,378 versus Rp 4,294) for the employment pattern, compared to the less than two to one ratio for rice (Rp 10,776 versus Rp 6,798), means that the utility is higher. In this case the middle group provides political support for the program because of its insurance value, and the employment/safety rope pay-offs are preferred by both the social planner and the voting public.

6 CONCLUSIONS

There are four main findings of this study.

First, with panel data dynamic benefit incidence can be measured and applied to compare programs following standard procedures that have been used widely for static benefit incidence.

Second, program design matters. Mechanisms of targeting that might be effective for static benefit incidence do not necessarily reach those who have been affected by shocks. There is strong evidence to suggest that the subsidized sale of rice to targeted households based on an administrative list compiled to identify poor households was not closely related to the "shock" in expenditures that households experienced. On the other hand, employment creation (*padat karya*) programs that used even weak self-selection mechanisms were better targeted to both expenditure levels and shocks.

Third, using these patterns of pay-offs, the trade-offs of different types of programs are illustrated from both policy and positive political economy points of view. The key policy issue is that the flexibility of the targeting criteria has to respond to changes in household fortunes as events unfold. Without this flexibility, even a well-targeted program that is based on established data on household living standards may have very little "safety rope" value for the bulk of the population. As pointed out by Jalan and Ravallion (1999*a*, 1999*b*), an important issue with proxy means testing is not just whether the proxies (say, assets) have a close fit with the desired but unobserved targeting variable (consumption expenditures) in some initial period, but also how variable consumption expenditures are for individual households. If, as studies are coming to show, a great deal of poverty is transitory, then programs with fixed criteria will necessarily be inadequate.

Fourth, the simply self-interested voting politics depend on not just which program targets the poor but also on the insurance value to middle groups, which depends on risk aversion.

Finally, let us repeat that patterns of targeting are of course just one piece of an extremely complicated puzzle. In the actual choice of programs, administrative complexity, the ability to protect program implementation from fraud and waste, the costs of targeting, institutional capacity to implement, political will, and the potential benefits of investments, must all be considered. These issues were not addressed here. When all of these are considered together, we believe that the analysis, if it were done, would show that the costs per dollar of benefits delivered to any poor recipient are actually much higher for an employment scheme than for OPK in the actual Indonesian context. Therefore, even though employment schemes with self-selection may have better patterns of targeting, weaknesses in other aspects of the program (high costs, administrative complexity and the like) may determine actual choices.

Notes

Reprinted from *World Development*, Vol. 31, no. 7, Sudarno Sumarto, Asep Suryahadi and Lant Pritchett, "Safety Nets or Safety Ropes? Dynamic Benefit Incidence of Two Crisis Programs in Indonesia", pp. 1257–1277, 2003, with permission from Elsevier.

1. This general definition of poverty covers any of the class of Foster et al. (1984) poverty measures which adjust for the intensity or depth of poverty, and is consistent with either absolute or relative poverty lines.
2. In OECD countries the distinction has been used to characterize different "systems": those that rely on means testing versus those that provide universal benefits (Esping-Andersen 1990; Goodin et al. 1999).
3. Economists would recommend poverty programs to a hypothetical benign social welfare maximizer if the social welfare function was built up from individual (household) utility functions with declining marginal utility, in which case a (costless) transfer from rich to poor is not a Pareto improvement but does raise social welfare. There is also an argument for poverty programs from an externality in altruism. In contrast, the normative case for government involvement in mitigation of risk is based on the argument that, if moral hazard and adverse selection are sufficiently large, then welfare-improving markets for insurance against these risks will not exist (and they would be 'too small' in any case). This is potentially the case in a wide variety of insurance markets — but particularly affect the market for insurance of incomes.

4. There are calculations of tax incidence in the UK as early as 1919 and in the USA before 1940. By the 1970s there were combined estimates of tax and expenditures incidence in the USA (Musgrave et al. 1974). There were also early estimates for developing countries (Selowsky 1979 for Colombia, Meerman 1979 for Malaysia).

5. When average public sector costs are used, the name "benefit incidence" is something of a misnomer as there is no valuation of the services received and, given that there is no reason to assume governments are fully efficient producers, there can be no assumption about a connection between the value of the expenditure by the government and the value of the service actually received. For instance, in the case of visits to health clinics, this can be particularly striking when, due to the poor quality of services, utilization of facilities is low such that the average cost per visit is very high even if value of benefits is low — so that the "expenditure" incidence and the "benefit" incidence clearly diverge.

6. In either case, one divides the income/expenditure distribution into percentiles and asks what fraction of the benefits accrues to households between various percentiles of the distribution. With benefit incidence these are standard percentiles (quartiles, quintiles and deciles), while for poverty incidence the percentiles are chosen by using a poverty line. So if p per cent of the population is below the poverty line, one is comparing benefit incidence above and below the pth percentile.

7. A recent addition to the benefit incidence literature distinguishes between marginal and average incidence and examines how the benefit incidence of programs evolves as programs expand, either across regions or over time (Lanjouw and Ravallion (1998) for education in India, and Lanjouw et al. (2000) in Indonesia). This recent approach examines dynamics of static benefit incidence—how it changes over time, while this paper examines how program incidence is related to the dynamics of household expenditures at a single point in time.

8. Indicator targeting is a subset of administrative targeting in which proxy variables are chosen based on an established relationship between some variable that is observed for all households (e.g., age)

and the underlying desired targeting criterion, which is not easily observed or could easily be manipulated (e.g., current household consumption).

9. By analogy with statistical terminology, undercoverage is sometimes referred to as "type I" error (e.g., rejecting a hypothesis that is true) while leakage is called "type I" error (failing to reject a hypothesis that is false).

10. The word "shock" is appropriate in the context of the Indonesian crisis as most of the innovations were negative, and the magnitude unexpected. One could also define the shocks as "unexpected" innovations to expenditures and use the panel to estimate some model of "unexpected" expenditures.

11. Another way to think of this is the difference between flows and stocks, which makes it clearer that the difference is a matter of the time period that the analysis considers. The current level of actual or expected household wealth is just the cumulated values of "shocks" to (actual or expected) wealth, beginning from some initial value (say, household formation). So, over a long enough period (and if initial differences are small relative to cumulated "shocks"), then the difference between "shocks" and "levels" is not valid, as the level is primarily determined by shocks. But one can still distinguish between stocks and flows, or between levels and innovations, over any given, relatively short, period. Here we are focused on a period of approximately a year, so the distinction between levels and shocks is reasonably clear.

12. More precisely, this is the one-period dynamic benefit incidence. Since levels at a point in time are the result of an initial condition plus the cumulation of all previous innovations, in some sense the static could be thought of as the long-run dynamic, while this is the one-period dynamic.

13. These are referred to as *keluarga pra-sejahtera* or KPS and *keluarga sejahtera* or KS I, KS II, and KS III. See Chapter 6 for further details.

14. The OPK program was expanded so that each eligible household was allowed to purchase 20 kg of rice per month.

15. A fifth criticism that is particularly important in Jakarta (and some other major cities) is that the list may include only those with a

valid identification card (KTP) for that location. Since these KTPs are difficult to obtain, a large fraction of the poor would be excluded by this criterion.

16. The official rules are specified in Menpangan and BULOG (1999).

17. BULOG (the National Logistics Agency) made the amounts of rice available to villages at the DOLOG (Logistics Depot) and SUB-DOLOG offices based on the eligibility lists, but responsibility for transporting the rice lay with the village head or designated official.

18. The impact of the use of "community" discretion in targeting and its impact on decisions is a new area of research. Galasso and Ravallion (2000) examine how it affected targeting in Bangladesh, while Olken et al. (2001) examine how the distribution of rice varied across villages in Indonesia.

19. This diversion from one set of households to others is in addition to less frequent reports of blatant corruption in which rice was diverted from household distribution altogether by local officials and sold on the local market (Suryahadi et al. 1999).

20. See Chapters 2 and 4 above for details of the 100 Village Survey.

21. The panel sampling was perhaps non-standard. In the May 1997 round, 60 households from each of two enumeration areas in each village were sampled. In the August 1998 round, the sample was changed to 40 households from each of three enumeration areas. The 80 panel households were chosen from the 120 first-round households. But if a chosen household was not present in the second round, it was replaced by another household. So the panel is complete but attrition is not observed, as there is no way of knowing how many of the 80 households were randomly chosen from the 120 and how many replacements were made.

22. Although $0.75 \times 56.2 = 42.15$ (and not 42.4), rounding of the actual number, which is 0.7544, has created what appears to be an error.

23. This more or less arbitrary figure is chosen because, if the total development budget for safety nets in 1999-2000 of Rp 5.6 trillion were distributed equally to each of the country's 45 million households, this would provide Rp 10,370 per household per month.

24. An equivalent procedure for comparing the programs would have been to scale up employment participation to the rice level on average, producing equivalent values across this table.

25. Another key hypothetical feature is that we ignore risk aversion within cells of the matrix and assume that each person receives the expected value, whereas in fact, even within cells, people received different amounts, from nothing at all to the program maximum.

Chapter 8

NEW APPROACHES TO THE TARGETING OF SOCIAL PROTECTION PROGRAMS

Asep Suryahadi, Wenefrida Widyanti,
Daniel Suryadarma, and Sudarno Sumarto

1 INTRODUCTION

The Indonesian experience of implementing social protection programs during the economic crisis of the late 1990s and also during the post-crisis period shows that targeting in programs of this kind is always difficult. As a consequence, social protection programs always suffer from the problems of undercoverage and leakage at the same time. Both problems cause these programs to become less effective and less efficient than they have potential to be (Sumarto et al. 2002). Hence there is a clear need to improve targeting at two levels simultaneously: the geographic and the individual levels. This paper describes attempts to develop more effective targeting tools than those already in use in Indonesia.

2 POVERTY MAPPING: A TOOL FOR BETTER GEOGRAPHIC TARGETING

2.1 The Advantages of Small-area Poverty Mapping

Ideally, geographic targeting should be based on a description of poverty incidence and other indicators of economic welfare in small areas or at low administrative levels. It is here that poverty mapping offers advantages. Detailed poverty maps of small areas can provide benefits to help address many of the shortcomings of aggregate poverty profiles and can greatly enhance and sharpen poverty analysis.

First, small-area poverty maps can obviously reveal the variations in local poverty levels. Almost all countries in the world have regions that are well off and others that have lagged behind. Such differences are often obscured in national-level statistics, a problem that is particularly critical in large and heterogeneous countries like Indonesia. Second, poverty maps can improve the targeting of interventions, which means that resources can be used more effectively. Poverty maps have the potential to reduce the risk that benefits may be leaked from a program to non-poor households. Similarly, they can also reduce the risk of undercoverage, that is, the possibility that poor households will be missed by a program.

Third, poverty maps can help governments to state their policy goals objectively. If allocation decisions are based on observed geographic poverty data rather than on subjective rankings of regions, the transparency and credibility of government decision-making is increased. Poverty maps can therefore help limit the influence of special interests in allocation decisions. This is particularly relevant in the context of currently decentralized Indonesia. By increasing transparency, poverty maps can help prevent regional autonomy policies from being hijacked by local elites. Fourth, poverty maps can form an important tool for local empowerment and decentralization. Disaggregated information on human welfare in conjunction with other locally relevant information is useful not only to governments and decision-makers but also to local communities. Poverty maps thus provide local stakeholders with the facts required for local decision-making and for negotiation with government agencies.

Fifth, poverty maps are useful tools for evaluating the impact of various interventions. In addition, they open up more opportunities to undertake detailed empirical research on the causal relationships between local poverty, income inequality, and various other social outcomes at both the individual and community levels. Sixth, the estimation of small-area indicators of poverty allows their incorporation into geographical information systems (GIS). This feature of poverty maps facilitates the combination of poverty information with other indicators from policy-relevant subject areas. Examples are geographic databases of transport infrastructure, public service centres, access to input and output markets, or information on the quality of natural resources. With geographic overlay techniques and spatial analysis methods, the newly constructed databases on poverty can be used to address a range of multidisciplinary questions. The databases can also be used by the private sector as a guide in determining locations for new investment opportunities.

In the context of Indonesia, however, the creation of poverty maps obviously requires village-level information on the distribution of economic welfare. Such information could be obtained by carrying out a household survey that is representative at the village level. But with a total of around 70,000 villages in Indonesia, a household survey of this kind would be prohibitively large and expensive to carry out. For comparison, current poverty statistics in Indonesia are based on the Consumption Module of SUSENAS, which has a sample size of only around 65,000 households.

As a result of recent methodological advances in small-area poverty mapping, a new methodology has been developed to estimate poverty using the statistical data collections that are normally available in a country (Elbers et al. 2001 and 2002; Hentschel et al. 2000). Following the names of its proponents, the method is called the ELL method, an acronym of Elbers, Lanjouw, and Lanjouw (Davis 2004). This method has been successfully implemented in a few countries, in particular South Africa and Ecuador (Elbers et al. 2001), where early applications have shown that it can be used if the required data sources are available. Since the maps produced have been found to be very useful for a range of purposes, these successful examples have encouraged the application of the method to other countries, including Indonesia.

2.2 Methodology

The principle of the method is to combine information obtained from a household survey with the information collected through a population census. A household survey usually collects very detailed information on household characteristics, including consumption level, but the coverage is generally limited and only representative for a relatively large geographical unit. On the other hand, a population census has complete coverage of all households but usually collects very limited information on household characteristics. The methodology that has been developed combines the advantages of detailed information on the household characteristics obtained from a household survey with the complete coverage of a population census.

The procedure (described in Appendix A) uses household survey data to estimate a model of per capita consumption expenditure (or any other household or individual-level indicator of well-being) as correlates of variables that are available in both the household survey and the population census. The resulting parameter estimates are then used in a simulation to predict per capita consumption for each household in the census. Using the predicted per capita consumption, household-level measures of poverty and inequality are calculated and aggregated for small areas such as districts/cities, subdistricts, or villages. Importantly, the method allows for the calculation of standard errors for whichever welfare measure is estimated. This feature is critical in that it offers a means to assess the statistical reliability of the estimates as well as of comparisons of estimates for different communities.

Through a grant from the World Bank and in cooperation with Statistics Indonesia (*Badan Pusat Statistik*, or BPS), the SMERU Research Institute successfully implemented a study for the creation of poverty maps in Indonesia. The objective was to test the feasibility of applying the new poverty-mapping method in the context of Indonesia. Until then, the method had never been applied in a large country. It was therefore decided that the effort would be initiated through a pilot study, where the method would be applied to data from only three of the total thirty provinces in Indonesia (Suryahadi et al. 2005*a*).[1]

At the conclusion of the pilot study, SMERU submitted a proposal to continue developing a poverty map of the whole of Indonesia to a research competition held by the Ford Foundation through its "Regional Research Initiative on Social Protection in Asia". The SMERU proposal was selected as one of the research projects to be funded under the initiative, which enabled SMERU to continue the application of the poverty-mapping method to the rest of Indonesia's provinces. This work has succeeded in achieving its objective of creating a poverty map for the whole country, disaggregated at provincial, district/city, subdistrict and village levels (Suryahadi et al. 2005*b*).

The first-time availability of accurate welfare indicators at district/city, subdistrict, and village levels is already an achievement. But the real power of poverty mapping lies in the presentation of the outcomes in a geographical map, which makes it possible to overlay the poverty data with all kinds of

FIGURE 8.1
Poverty Map of East Kalimantan by District/City, Subdistrict,
and Village

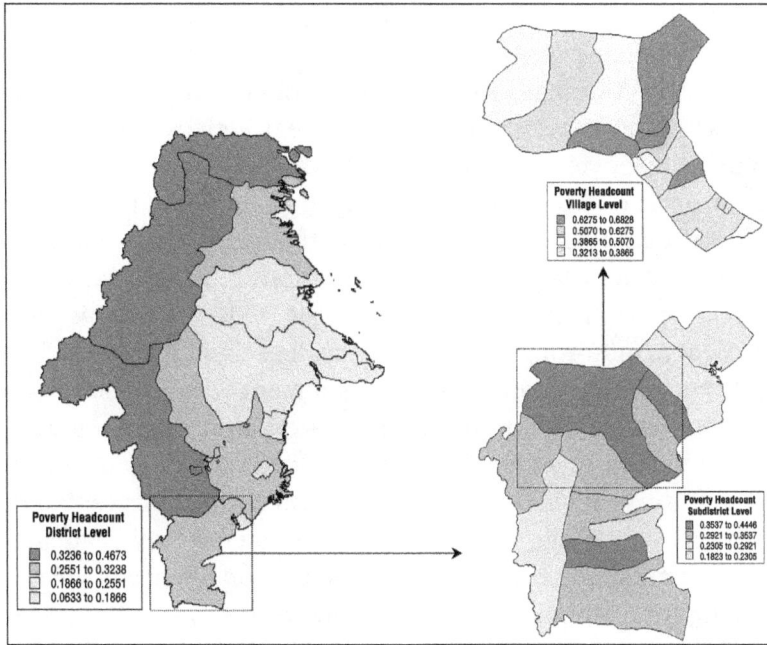

Source: Suryahadi et al. (2005*a*)

spatial characteristics. Figure 8.1 provides an example of the level of detail of the poverty map that has been developed. With the district/city poverty rates in the province of East Kalimantan as the starting point, it is possible to examine the distribution of poverty across subdistricts within a district/city. It would also be possible to study the distribution of poverty across villages within one subdistrict.

2.3 Verification of Poverty Mapping

In order to test the accuracy of the estimation results of the poverty map that had been developed, verification was undertaken through a qualitative study (Suharyo et al. 2005), which was carried out by a different group of SMERU researchers who did not know the poverty-mapping results when they went to the region. In this way bias in making qualitative judgements was avoided. Ranking of regions was based on the perceptions of local stakeholders through focus group discussions (FGDs), which are assumed to reflect real conditions in the field. Verification involved comparing poverty rankings across districts and subdistricts based on the two methods, poverty mapping and FGDs. The consistency of results suggests that quantitative estimates at district and subdistrict levels reflect real conditions relatively well. The correlation with the FGD results for the 2004 situation is also fairly high, indicating that the poverty map could still be used at that time, although any major development with the potential to affect welfare conditions in certain areas after 2000 should be taken into consideration in using this poverty map.

In the case of villages, however, consistency between rankings derived from FGDs and rankings based on poverty mapping varies across subdistricts. Evidence that the consistency of village ranking is quite high in some subdistricts reflects the ability of the small-area estimate model to provide reliable poverty estimates down to village level, particularly for villages with agricultural communities. A comparison between poverty estimates based on poverty mapping and rankings based on local community perspectives also reconfirms this. But in spite of this, village-level poverty estimates should be used with caution in regions with distinct characteristics as well as in regions with urban and semi-urban characteristics. This indicates that there is room for further improvements in the poverty-mapping method.

Ideally, the verification of maps that provide poverty estimates of small administrative areas should be based on a household-level census or survey that collects consumption data and can provide poverty estimates at the village level in at least some areas as a sample. These estimates could then be used for comparison with the poverty estimates produced by poverty mapping. This kind of undertaking, however, would be both expensive and impractical. From an academic point of view, it could be questionable to compare the poverty situation based on local people's perceptions — whether it involves poverty ranking or the poverty rate — with poverty estimates based on quantitative calculations. Such a comparison is like comparing two different animals, as the two estimates use different indicators and benchmarks. From the point of view of practical application, however, this kind of comparison could be of particular importance, since no one will trust an estimation that appears to be completely different from what local people perceive from their personal observations. Consistency between relative-wealth estimates produced from poverty mapping and observable conditions could imply that poverty mapping is reliable and could increase the acceptability of mapping results.

The inconsistencies uncovered in the verification study indicate some potential problems in the application of both the poverty-mapping approach and the FGD method. It is well known that the capacity of the small-area estimation method to provide good estimates is limited by the availability of the data needed to develop the estimation model. Since this study has pointed to the weaknesses in estimating poverty in urban and semi-urban communities and in communities other than those that are rural and agricultural in nature, there is need to expand the indicators covered in the data sources to reflect poverty conditions in these communities in a better way. Another potential weakness in poverty mapping could stem from the quality of survey and census data used in the calculations, including the rural/urban categorization of a village. This problem is evident from the finding that in a small number of cases poverty mapping has produced quite different poverty estimates for two villages with very similar conditions. This points to the importance of improving the quality of the data sources, namely, SUSENAS and PODES.[2]

2.4 The Use of Focus Group Discussions

It is widely acknowledged that, despite the benefits of the interactive nature of FGDs, this method also has some limitations. Although the FGDs in this study had been carefully planned in accordance with the study objectives, there were still some weaknesses in the discussion process. These weaknesses included judgements biased towards the physical accessibility of regions, judgements based on temporary shock, and difficulties in ranking similar regions, which led to the use of indicators not directly related to welfare levels such as security or the divorce rate. There were also some shortcomings in the recall of past conditions and the limited knowledge of FGD participants about community conditions in certain regions, even though the FGDs discussed only the perspectives of the participants regarding poverty and relative welfare in their own region. FGDs were also found to be more difficult at higher administration levels. It might be better to use FGDs at district, subdistrict, and village levels, where the participants are more likely to have sufficient knowledge of the region being discussed. It also seems that FGDs are more suitable for discussing current than past conditions. In addition, given that the relatively high standard errors of poverty estimates at village level in some regions limited the ability of poverty mapping to provide reliable poverty comparisons across villages, the holding of an FGD at subdistrict level is highly recommended to sharpen the geographical targeting.

In a sense, the qualitative and quantitative approaches were applied separately. It became apparent in analysing the field verification results that it might have been useful to conduct an FGD to discuss the inconsistencies between the results obtained from these two measures. This kind of discussion could potentially enrich knowledge and understanding about poverty in the region. Nevertheless, based on field experience in conducting this study, a combination of the quantitative and the qualitative approaches is highly recommended for a more comprehensive poverty assessment.

3 CBMS: A TOOL FOR BETTER INDIVIDUAL TARGETING

3.1 The BPS and BKKBN Methodologies

After geographic targeting, the identification of beneficiaries is one of the most crucial aspects in the implementation of social protection programs. In Indonesia, government assistance programs have normally used a two-step targeting process. The central government first allocates the programs at the district level using geographic targeting. Although the exact targeting process varies by program, poorer districts generally receive a larger quota under the program. The second step is individual targeting, where each district government is responsible for ensuring that the intended recipients receive the programs.

District governments have normally used family welfare data collected annually by the National Family Planning Coordinating Board (BKKBN) in the context of its own programs. Since implementation of the Regional Autonomy Law began in 2001, several districts and provincial governments have tried to define their own individual targeting methodology. The indicators used to identify the poor are mainly adapted from the BKKBN indicators, with some minor adjustments.[3]

There are two obvious differences between the BPS methodology, which has been used in the Unconditional Cash Transfer (BLT) program,[4] and the BKKBN methodology. The first is that BPS uses a much more sophisticated methodology to identify district-specific poverty indicators, whereas BKKBN uses a simple nationwide checklist. The second difference is that BPS mostly uses its own personnel for enumeration, whereas BKKBN uses local residents. While these differences mean that each methodology has its own strengths over the other, it also means that both have weaknesses that could cause both undercoverage and leakage in program implementation.

The first weakness of both methods is the ease with which the data can be manipulated. Since the indicators are determined prior to actual data collection, it is relatively simple to alter a family's characteristics in order to classify the family as poor or not poor. Secondly, poverty is a localized phenomenon in which the characteristics of the poor differ among villages. Therefore, having a single checklist for an entire district, let alone a single list of indicators for the whole country, would certainly introduce bias. The ideal system would be one that has the strength of both methods — that is, the advantage of local knowledge and the use of sophisticated methodology — and none of the weaknesses described above.

3.2 The Community Based Monitoring System

With this in mind, the SMERU Research Institute set out to design and test a new method to identify the poor. Using BKKBN's strength, the new system, which is aptly called the Community Based Monitoring System or CBMS, involves the local residents of an area. Drawing on the strength of the BPS approach, poverty indicators are designed to be sensitive to local conditions using a relatively modern statistical calculation. Improving on the weaknesses of the two methods, poverty indicators are determined *after* data collection is finished, thus removing any possibility of data manipulation. In this way specific poverty indicators at the village level can be determined. Identification of the poor through the CBMS approach makes it possible to achieve greater accuracy in the targeting of program beneficiaries.

The CBMS uses two questionnaires, based on family and village characteristics, for data collection. The family questionnaire has eighty-six questions and records basic family conditions, while the village questionnaire, which consists of thirty-one main questions, records available facilities in the village. Since the family questionnaire is completely enumerated by local residents, it consists mostly of simple questions with a yes/no answer. Although relatively simple, the questionnaire is quite thorough. Given enough training, local residents can use it to calculate figures such as school enrolment rates, contraception usage, and the unemployment rate, to name only a few. The questionnaire can thus be used as a data source for other purposes in addition to poverty identification.

The CBMS involves local people because local residents always know more about conditions in their village than outsiders do. Furthermore, local participation ensures that data are less likely to contain wrong information because residents usually find it harder to give false information to their own neighbours. Therefore, the data are of high quality. Insistence on local involvement, however, means that the system must be very simple at the enumeration stage, given the wide variations in educational level and data collection capacity among local people. Furthermore, it is imperative to have a rigorous but straightforward training session for the enumerators. It is also important that the enumerators receive support and that their work is checked during the initial enumeration period to ensure mistakes are corrected and not repeated.

3.2.1 Principal Components Analysis (PCA)

In order to identify objectively which residents are poor by comparison with the other residents of an area, the CBMS uses a method called Principal Components Analysis (PCA). PCA is basically a statistical method that reduces the multidimensionality of a dataset while retaining the variation in the dataset as much as possible. For example, in a two-dimensional problem, there are two variables X and Y. The first principal component score shows a line that best represents the common variability of X and Y. PCA is therefore able to calculate a multidimensional welfare concept, where a family's welfare is determined by many factors. Furthermore, the use of PCA does away with the problem of data tampering because it is impossible for anyone to know prior to analysis which data will be used as indicators. The poverty situation and family welfare ranking in the village are known only at the end of the data analysis phase.

For the purpose of analysis, the questionnaire data must be entered into a computer to be processed using PCA. This obviously cannot be done by local residents but has to be carried out at district level. Being a relative poverty indicator, PCA does not determine whether a family is poor or not but indicates where a family is placed when every family in the village is ranked from poorest to richest. By contrast, the BKKBN method uses an absolute poverty indicator, where a family's welfare is compared to a pre-established poverty or welfare standard.

3.2.2 Pilot Testing of the CBMS

In 2005 SMERU pilot-tested the CBMS in four villages: Cibulakan and Parakantugu in Cianjur District, West Java, and Kedondong and Jungpasir in Demak District, Central Java (Suryadarma et al. 2005). The pilot was undertaken in conjunction with the BKKBN, which was an ideal partner because it already had local enumerators in most parts of the country. Some BKKBN district offices, however, have been in an uncertain position since the regional autonomy era began, when their authority was delegated to the district government. This was also the reason for choosing Cianjur and Demak Districts. While the BKKBN in Cianjur District is already institutionalized, the BKKBN in Demak District still had no official status in the district government structure.

In Cianjur the task of recruiting enumerators was left to BKKBN officials, but in Demak, where the BKKBN district office is severely underfunded, the task was mostly undertaken by village heads. Thus in Cianjur most of the enumerators were BKKBN cadres, while in Demak they included ex-cadres, teachers, midwives, and members of village-level women's groups. Enumerators had to have at least nine years of education and had to be socially active. While the latter requirement was largely met, the former had to be waived because it turned out that there were not enough people with the required level of education in the villages.

The training of enumerators took place in the village offices in one session of approximately three to four hours. Enumeration started the next day and was completed in around two weeks, with SMERU researchers supervising for the first two days. Each enumerator was in charge of collecting data in the neighbourhood where she or he was living. After the enumeration was finished, the questionnaires were sent to SMERU, where they were entered into a database. In the actual CBMS, this process would take place in the district BAPPEDA (Regional Development Planning Board) or BKKBN office. Following the entry of data from 500 questionnaires, which took some 200 man-hours, implementation of PCA required only one to two days for all four villages. In total, the CBMS took only a little more than three months from recruitment of enumerators to production of the PCA results.

From the eighty-six questions in the family questionnaire, SMERU determined sixty-three welfare indicators, including education levels, employment, health practices, immunization for infants, consumption patterns, asset ownership, political participation, and access to information. Each of the sixty-three indicators had its own weighting in each village, which showed the importance of that indicator in measuring family welfare in that village. A variable with higher absolute weight is a more important welfare determinant than variables with lower absolute weights. Table 8.1 shows the ten indicators with the highest weight for the two villages in Cianjur District. It should be noted that a negatively weighted variable means that families with that

TABLE 8.1
The Ten Variables with the Greatest Weight in CBMS Pilot Project Villages

Parakantugu Village		Cibulakan Village	
Variable	*Weight*	*Variable*	*Weight*
Own refrigerator	0.26	Own refrigerator	0.26
Own telephone	0.25	Own colour television	0.26
Own savings	0.24	Own cellular phone	0.26
Own fan	0.24	Own DVD/VCD player	0.23
Own satellite dish	0.24	Own fan	0.22
Own DVD/VCD player	0.24	Own savings	0.22
Own colour television	0.24	Own tape recorder	0.20
Own motorcycle	0.21	Use private toilet	0.20
Family head education: elementary	−0.20	Eat meat at least once a week	0.18
Own tape recorder	0.19	Own motorcycle	0.18

Source: Suryadarma et al. (2005)

characteristic tend to have a lower level of welfare than families without it.

In general, asset ownership variables provided the best predictions of poverty in each village, although there were quite discernible differences in the types of assets. There were also non-asset poverty indicators. In Parakantugu only one non-asset variable (the educational level of the family head) was in the top ten, while in Cibulakan the consumption pattern was among the ten variables with the greatest weight. Thus the pilot project provided evidence that poverty indicators certainly differ among villages.

One way of testing the robustness of the welfare score is to isolate the richest and the poorest families in a village and compare their characteristics. As noted above, PCA is a relative poverty indicator and indicates where a family is placed when all families are ranked from poorest to richest. In all of the sample villages a wide gap was found to exist between families regarded as rich and those considered poor in almost every indicator. Table 8.2 presents a comparison of the characteristics of the ten per cent richest families and the ten per cent poorest families in Cibulakan village. As there are 1,430 families in Cibulakan, the characteristics of the richest 143 families are compared with those of the poorest 143 families.

Almost all families in Cibulakan, rich and poor alike, eat two meals a day. Since the village has a supply of power, both rich and poor have access to electricity. Most families have a house of at least eight square metres per capita and hardly anyone in the village lives in a house with a dirt floor. Political participation is equally high among rich and poor, confirming that voting in national elections has no connection with economic status.

This is where the similarities cease. As Table 8.2 shows, although most families eat twice a day, protein intake is very different since most rich families eat meat, fish, and eggs at least once a week. At the same time the proportion of rich families that

TABLE 8.2
Characteristics of the Richest and Poorest Families
in Cibulakan Village

Variable Group	Variable	Share of 10% Richest Families (%)	Share of 10% Poorest Families (%)
Marital status	Family head is married	99.31	33.57
Sex of family head	Family head is female	1.39	58.04
Education	Family head education: elementary school	34.72	60.14
	Family head education: junior secondary school	10.42	0.7
	Family head education: senior secondary school	33.33	0
	Family head education: diploma	9.72	0
	Family head education: university	10.42	0
	Spouse education: elementary	2.08	20.98
	Spouse education: junior secondary school	43.06	12.59
	Spouse education: senior secondary school	13.19	0
	Spouse education: diploma	30.56	0
	Spouse education: university	5.56	0
Occupation	Family head is working	100.0	60.84
	Spouse is working	27.78	11.89
	At least one school-age child is working	1.39	2.8
Sector of employment	Family in agriculture sector	9.03	54.55
	Family in industrial sector	2.78	1.4
	Family in trade sector	22.92	4.9
	Family in services sector	60.42	2.8
	Family receiving transfer (unemployed)	4.86	36.36
Access to financial institutions	Own savings	67.36	0.7
	Received credit from a formal financial institution in the past three years	32.64	0
	Mortgaged assets in the past three years	6.25	0
	Had to sell assets to pay debts	4.86	0

TABLE 8.2 (continued)
Characteristics of the Richest and Poorest Families
in Cibulakan Village

Variable Group	Variable	Share of 10% Richest Families (%)	Share of 10% Poorest Families (%)
Food consumption and health indicators	Eat two meals a day	97.92	97.2
	Eat meat at least once a week	90.97	13.99
	Eat fish at least once a week	96.53	33.57
	Eat egg at least once a week	98.61	40.56
	Seek modern medical treatment when sick	95.14	74.83
	Drink water from protected source	94.44	49.65
	Have private toilet	95.14	13.29
	Per capita family house size more than 8 sq. metres	94.44	82.52
	Live in a house with a dirt floor	0	0.7
	Experienced death of an infant in past three years	5.56	0.7
Other welfare indicators	Have access to electricity	100	94.41
	At least 1 school-age child dropped out of school	14.58	21.68
	High dependency rate (more than half of family members are younger than 15 years old)	10.42	7.69
	Most members buy new clothes at least once a year	95.14	41.96
	Victim of crime in the past year	4.86	1.4
Political participation	At least one family member voted in the last general election	99.31	92.31
Access to information	See television or newspaper at least once a week	100	44.06

Source: Suryadarma et al. (2005)

drink safe water is twice that of the poor and sanitation facilities are more available among the rich. Almost all rich family heads had completed at least six years of formal schooling and many had gone on to high school and tertiary-level education, whereas the majority of poor family heads had only six years of education and none went beyond junior secondary level. The gap between the educational levels of rich and poor is even wider among the spouses of family heads. At the same time, far more poor than rich families have a female head. Not surprisingly, every rich family head is employed while almost half of poor family heads do not have a job. Rich families tend to be engaged in services, trade, and industry rather than in farming. The opposite is true of poor household heads, a far greater percentage of whom work in agriculture.

Reflecting asset ownership, rich families have greater access to formal financial institutions. The majority have savings and many have received credit from formal institutions. Almost all rich families seek modern health services during sickness, whereas only three-quarters of poor families do so. Almost all rich families buy clothes at least once a year while less than half of poor families do so. In the case of access to information, while every rich family sees television or a newspaper regularly, less than half of poor families do.

Further verification of the accuracy of the CBMS in targeting poor households in Cianjur and Demak Districts was undertaken in two of the four sample villages that had participated in the original pilot test. Using the focus group discussion (FGD) method, Akhmadi et al. (2006) found that the CBMS had correctly ranked neighbourhoods and hamlets in each area by level of family welfare. The FGDs showed that households in Cibulakan village had exactly the same inter-neighbourhood ranking order that had been obtained from the CBMS methodology. The CBMS was able to predict the ranking of families with quite high accuracy, a feature that enables subjectivity in the targeting of programs to be minimized.

4 CONCLUSION

Accurate targeting is essential if cost effectiveness is to be achieved in social protection programs, but it is not as easy to implement as is often suggested. Targeting of program beneficiaries requires detailed administrative guidance as well as community involvement if it is to be effective and at the same time socially and politically acceptable. While effective geographic targeting requires up-to-date, complete, and accurate data, even static administrative targeting is unable to catch newly poor households when such data are unavailable. Two major attempts have been made recently to develop more effective tools for the identification of beneficiaries in poverty reduction programs in Indonesia, namely, poverty mapping as a way to improve geographic targeting and the Community Based Monitoring System (CBMS) as a means to ensure better individual targeting.

Poverty maps can play a major role in efforts to overcome the weaknesses inherent in aggregate poverty analyses. The fact that differences in small administrative areas often go unnoticed in national statistics is a common but serious problem for planners in countries of the size and diversity of Indonesia. Poverty maps can assist in identifying those differences while at the same time they can enable resources to be used more effectively by reducing the leakage of program benefits to non-poor households and by lessening the risk of poor households being overlooked by program planners, that is, undercoverage.

The simplicity of data collection and the analysis process associated with use of the CBMS enables this method to be initiated by district governments using local capacities and resources. It also means that the flexibility of local governments can be more accommodated in determining relevant requirements such as instrument variables, cost structure, the time of implementation, and possibilities for updating. In future, a planner at the district level can know exactly which families should receive assistance from the quota allocated by the national government.

APPENDIX A: POVERTY MAPPING METHODOLOGY

Poverty mapping uses household survey data to estimate a model of per capita consumption (or other indicators of welfare) as a function of variables that are available in both the SUSENAS and the Population Census. The resulting parameter estimates from this procedure are then used in a simulation to predict per capita consumption for each household in the census. Using the predicted per capita consumption, household measures of poverty and inequality levels are then calculated and aggregated for small areas such as districts, subdistricts, and villages. The fact that this method allows for the calculation of standard errors for whichever welfare measure is estimated is important in that it offers a means to assess the statistical reliability of the estimates and also allows for comparisons to be made among different regions.

Stages in the Poverty Mapping Process[5]

Stage 1: Matching Variables in the Survey and the Census

In order to obtain rigorous estimates of consumption levels of the households in the Population Census, the explanatory variables selected in the consumption determination model have to exist and be measured in the same way in both the household survey and in the census. If the sample of the household survey was randomly selected and nationally representative, the distribution of each explanatory variable in the household survey could be expected to be the same as its distribution in the census.

Stage 2: Selecting Explanatory Variables for the Consumption Model

Following Elbers et al. (2001, 2002), the empirical model of household consumption is defined as:

$$\ln y_{vh} = E(y_{vh} \mid x_{vh}) + u_{vh} \tag{8.1}$$

where $\ln y_{vh}$ is the logarithm of per capita consumption of household h in village v, x_{vh} is a vector of the observed characteristics of this household (including village-level variables), and u_{vh} is the error term. Note that u_{vh} is uncorrelated with x_{vh}. This model is simplified by using a linear approximation to the conditional expectation $E(y_{vh} \mid x_{vh})$ and decomposing u_{vh} into uncorrelated terms:

$$u_{vh} = \eta_v + \varepsilon_{vh} \tag{8.2}$$

where η_v represents a village-level error term common to all households within the village and ε_{vh} is a household-specific error term. It is further assumed that the η_v are uncorrelated across villages and the ε_{vh} are uncorrelated across households.

With these assumptions, equation (8.1) reduces to:

$$\ln y_{vh} = x_{vh}\beta + \eta_v + \varepsilon_{vh} \tag{8.3}$$

The procedure in selecting the explanatory variables of equation (8.3) starts by running a regression of log consumption on the matched variables identified in Stage 1, plus some variables that can be created from those variables such as the square and cube of household size or the square and cube of the age of the household head.[6] In order to obtain a robust specification, variables are only selected for inclusion in equation (8.3) if they contribute significantly to the explanation of (log) per capita consumption. Hence variables with low t-values are dropped.

After a promising set of variables has been selected in this way, the regression is run again and the residuals of this regression are saved. These residuals need to be scrutinized to check if there are some outliers in the observation. If indeed there are some residual values that are far out of the range of most residual values, then these observations must be checked for coding or other errors. Ultimately it may be necessary to delete them from the data. Fortunately, this is extremely rare.

The next step is to select village-level independent variables to complete the consumption model specification. The village-level variables are obtained from either the census data aggregated at the village level (for example the total number of individuals in the population or means of the ages of household heads in each village) or from the PODES data. These variables are then grouped into several sets such as demographic variables, village infrastructure variables, and village economic variables.

The residuals of the last regression are aggregated at the village level to calculate the mean of these residuals for each village. The variable selection is then done by running separate regressions of the village-level mean of residuals on each set of the village-level variables. The variables with significant t-values are selected as the candidates for inclusion in the consumption model.

The feasibility of including these candidates for village-level variables in the consumption model is tested by running regressions of village dummy variables on these variables. One regression is run for each independent variable candidate. If the coefficient of a certain variable in a regression is one, it shows that there is a perfect multicollinearity between this variable and the village dummy variable. This will happen if, for example, a village has a certain infrastructure that no other villages have or, on the other hand, all villages except one have a certain infrastructure. Such variables are necessarily excluded from the model. This test may explain why, for example, electricity is included in the model for rural areas but excluded from the model for urban areas.

Stage 3: Estimating the Consumption Model

The result of Stage 2 is a complete specification of the consumption model, incorporating both household-level and village-level independent variables of the model. The next step is to test whether there is heteroscedascity in the data. This will determine the method to be employed for estimating the model. The first step in doing this is to estimate the model of equation (8.3) using Ordinary Least Squares (OLS) and save the residuals as a variable $\hat{u}_{vh}$. Based on equation (8.2) the residuals $\hat{u}_{vh}$ are then decomposed into uncorrelated components as:

$$\hat{u}_{vh} = \hat{u}_{v\bullet} + \left(\hat{u}_{vh} - \hat{u}_{v\bullet}\right) = \hat{\eta}_v + e_{vh} \tag{8.4}$$

To investigate the presence of heteroscedascity in the data, a set of potential variables that best explain the variations in e_{vh}^2 is used to estimate the following logistic model:

$$\ln\left[\frac{e_{vh}^2}{A - e_{vh}^2}\right] = z_{vh}^T \hat{\alpha} + r_{vh} \tag{8.5}$$

where we take A equal to $1.05*\max\{e_{vh}^2\}$ as in Elbers et al. (2002). This specification puts bounds on the predicted variance of ε_{vh}^2. In the case where homoscedascity is rejected, a household-specific variance estimator for ε_{vh} is calculated as:

$$\hat{\sigma}_{\varepsilon,vh}^2 = \left[\frac{AB}{1 + B}\right] + \frac{1}{2}\hat{\mathrm{V}}\mathrm{ar}(r)\left[\frac{AB(1 - B)}{(1 + B)^3}\right] \tag{8.6}$$

where $B = \exp\{z_{vh}^T \hat{\alpha}\}$. The consumption model is then re-estimated using the Generalized Least Squares (GLS) method, utilizing the estimated variance-covariance matrix, $\hat{\Sigma}$, resulting from equation (8.6) and weighted by the population weight, l_{vh}. The estimated parameters, $\hat{\beta}_{GLS}$, and their variance, $\mathrm{Var}(\hat{\beta}_{GLS})$, are saved for use in the simulation.

Stage 4: Simulations on Census Data

The purpose of this procedure is to apply the parameters estimated in the previous procedure to the census data. However, since the values of these parameters are obtained through estimations, they are not precise values and are subject to sampling error. This needs to be taken into account in applying the parameters to the census data, i.e., by incorporating the standard errors of the coefficient estimates in the application process. To start, recall that the purpose is to calculate the simulated version of equation (8.3):

$$\ln y^s_{vh} = x_{vh}\beta^s + \eta^s_v + \varepsilon^s_{vh} \tag{8.7}$$

where the superscript s refers to the simulated version of each parameter or variable and now x_{vh} refers to characteristics of the households in the Population Census data.

Simulation of β

The simulated value of β is obtained through a random draw, assuming $\beta \sim N\left[\hat{\beta}_{GLS}, \text{Var}\left(\hat{\beta}_{GLS}\right)\right]$. Note that the draw has to take into account the covariance across β's. The randomly drawn parameter is defined as β^s. The next step is then to apply this simulated parameter to each household in the census data to calculate the value of $x_{vh}\beta^s$.

Simulation of η_v

The process of obtaining the simulated value of η_v requires two steps of simulations. This is because the variance of η itself is estimated with error. Hence, the first step is to obtain the simulated variance of η, σ^{2s}_{η}. Elbers et al. (2002) propose to draw σ^{2s}_{η} from a gamma distribution: $\sigma^{2s}_{\eta} \sim G\left[\hat{\sigma}^2_{\eta}, \text{Vâr}\left(\hat{\sigma}^2_{\eta}\right)\right]$. Accordingly, a random draw of the variance for the whole sample is exercised and its mean is defined as σ_η^{2s}. Then the second step is to randomly draw η_v^s for each village in the census data, assuming $\eta_v \sim N(0, \sigma_v^{2s})$.

Simulation of ε_{vh}

The process of obtaining the simulated value of ε_{vh} requires use of the results of estimation of equation (8.5). Assuming $\alpha \sim N[\hat{\alpha}, \text{Var}(\hat{\alpha})]$, a random draw of α is made and defined as α^s. As in the case of β, the draw has to take into account the covariance across α's. The simulated parameter is then used to simulate the household-specific variance estimator for ε_{vh} as defined in equation (8.6) for each household in the census data. Finally, the simulated value of household-specific, idiosyncratic shock, ε_{vh}^s, for every household in the census data is obtained by taking a random draw, assuming $\varepsilon_{vh} \sim N(0, \sigma_{vh}^{2s})$.[7]

Now that all the three components of equation (8.7) have been simulated, the value of $\ln y_{vh}^s$ for all households in the census data can be calculated by summing up the values of $x_{vh}\beta^s$, η_v^s, and ε_{vh}^s that have been obtained. The whole set of simulations is then repeated a number (one hundred) of times, so that in the end a database of a hundred simulated values of (log) per capita household expenditure for all the households in the census data is created.

Stage 5: Calculation of Poverty and Inequality Indicators

The final output of Stage 4, a database of one hundred simulated values of household expenditure for all households in the census data, is used as the basis for calculating various poverty and inequality measures at the provincial, district, subdistrict, and village levels. The point estimate of each measure is the mean of the calculated measure over the hundred simulation values. Meanwhile, the standard error of this estimate is equal to the standard deviation of the calculated measure over the hundred simulation values.[8]

A word of warning should be issued here on interpreting the results obtained from this exercise. Suppose a headcount poverty indicator of 0.10 is listed for a location, along with a standard error of 0.03. This should be taken to mean that if there were to be found other locations with similar patterns of household characteristics, and if one had direct measurements of poverty headcounts in these locations, then we would predict that the poverty headcounts in these locations are likely to fall between 0.07 and 0.13 (with a 70 per cent confidence interval). In particular, we do not claim that all these similar locations share the same headcount, nor is there a good reason to attach too much significance to the "point estimate" of 0.10.

The pairing of point estimate *and* standard error expresses the fact that, conditional on the information about the location that we have, it is just as likely that its headcount is between 0.07 and 0.13 as that it would be "centred" in the slightly narrower interval between 0.095 and 0.105. This uncertainty in the poverty estimates reflects the fact that the parameters of the consumption model (8.3) cannot be estimated with infinite precision and that there is no way to deduce the error terms u_{vh} from the available data.

Similarly, to conclude that the headcount in one location (A) is greater than in another (B), it is not sufficient to note that the point estimate for the headcount in A is higher than the one for B. Again, one has to take into account the error margins on the point estimates. For example, suppose that the headcount in A is h_A with a standard error of S_A and similarly for location B with h_B and S_B, where A's point estimate is higher: $h_A > h_B$. Then one can only conclude with reasonable confidence (more than 70 per cent) that A's true headcount is higher than B's if $h_A - S_A > h_B + S_B$. In other words, one should account for the possibility that the estimated headcount for A is an overestimate, while B's estimate is an underestimate.

Notes

1. The number of provinces in Indonesia is now thirty-three, but it was thirty when this chapter was written.
2. See notes 5 and 6 in Chapter 2 for details of SUSENAS and PODES.
3. See note 16 in Chapter 2 for details of the BKKBN methodology.
4. See Chapter 9 for details of the Unconditional Cash Transfer (BLT) program.
5. The stages and procedures in applying the model to create poverty maps are from Suryahadi et al. (2005a). For each province, the estimations for urban and rural areas are implemented separately except for Jakarta, which is a wholly urban area. The poverty line for each region is taken from Pradhan et al. (2001).
6. Experience with poverty mapping in other countries suggests that these regressions should be weighted using cluster expansion factors. In the case of the SUSENAS, cluster expansion factors within urban or rural areas in a province are all equal. Since the estimations are implemented at this level, the issue of weighting does not arise.
7. Elbers et al. (2002) mention alternatives for the assumption that the error component terms follow normal distributions. In separate sets of simulations we have experimented with these alternative assumptions. In no case did this lead to significantly different results.
8. The application of this poverty-mapping exercise from Stages 3 to 5 is implemented using a software package called PovMap (Version 1.0 BETA), developed by Qinghua Zhao at the World Bank.

Chapter 9

POST-CRISIS SOCIAL PROTECTION PROGRAMS IN INDONESIA

Sudarno Sumarto and Asep Suryahadi

1 INTRODUCTION

In response to the economic crisis of 1997–1998, the Indonesian Government introduced a series of poverty alleviation programs that together constituted the so-called Social Safety Net (JPS). But although the negative effects of the crisis on social welfare began to decline as the economy slowly recovered and macroeconomic stability was restored, the poor and vulnerable still very much needed assistance in the post-crisis period. Most of the components of the JPS programs were retained in the social protection programs that were adopted in and after 2000, although some underwent modifications in design. The JPS program itself was gradually phased out and by 2003 had ceased to exist in its original form.

2 POST-CRISIS SOCIAL PROTECTION INITIATIVES

2.1 Fuel Subsidy Reductions

In the year 2000 policy-makers launched the first phase in a lengthy process of reductions in the subsidy for fuel (gasoline, diesel fuel, and kerosene, known collectively as *Bahan Bakar Minyak*, BBM). The BBM subsidy, which had been increased in May 1998, had drastically reduced the cost of fuel products relative to international prices. The subsidy was highly regressive in absolute terms, however, as the majority of cumulative benefits accrued to non-poor households. It was only mildly progressive in relative terms in that BBM, particularly kerosene, comprised a slightly larger proportion of total expenditures among poorer households. The first subsidy reduction occurred near the end of 2000 and over the following years the price of BBM was gradually increased, but no government was willing to make adjustments on a scale that would have significantly altered this extremely regressive form of public spending. It was largely for reasons of political expediency that subsequent governments did not substantially reduce the subsidy on kerosene until several years later in the context of more dramatic overall price adjustments.

In October 2000 the Indonesian Government cut the fuel subsidy by approximately 12 per cent. It then reallocated Rp 800 billion in savings to a package of short-term compensatory programs known as PKPS-BBM (*Program Kompensasi Pengurangan Subsidi Bahan Bakar Minyak* or the Fuel Subsidy Reduction Compensation Program). Funding was made available for three separate short-term programs that were designed to alleviate poverty and increase prosperity within the community, namely, cash transfers that provided direct subsidies to poor households, revolving funds that encouraged the development of small businesses and micro-enterprises, and community empowerment programs that supported the development of infrastructure projects.

With identification based on BKKBN criteria, approximately 6.6 million poor households across the country received a cash transfer of Rp 10,000 per month for three months, from October until December 2000. In the case of the revolving funds program where the aim was to increase the capital available to small enterprises through existing financial institutions, the program distributed Rp 100 million to savings and loan cooperatives and Rp 50 million to micro-finance institutions. The third program, community empowerment, involved an infrastructure development and employment generation program known as PPM Prasarana *(Program Pemberdayaan Masyarakat — Prasarana*, or Community Empowerment Program and Infrastructure), which targeted low-income rural communities with priority given to regions outside Java. Each of 250 subdistricts across fourteen provinces received between Rp 750 million and Rp 1.1 billion for maintenance, rehabilitation, and development projects. Like the guidelines for *padat karya* programs, directions for the new program stipulated that wages were not to exceed the official minimum wage in each locality.

One of the major JPS programs, the sale of subsidized rice (*Operasi Pasar Khusus*, or OPK), was maintained largely as it had been during the crisis, although in mid-2001 program planners introduced a set of primarily cosmetic changes, including the new program title of *Raskin*, an acronym for *Beras untuk keluarga miskin* or "rice for poor families". The purpose of the name change was to discourage the non-poor from seeking to obtain the benefits provided by this program. At the same time, the amount of rice that a poor family could purchase each month was increased from between 10 and 20 kg to exactly 20 kg (Hastuti and Maxwell 2003). Many experts and policy-makers, however, have strongly questioned the wisdom of continuing the program without substantial reforms to Indonesia's rice production and import policies, which are a persistent source of consumption volatility for poor households.

2.2 Education

During the post-crisis period policy-makers implemented new programs in the education sector. Following the fuel subsidy reduction of October 2000, a large-scale educational assistance program was provided in 2001 through the PKPS-BBM program as a follow-up to the JPS scholarship and block grant program (Rahayu et al. 2003). Introduced in the 2001–2002 school year and known as BKM (*Bantuan Khusus Murid*, or Special Assistance for Students), it was a new scholarship program for students in primary (SD), junior secondary (SMP) and senior secondary (SMA) schools. Operating alongside the JPS scholarship program until the end of the 2002–2003 school year, the BKM program provided scholarships for many more students and stipulated how scholarship funds could be spent.

Scholarships were of the same value as the JPS scholarships — Rp 10,000 per month for primary school pupils and Rp 20,000 per month for junior secondary school pupils — although the total amount of funding provided for scholarships under the BKM program was much greater than it had been under the JPS. Nearly 20 per cent of primary school students and 26 per cent of junior secondary school students received scholarships in 2004. School committees were asked to indicate students' eligibility based on flexible criteria similar to those of the JPS system. School administrators could direct scholarship funds towards any of the following: monthly tuition, the purchase of schoolbooks or other supplies, transportation costs, and daily living costs. Associated with BKM was the BKS (*Bantuan Khusus Sekolah*, or Special Assistance to Schools) program, which operated only in 2001.

2.3 Health

In the health sector the health card program was also retained but several changes were made in program management. In 2001 the government provided additional subsidies for health services for the poor through the PDPSE-BK program (Reduced Energy Subsidy Impact Alleviation program — Health Sector). In 2002 the source of funds was replaced by the PKPS-BBM program, although the nature of the health program did not change. Implementation of the health card program was aimed at increasing access to health services by the poor. The program experienced many problems, however, including identification of the poor and distribution of the health cards as well as administrative constraints. Because of the limitations of the health card program, the government sought a more effective, efficient, and sustainable mechanism.

In August 2003, some two years after regional autonomy had been established throughout Indonesia, the government launched the program known as JPK-Gakin (*Jaminan Pelayanan Kesehatan untuk Keluarga Miskin*, or Health Service Insurance for Poor Families), which was intended to be a local health financing scheme based on the principles of health insurance. Finance for the program came from two sources: PKPS-BBM funds and special regional budgetary allocations (DAU). General program guidelines stipulated that poor households were to receive guarantees in the form of health cards for free health services at public health clinics and hospitals. While evidence suggests that hospital utilization among beneficiaries was low, this was the first time that a safety net program in the health sector had guaranteed hospital services for the poor. In early 2005, the government allocated approximately Rp 3.87 trillion of PKPS-BBM funds to expand and strengthen the JPK-Gakin program, which had initially aimed to provide 12 million households with health service guarantees worth Rp 5,000 per person per month.

Two unique aspects of the JPK-Gakin program set it apart from the previous JPS health card program. First, district (*kabupaten*) governments had the flexibility to design targeting and benefit schemes. Secondly, in line with the decentralization policy that had commenced in 2001, the government transferred the authority to manage this program to the district level. Program planners in Jakarta established management units (*Badan Pelaksana*, or *Bapel*) whose task was to oversee local design and implementation in each district. In late 2004, however, with the enactment of a new Social Security Law, the government recentralized program management under PT Askes (a state-owned health insurance company), which, with very little experience in implementing safety net programs, was authorized to provide JPK-Gakin benefits alongside the *Bapel*. This created a competitive process among service providers with two rather different ways of operating (Arifianto et al. 2005).

The PKPS-BBM programs built on the lessons of previous programs. Given the large and flexible budget, funded primarily by flows of savings due to BBM subsidy reductions, these programs achieved a degree of national coverage that had not been possible with the JPS programs. This in itself established credibility among stakeholders at all levels of government.

3 POLICIES AND PROGRAMS SINCE 2005

A massive reduction in the fuel subsidy took place near the beginning of 2005. At that time, spending on fuel subsidies absorbed nearly 2.9 per cent of GDP (or Rp 76.5 trillion) in the revised budget for 2005. In March 2005 the government raised the price of fuel products by a weighted average of 29 per cent and promised to reallocate half of the expected savings to a compensation fund worth Rp 11 trillion that would comprise a number of programs. Most of the budget was reallocated to four large-scale programs in the fields of education, health, direct cash transfers, and rural infrastructure.[1]

3.1 Education: School Operational Assistance

In the education sector the government developed a new assistance program called BOS (*Bantuan Operasional Sekolah*, or School Operational Assistance), which commenced at the start of the 2005–2006 school year in July 2005. The BKM scholarship program for primary and junior secondary schools was dramatically changed to become a block grant program provided to schools instead of to poor students. The size of the fund for each school was determined on the basis of the number of students. Schools that received BOS funds could use the funds for any school operational costs excluding the salaries of permanent teachers and school construction activities. Meanwhile, the BKM scholarship program at senior secondary school level continued as before (Suharyo et al. 2006).

As part of the government initiative to achieve nine years of compulsory education, the Department of Education had calculated that Rp 50 trillion would be required annually to provide free primary and junior secondary schooling. Unlike the JPS operational grants that had gone to the poorest 60 per cent of schools in each district, the BOS program provided funds to all schools across the archipelago. Together with the implementation of BOS, education planners refocused the BKM program on senior secondary schools, increasing scholarships to Rp 60,000 per month for nearly 700,000 SMA students. BOS planners also allocated approximately Rp 5.136 trillion to all state and private schools based on the total enrolment at each school. Primary schools received Rp 235,000 and junior secondary schools Rp 324,500 per student per year for a total of approximately 39.6 million students.

In contrast to the BKM/JPS program, which had provided scholarship funds directly to poor students, BOS funds were provided to schools to be managed in accordance with requirements set out by the government. The program enabled schools to reduce or even cancel tuition fees without adversely affecting the quality of education. School committees had the task of allocating funds among any of the eleven expenditure categories stipulated in program guidelines. Guidelines mandated the elimination of tuition fees in schools that, prior to receiving BOS, had charged tuition rates less than BOS funds. If pre-program tuition rates exceeded BOS funds, schools had to exempt poor students from fees and reduce tuition fees for other students.

Schools provided additional assistance to poor students in the form of transportation, uniforms, school bags, stationery, and reductions in other fees.

In practice, the BOS program has functioned as a generalized education subsidy targeting both supply-side and demand-side outcomes. The government reduced the overhead costs of education, allowing providers to allocate greater resources towards the variable costs generally borne by students' families. There is evidence that poor students have benefited, though not substantially, from the BOS program. Ultimately, the BOS program has generated clear benefits to schools with extremely limited sources of revenue. In some primary schools BOS funds have led to a near tripling of school revenue, which has allowed schools to purchase writing utensils, supplementary teaching tools and textbooks, as well as to pay the salaries of temporary teachers.

While Indonesia has achieved significant results in maintaining high primary and junior secondary enrolment rates since the crisis, many people have asked whether there have been quantity-quality trade-offs. The BOS program directly addressed supply-side weaknesses by advancing the quality and quantity of educational resources available to students, in the form of better-paid, non-permanent teachers and more abundant school supplies in particular. Given credible assumptions about program continuity, school officials have had an incentive to maintain high enrolment and educational quality to ensure steady or increasing flows of BOS funds. Assuming student mobility across schools, this would provide incentives for competition among schools for a fixed program budget allocated according to student enrolment.

3.2 Health: Insurance for the Poor

In the field of health services, starting in 2005 the government authorized PT Askes to manage all health funding for the poor. This program is being implemented as a social health insurance mechanism, popularly known as Askeskin (*Asuransi Kesehatan untuk Masyarakat Miskin,* or Health Insurance for the Poor). The program targets 60 million poor people whose premiums are paid by the government. The launching of this program drew protests from some regional governments, however, because it meant that initiatives on health financing for the poor in the regions no longer received financial support from the central government.

Under the program Askeskin holders can receive basic outpatient health care at community health centres (*puskesmas*) and third-class hospital care for free. In addition, Askeskin coverage includes an obstetric service package, mobile health services and special services for remote areas and islands, an immunization program, and medicines. In 2005, the Askeskin budget reached US$162 million for basic health services and US$237 million for hospital care.

Despite some similarities, the Askeskin program is different from the earlier JPS health card program in two respects. First, Askeskin targets individuals, whereas the JPS health card program targeted households. Second, Askeskin links financial and operational support for health care providers to provision of services to the poor, while in the health card program this link was absent.

Initially, Askeskin aimed to cover 60 million poor people in 2005. Districts were responsible for identifying and counting the eligible participants and reporting this to PT Askes and the Ministry of Health. Most districts used household-level poverty data collected by BPS that was also used for identifying participants for other anti-poverty programs (in particular, the unconditional cash transfers). Some districts, however, opted to use the household welfare indicator constructed by the BKKBN. Based on the data submitted by the districts, PT Askes issued Askeskin cards to all eligible participants.

Due to delays in providing Askeskin cards in the first year, health cards and village poverty letters (*Surat Keterangan Tidak*

Mampu, or SKTM) also provided access to health care. A person requiring health care but unable to cover the costs could apply for a SKTM poverty letter from the village head. With this letter, services covered by Askeskin could be obtained at community health centres. For hospital referrals, SKTM holders would be issued first with an Askeskin card at the local health centre. The drawback in this procedure is that Askeskin coverage through health cards and SKTM letters is overlooked in the Askeskin fund allocation to districts, hence putting extra pressure on district budgets and creating insecurity with hospitals as to whether all costs of Askeskin services will be reimbursed.[2]

3.3 Direct Transfers: the Unconditional Cash Transfer Program

In October 2005, six months after the first large-scale reduction in the fuel subsidy in March 2005, the same government again slashed the BBM subsidy, extending the cuts to premium gasoline, automotive diesel, and household kerosene. Before the reduction was made, the potential shocks to the economy in general and to household purchasing power in particular were already apparent to policy-makers. The challenge for the government was to reallocate resources immediately to social programs so as to mitigate the impact of the price shocks on welfare.

On 1 October 2005 the Indonesian Government launched its most ambitious social protection program to date, a one-year unconditional cash transfer program known as BLT (*Bantuan Langsung Tunai*, or Direct Cash Assistance). Prior to the October price increase, the government had already allocated Rp 5 trillion to education, Rp 3 trillion to health, and Rp 3 trillion to infrastructure. Initial estimates placed the expected savings from the October fuel subsidy cut at Rp 25 trillion, of which the government planned to allocate Rp 4.7 trillion to the first of four quarterly tranches of the transfer program. The first tranche was to reach 15.5 million households or approximately 62 million people, making BLT the largest program of its kind in the world. Even so, the national poverty rate still increased from 15.97 per cent in February 2005 to 17.75 per cent in March 2006.

The widely publicized BLT program provided nearly a quarter of Indonesian households with Rp 300,000 per household every three months from the fourth quarter of 2005 to the third quarter of 2006. The central government and particularly regional administrations demonstrated the institutional capacity required to conduct such a massive transfer program. Indonesia's experience in the first tranche of the program yielded important insights for subsequent tranches and also gave rise to much-needed policy debate about the future of transfer programs.

Given the time and administrative constraints facing policy-makers, the program unfolded quite smoothly. Crude simulations had initially suggested that the proposed subsidy cuts would lead to a 5.5 per cent increase in poverty in the absence of a transfer program. Although the magnitude of real-income shocks varied widely across regions, the poverty headcount rate increased roughly by only two per cent to 18.2 per cent in 2005, according to BPS figures. In general, the BLT program proved to be an effective and equity-enhancing means of reallocating savings from the BBM subsidy cutbacks.

The targeting mechanism used in the BLT program differed from the BKKBN checklist approach. In the new program BPS conducted individual targeting through a method called proxy means testing. There were several steps in identification of the poor for purposes of the BLT. First, BPS used SUSENAS Core data from 2002 to 2004 to identify poverty proxy indicators in each district. It then deployed its personnel throughout the country to enumerate household characteristics using a newly created questionnaire. Finally, data for each family's characteristics were entered into a computer where the welfare score of each family was calculated, hence the term "proxy means test". Through this process BPS determined the families eligible to receive the direct cash transfer (Hastuti et al. 2006).

Targeting for the BLT program was quite accurate at the subdistrict level, but some significant mistargeting took place at the household level. The main causes of mistargeting were local capture by relatively well-off households linked to local officials and weak proxy indicators in the household survey. This was the first time that proxy means tests had been used to target poor households in a national social protection program. But although the fourteen proxies used by official enumerators moved beyond the limitations of previous BKKBN targeting criteria, they ultimately failed to capture sufficient variation between poor and non-poor households, particularly in areas where there was a concentration of households around the poverty line.

In later tranches the government expanded the number of eligible households from around 15.5 million to approximately 19.2 million households, partly in response to the overwhelming number of supplementary eligibility requests. Given the inevitable mistargeting of non-poor households, the emergence of social jealousies, and popular perceptions of entitlement to benefits after the fuel subsidy cuts, local governments faced mounting pressure to spread BLT benefits to more households. Drawing on continued savings flows from the subsidy reductions, the government was able to defuse these social and political pressures directly by expanding the reach of the program. The swift implementation of the BLT program ensured the irreversibility of the October 2005 subsidy reductions, despite the high potential for a popular backlash. A basic political economy model suggests that the post-crisis Indonesian approach of gradual subsidy reductions coupled with compensation programs reduced the likelihood of the policy reversals that had taken place in several countries in the Middle East and North Africa, where governments attempted drastic subsidy cuts in one go.

By most accounts, the BLT program prevented the sudden increase in poverty that many had been predicting prior to October 2005. Nearly 27.1 per cent of Indonesian households received BLT funds in late 2005 and the program was relatively well targeted towards the poor. Targeting was more pro-poor, however, in urban areas where 28.2 per cent of program benefits reached the poorest decile compared to only 17.5 per cent in rural areas. This differential reflects the relative ease of targeting in urban areas where the distinction between poor and non-poor is more striking than in rural areas, where the majority of poor Indonesians reside. The program reached 55.6 per cent of households in the poorest decile and 39.4 per cent in the second poorest decile.

The government has subsequently justified the targeting outcomes on the grounds that the program aimed to reach not only poor households but also those vulnerable to poverty. Between February 2005 and March 2006, that is, the period during which the BBM subsidy was cut on two occasions, 56.5 per cent of initially poor households remained poor, 19.4 per cent became near poor, 17.7 per cent became near non-poor, and 6.5 per cent escaped poverty altogether, moving to the non-poor category. Meanwhile, only 6 per cent of households that were non-poor in February 2005 became poor or near poor a year later. The BLT funds constituted a significant proportion of monthly expenditures for the poorest households, covering 24 per cent of average monthly household expenditures in rural areas and 17 per cent in urban areas among households in the poorest decile. Furthermore, survey evidence suggests that for certain households, the funds were sufficient to cover not only consumption goods but also some health and education expenditures.

The BLT program addressed three fundamental concerns: (i) the need to ensure that poor households did not fall more deeply into poverty as a result of income and purchasing power shocks, (ii) the need to protect near- and non-poor households from slipping into poverty, and (iii) the need to promote welfare improvements among poor households, pushing them to higher expenditure gradients. The challenge now is to integrate an incentive structure into the transfer program in order to generate and maintain the human capital investments vital for sustained growth and poverty reduction. Careful restructuring of existing targeting and transfer arrangements will be required to secure the potential gains of a more equitable and efficient cash transfer program.

4 CONCLUSION

As the BLT program approached its final stages in 2006, policy-makers were occupied in formulating a new approach to social protection and poverty reduction in the form of a conditional cash transfer (CCT) program that will unite the health, education, and cash transfer components of the PKPS-BBM programs. In their attempts to design an effective conditional cash transfer program that responds to Indonesia's diverse environment, social planners must address the following issues:

- The conditional cash transfer program should adequately link the supply and demand sides of social protection. Policy-makers should search for the most welfare-enhancing mix of transfers to households and subsidies to service providers. Evidence suggests that demand-constrained, poor households benefit more from direct transfers such as scholarships or health cards than from general operational support to service providers.
- On the supply side, the government should create incentives among suppliers to improve the quality of their services by experimenting with different service providers as in the JPK-Gakin program.
- Policy-makers must effectively weigh the costs of identifying the poor against the benefits of excluding the non-poor

from social programs. Because there is likely to be a trade-off between the precision of targeting and the quantity and size of transfers, these analyses are vital in shaping budget allocations.

• Similarly, the costs of monitoring and enforcing conditionality can be extremely high in the absence of strong administrative capacity. Conditionality presumes one or both of the following: (i) that the government cares more about the welfare of future generations than parents care about their children's long-term welfare or (ii) that the government has more information about the potential returns to health and education than parents. Consideration of the costs and benefits of unconditional versus conditional cash transfers must ultimately underlie decisions about conditionality.

Drawing lessons from both the JPS and PKPS-BBM programs, policy-makers and researchers are now endeavouring to create a more efficient, equitable, and coherent social protection policy. The aim is not merely to provide risk-coping mechanisms in response to crises but also to institute sustainable programs that will enable the children of poor households to move out of poverty permanently. The PKPS-BBM programs have helped to maintain the gains of the JPS programs in the post-crisis period despite periodic bouts of economic fluctuations and, more importantly, they have enabled the central government to make the transition to a more progressive public spending regime. Today, however, Indonesia's budgetary allocations to social and human development priorities as a proportion of Gross Domestic Product still remain among the lowest in Southeast Asia and policy-makers face a critical trade-off between further assisting the state budget and making necessary social investments.

Notes

1. The rural infrastructure program is not discussed in the present paper as it is not a social protection program.
2. In September 2008 the Askeskin program is to be replaced by *Jamkesmas* (*Jaminan Kesehatan Masyarakat,* or Community Health Insurance). There will be no major changes in services for the public but the role of PT Askes will be reduced considerably.

Chapter 10

CONCLUSION: COPING WITH THE CRISIS

Sudarno Sumarto and Asep Suryahadi

Before the onset of the economic crisis in 1997, Indonesia was one of the fastest growing economies in the world. During the three decades before the crisis, the economy had grown at an average of around 7 per cent annually. This rapid growth had generated an unprecedented reduction in poverty within a relatively short period of time. Between 1970 and 1996, absolute poverty fell by around 50 percentage points, accompanied by substantial gains in education and health outcomes.

In mid-1997, however, after nearly a quarter of a century of rapid growth and welfare gains, a currency crisis struck Indonesia and by early 1998 the country was suffering from the combined effects of financial, economic, and political crises. Within one year, the value of the rupiah fell by 85 per cent, domestic prices soared by 78 per cent, nominal food prices increased threefold, and the economy contracted by almost 14 per cent. As the crisis worsened, mass rioting occurred in the capital Jakarta and in a few other major cities, culminating in the May 1998 fall of Soeharto, who had been in power for three decades.

The social impact of the crisis was enormous. By one account, the poverty rate doubled between mid-1997 and the end of 1998, implying that an additional 36 million people were pushed into absolute poverty by the crisis. More than half of the increase in poverty between 1996 and 1999 was due to an increase in chronic poverty, as the proportion of the chronic poor within the total population tripled during this period. Similarly, the vulnerable, that is, non-poor households that have a high probability of falling below the poverty line, tripled in number between 1996 and 1999. The crisis primarily affected the poor and the vulnerable through falling real wages and a large increase in the prices of basic commodities.

To reduce the adverse social impact of the crisis, the Indonesian Government introduced Social Safety Net (*Jaring Pengaman Sosial*, or JPS) programs aimed at preventing the poor from falling more deeply into poverty and at reducing the exposure of vulnerable households to risks. The Social Safety Net was focused towards ensuring that food, in particular rice, was available at affordable prices, raising the purchasing power of households through job creation, enabling the poor to continue to obtain major social services like health and education, and maintaining local economic activity through regional block grants and the extension of small-scale credits. It was hoped that the implementation of the JPS programs would prevent or at least significantly reduce the worst effects of the crisis.

During the pre-crisis period of high growth, government social safety net programs had been almost non-existent in Indonesia. The anti-poverty strategy at that time included general social spending on health, family planning, education, development programs aimed at increasing productivity among the poor, and some small programs for disadvantaged groups such as the handicapped and orphans. There were also mandatory social security and health insurance schemes for employees in medium and large enterprises, the public service, and the military. These schemes, however, proved largely ineffective during the crisis because they excluded most of the population and in particular the poor, as two-thirds of Indonesian workers were employed in the informal sector, where the compulsory social security schemes did not apply.

The Indonesian people, having never known public safety net programs in the past, turned to their own coping measures at a household level when the economic crisis occurred. The main coping strategies they adopted were reductions in expenditures, borrowing, and attempts to raise incomes. Clothing and recreation expenditures were cut most frequently, followed by transportation expenses, while reductions were also made in the quality or in some instances even the quantity of food. At the same time some households maintained expenditures by borrowing or selling assets, while many increased their incomes by taking additional jobs, working longer hours, or increasing the number of family members who worked. Children often augmented family income by engaging in labour activities in addition to attending school.

There is also evidence that a form of insurance took place among Indonesian households during the crisis. Village-level income shocks only partially yielded lower household consumption, which points to the presence of some inter- and/or intra-household insurance or redistributive mechanism at work. Undoubtedly this "moral economy" or "informal social safety net" within families and communities complemented the official JPS programs in limiting the worst effects of the crisis.

The JPS programs covered food security, education, health, community empowerment, and employment creation. Without a clear institutional precedent, policy-makers faced a challenging task in striving to undertake these social interventions amidst severe political instability and an increasingly unfriendly fiscal environment. In July 1998, with financial support from international donors, the Indonesian Government allocated Rp 3.9 trillion directly to JPS programs out of a total development budget of Rp 14.2 trillion, at a time when the exchange rate was around Rp 10,000 to the U.S. dollar. The magnitude of this social protection initiative was quite unprecedented in Indonesian history.

In the food security sector, the government introduced a subsidized rice program known as OPK (*Operasi Pasar Khusus*, or Special Market Operation) in July 1998 to ensure continued access among the poor to affordable rice. After a successful pilot program in Jakarta, it was expanded to the rest of the country. The OPK program was the largest and arguably the most critical component of the JPS programs during the crisis and was particularly effective in ensuring staple food intake among poor households. The initial target population took in around 7.4 million households or roughly 15 per cent of all households in the country. By far the most important commodity for poor households, rice comprises nearly a quarter of average monthly expenditures in poor households and contributes 34 and 26 per cent respectively to the official rural and urban poverty lines. By mid-1999, over 50 per cent of households in all but the richest quintile reported receiving OPK rice.

The OPK program shared some similarities with traditional commodity subsidy programs in other developing countries. As an indirect income transfer, the program reduced the price of the largest component of most poor households' monthly expenditures. The OPK "transfer" constituted 9 to 11 per cent of the total pre-program monthly expenditure of the median participant household. Econometric evidence suggests that OPK recipients experienced an increase in per capita household consumption that was in the order of 4 per cent higher than that of non-recipients at similar welfare levels.

Although poor households were explicitly targeted, the program also had an element of implicit self-selection by restricting the quality of OPK rice to that of medium quality rather than the higher quality rice traditionally purchased by wealthier households. Neither the explicit nor implicit targeting, however, was effective in limiting program participation to solely the poor. In 2001, 20.2 million households received subsidized rice — nearly double the target population — and yet only 52.6 per cent of the poor participated. To counter mounting criticism and perhaps the de facto distributional incidence, the official eligibility criteria were expanded to include both the lowest and the second-lowest family welfare categories in the system of household classification used by the National Family Planning Coordinating Board (BKKBN).

Another large component of the JPS was the employment-creation initiative known as the *padat karya* or labour-intensive program, which was launched in late 1997 and funded primarily through the state budget. Although some of the employment-creation activities were targeted at specific areas, particularly hard-hit urban areas, during the initial stage of the crisis, there was a notable lack of implementation guidelines. To the extent that there was household targeting, it was mainly through self-selection, as workers chose to work or not to work based on the going wage rates. There was no fixed minimum wage but in some regions the rate was actually set higher than the prevailing local wage rate, thus inducing those already working to switch jobs or to take additional jobs.

Households with at least one member participating in the program experienced an increase in per capita consumption approximately 4 per cent higher than that of non-participant households. The dynamic benefit incidence of the labour programs fared better than that of other JPS programs in health and education, largely due to the self-selection mechanism, which naturally responds to welfare changes more effectively than do administratively assigned benefits. In this regard, the labour programs may have effectively reached not only the chronic poor but also vulnerable, near-poor households that were facing transitory shocks.

Fearing deterioration in public and family health as a result of the crisis, the Indonesian Government established a social security program known as JPS-BK (*JPS Bidang Kesehatan*) in the health sector. The components consisted of a targeted consumer price subsidy, nutritional supplements, and operational support for public health facilities and village midwives. The purpose was to enable public health providers to maintain the quality and availability of services and poor households to afford the higher costs of medical services. Based on BKKBN criteria and quite irrespective of health status, poor households that were eligible received health cards, which could be used to obtain free medical services at public health clinics.

Impact evaluations of the health program have produced mixed findings. First, targeting was progressive as the poorest two quintiles received nearly 60 per cent of the health cards. Approximately 18.5 per cent of the poorest quintile received cards by comparison with only 3.7 per cent of households in the richest quintile. Despite the pro-poor distribution of health cards, the actual utilization of the cards for outpatient care was limited by comparison with the number of cards distributed. The low utilization rates among recipients perhaps originated in the same constraints that the poor face in non-crisis times, such as the high cost of travel and the time needed to reach health facilities as well as limited access to information regarding health service quality and availability. The high rate of underutilization also reflected the weak linkage between the disbursement of health cards and the allocation of operational grants.

Nevertheless, among the poor the health card program led to increased health care utilization and a moderate shift from private to subsidized public facilities. For the non-poor, a similar shift in utilization was observed. Quasi-experimental evidence suggests that the operational grants had a relatively stronger impact on overall utilization than did the actual receipt of health cards. While household recipients of health cards may have experienced a 4 per cent increase in consumption relative to similar non-recipient households, the poorest non-recipients were still demand-constrained and hence unable to utilize the expanded health services. In this aggregate sense, nearly all of the social safety net programs were plagued by undercoverage due to the compounding fiscal constraints imposed by the crisis.

The JPS education program had its origins in government concern that parents might withdraw their children from school as one way to cope with falling incomes and rising costs. The government responded to the possibility of a large increase in drop-out rates by establishing an educational funding program in the 1998–99 school year. The program consisted of scholarships for students from poor families and block grants for schools to facilitate continuity in their operations. The scholarships covered nearly 8 per cent of average monthly per capita expenditure among recipient households in the poorest quintile. Meanwhile, 60 per cent of schools in each district received operational grants (*Dana Bantuan Operasional*, or DBO), which could be used to purchase school materials, make physical repairs, and cover other operational costs.

Although program coverage of the poor was rather limited, the scholarship program generated welfare improvements at both household and aggregate levels. The households in which there was a JPS scholarship recipient experienced a substantial increase in consumption that was almost 10 per cent higher than that of similar non-recipient households. Despite the severe impact of the crisis on household welfare, a large-scale withdrawal of students from schools was prevented. Although the JPS scholarships reached only 4.96 per cent of all students in primary, junior, and senior secondary schools in the first year, strong econometric evidence suggests that the program succeeded in returning enrolment to pre-crisis levels, especially among children of primary school age in rural areas. Approximately 13 per cent of recipients would have dropped out of school if they had not received a scholarship, yielding an increase in overall enrolment of 0.6 per cent. Unlike the JPS health programs, though, the demand side (scholarships) had a larger impact on enrolment than did the supply side (DBO operational grants). Furthermore, by raising the reservation wages of poor students, the JPS program reduced the use of child labour as a consumption-smoothing mechanism in recipient households.

Meanwhile, the PDM-DKE program (*Pemberdayaan Daerah Mengatasi Dampak Krisis Ekonomi*, or Regional Empowerment Program to Overcome the Impact of the Economic Crisis) provided open-menu funds for villages across Indonesia. The program permitted maximum discretion at the local level with regard to the use of these funds. Decisions about who would benefit were left entirely in the hands of the village-level representative body, which at that time was the LKMD *(Lembaga Ketahanan Masyarakat Desa*, or Village Community Resilience Institution). As the official guidelines on targeting were sufficiently general, almost any decision could be justified as consistent with the program. Since the PDM-DKE program had been introduced as a "crisis program", however, local officials often made decisions without adequate time for a proper public information campaign, training of program administrators, and community consensus-building. In some communities the PDM-DKE program appears to have reached the poor reasonably effectively, while in other places the local community had never heard of the program, suggesting poor socialization and/or local elite capture.

As one of the important determinants of program effectiveness, the issue of targeting has received considerable attention in Indonesia since the crisis began a decade ago. Although the socioeconomic heterogeneity of the Indonesian archipelago has made targeting difficult for social planners, the distributional outcomes of the JPS programs described above compare favourably with similar programs in Latin America and elsewhere. Similarly, the distributional incidence of most JPS programs is progressive relative to the kerosene subsidy and hypothetical uniform transfers.

The difficulty of targeting the poor in Indonesia stems from a combination of several factors. First, inequality in this country has been historically low relative to other developing countries with large targeted social programs in Asia and Latin America. In countries like Indonesia with relatively lower inequality, the distinctions between poor and non-poor tend to be less sharp. Second, as in many developing countries, the majority of the Indonesian labour force works in the informal sector, rendering the full income reporting required for a traditional means test generally unreliable. Household expenditure can be used as a reasonable proxy for income, but with high income volatility during crises, expenditures can vary wildly over a short period of time, making it difficult to assign accurate welfare scores at the household level. Predicting consumption-based poverty using non-consumption indicators also poses numerous challenges. Third, although the absolute majority of the poor resides in rural areas, poor areas do not perfectly identify poor people. Hence geographic targeting through allocation quotas at the district or subdistrict level becomes ineffective without the availability of timely and accurate household data needed for reliable upward aggregations.

At the time of the crisis there were no up-to-date, sufficiently complete, and administratively acceptable data on its impact. Effective targeting required much more precise information than was available from previous SUSENAS and BKKBN data. The BKKBN classification of households was basically inadequate for the targeting of social safety net programs, one weakness being that its criteria were not all of an economic nature. Another shortcoming was the fact that it was based on the relatively fixed assets of households, which do not reflect temporary shocks to income. Furthermore, data collection for preparation of the list had been carried out by BKKBN's village-level workers, who were not trained for tasks of this kind. At the same time local officials were in a position to alter data concerning the economic status of households in their village. In a development setting where the enrichment of data sources is essentially a public good, the government should intervene by funding innovative data collection initiatives and the expansion of existing data sources.

A major feature of the JPS undertakings was the wide range in the targeting performances of the programs. The factors contributing to these differences in outcomes included variations in the design of programs, the scale of regional budget allocations, and local institutional capacity. When targeting mechanisms are being designed, it should be remembered that the vulnerable and the chronic poor may respond differently to different types of welfare-enhancing interventions. The actual sources of vulnerability ultimately matter most when designing effective interventions. Vulnerability due to low mean consumption prospects, which tends to predominate in rural areas, might best be addressed through cash transfer programs. On the other hand, vulnerability due to consumption fluctuations, a relatively more common finding among the urban population, might best be addressed through interventions aimed at consumption-smoothing. In the final analysis, improvements in targeting will require not only finer methodological innovations but also strong political will and public institutional support.

While the targeting of the JPS programs has been called into question by numerous researchers, social welfare would not have recovered in such a relatively short time without programs of this kind. On balance, the JPS programs prevented the economic crisis of 1997–98 from creating the losses in welfare that might have been expected in a situation of rapid decline in purchasing power and widespread unemployment. With a very limited prior institutional foundation for formal social protection programs, the government utilized existing village-level institutions including BKKBN cadres, health centre administrators, school committees, and local government officials to implement education, health, community empowerment, and rice subsidy programs. In all of the JPS programs, with the exception of the small nutrition component of the health programs and the subsidized credit programs, participation in programs helped to increase household consumption.

The most valuable lessons from Indonesia's Social Safety Net programs include the following:

- Informal coping mechanisms complement formal social interventions but are independently insufficient to mitigate the worst effects of a major shock or crisis. Real spending on formal social safety net programs must rise unambiguously during crisis periods.
- All programs suffered to varying degrees from targeting problems and inefficient delivery of benefits. Nevertheless, leakage may constitute a positive externality if near-poor households receive program benefits preventing them from falling into poverty and/or if the leaked benefits generate and sustain greater political support from a larger portion of the population.
- An improved real-time data collection and information processing system is vital for targeting vulnerable and newly poor households during periods of high income and price fluctuations. The best promise for Indonesia's particular socioeconomic environment would be to develop rigorously tested proxy welfare indicators further. While these indicators must capture sufficient variation among the poor, near poor and non-poor, it is most important that data collection guidelines allow for flexible survey designs that take interregional heterogeneity into account. To avoid potential moral hazards, household welfare data should be collected

regularly and not merely in hurried preparation for safety net targeting.

- On the institutional side of social protection in Indonesia, it is essential to give regional governments the policy space to design their own social programs within certain limits so as to support capacity-building in the context of further decentralization.
- Long-term poverty alleviation and development strategies are not suitable as JPS programs during a crisis. In particular, micro-credit programs are not suitable as social protection programs. Not only are new micro-enterprises unlikely to be successful during a crisis, but also the hurried expansion of credit can undermine the slow, patient, and painstaking groundwork that successful micro-credit programs require.
- During crises there is great potential in scholarship programs for keeping children in school and in measures that maintain access to health services among poor households.

While social protection is always a dynamic and complex challenge, the Indonesian experience since the financial crisis of 1997–98 has demonstrated the importance of careful planning and learning-by-doing. The success of social protection programs in sustaining household welfare and human capital investments will depend on getting the incentives "right". The JPS scholarship program, for example, concentrated resources on junior secondary schools because at this educational level the likelihood of attrition is highest. Also, the variable size of scholarships in the JPS program reflected the higher opportunity costs of post-primary education. With adequate data and administrative capacity, planners can improve program efficiency by determining eligibility and transfer size simultaneously.

Indonesia's social protection policies during the last decade reflect a clear progression towards greater equity and efficiency. The JPS programs set the stage for the institutionalization of a social protection framework at all levels of governance. In the years following the crisis, policy-makers introduced new social safety net programs to manage a gradual transition away from regressive fuel subsidies. Throughout this process there has been a steady growth in progressive public spending. The government has an obligation to intervene in protecting the most vulnerable members of Indonesian society against the effects of market failures, many of which are driven by the inability of poor households to articulate demand for social services through formal market mechanisms.

In the final analysis, a sustainable reduction in poverty requires deeper investment in rural areas where the majority of the poor lives, a reduction in the instability of food commodity prices and particularly rice prices, serious labour market reforms, and a secure financing scheme for a permanent social safety net for poor households. An equitable and efficient social safety net is one of the vital mechanisms in halting the transmission of poverty from one generation to the next. Sustainable social protection is no easy task, but Indonesia's policy-makers have the tools and the experience to enable Indonesia to emerge as a leader among developing countries in an increasingly crisis-prone global economy.

BIBLIOGRAPHY

Akhmadi, Daniel Suryadarma, Hastuti, and Rizki Fillaili. "Verifying the Accuracy of the Community Based Monitoring System in Targeting Poor Households". Field Report, December 2006. Jakarta: The SMERU Research Institute, 2006.

Amemiya, T. "The Maximum Likelihood Estimator and the Non-linear Three Stage Least Squares Estimator in the General Non-linear Simultaneous Equation Model". *Econometrica* 45 (1977): 955–68.

Arifianto, Alex, Ruly Marianti, Sri Budiyati, and Ellen Tan. "Making Services Work for the Poor in Indonesia: A Report on Health Financing Mechanisms (*JPK-Gakin*) in the Districts of Purbalingga, East Sumba and Tabanan". Research Report, September 2005. Jakarta: The SMERU Research Institute, 2005.

Arndt, H.W. and H. Hill, eds. *Southeast Asia's Economic Crisis: Origins, Lessons, and the Way Forward.* Singapore: Institute of Southeast Asian Studies, 2000.

Baker, Judy L. "Evaluating the Impact of Development Projects on Poverty: A Handbook for Practitioners". Washington, DC: The World Bank, 2000.

Balisacan, Arsenio M., Ernesto M. Pernia, and Abuzar Asra. "Revisiting Growth and Poverty Reduction in Indonesia: What do the Subnational Data Show?" *Bulletin of Indonesian Economic Studies* 39, no. 3 (2003): 329–51.

Bane, Mary Jo and David T. Ellwood. "Slipping Into and Out of Poverty: The Dynamics of Spells". NBER Working Paper No. 1199. Cambridge, MA: National Bureau of Economic Research, 1983.

Basri, M. Chatib and Arianto A. Patunru. "Survey of Recent Developments". *Bulletin of Indonesian Economic Studies* 42, no. 3 (2006): 295–319.

Baulch, Bob and John Hoddinott. "Economic Mobility and Poverty Dynamics in Developing Countries". *Journal of Development Studies* 36, no. 6 (2000): 1–24.

Besley, Timothy. "Political Economy of Targeting: Theory and Experience". Paper prepared for the Annual Bank Conference on Development Economics. Washington, DC: The World Bank, 1996.

Bidani, Benu and Martin Ravallion. "A Regional Poverty Profile for Indonesia". *Bulletin of Indonesian Economic Studies* 29, no. 3 (1993): 37–68.

Blustein, Paul. *The Chastening: Inside the Crisis that Rocked the Global Financial System and Humbled the IMF*. New York: Public Affairs, 2001.

Booth, Anne. Review Article: "The World Bank and Rural Poverty". *Journal of International Development* 24 (1992): 633–42.

Booth, Anne. "Survey of Recent Developments". *Bulletin of Indonesian Economic Studies* 35, no. 3 (1999): 3–38.

Booth, Anne. "The Indonesian Crisis of 1997–1999 and the Way Out: What are the Lessons of History?" *Lembaran Sejarah* 3, no. 1 (2000): 1–27.

BPS. *Statistical Yearbook of Indonesia 1998*. Jakarta: Badan Pusat Statistik, 1998.

BPS and UNDP. *Crisis, Poverty and Human Development in Indonesia*. Jakarta: Badan Pusat Statistik, 1999.

Cameron, Lisa. "Survey of Recent Developments". *Bulletin of Indonesian Economic Studies* 35, no. 1 (1999): 3–40.

Chaudhuri, Subham. *Empirical Methods for Assessing Household Vulnerability to Poverty*. Mimeographed. New York: Department of Economics, Columbia University, 2000.

Cunningham, Wendy and William F. Maloney. *Measuring Vulnerability: Who Suffered in the 1995 Mexican Crisis?* Mimeographed. Washington DC: The World Bank, 2000.

Daimon, Takeshi and Erik Thorbecke. "Mitigating the Social Impact of the Asian Crisis: Lessons from the IDT Experience". Unpublished paper. May 1999.

Davis, Benjamin. "Choosing a Method for Poverty Mapping". Paper presented at the International Seminar on Mapping Poverty in Southeast Asia, The SMERU Research Institute and Ford Foundation: Jakarta: 1–2 December, 2004.

Dercon, Stefan and Pramila Krishnan. "Vulnerability, Seasonality and Poverty in Ethiopia". *Journal of Development Studies* 36, no. 6 (2000): 25–53.

Deuster, Paul R. "Survey of recent developments". *Bulletin of Indonesian Economic Studies* 38, no. 1 (2002): 5–37.

Dick, Howard, Vincent Houben, J. Thomas Lindblad, and Thee Kian Wie. *The Emergence of a National Economy: An Economic History of Indonesia, 1800–2000*. Sydney: Allen & Unwin, Sydney; Leiden: KITLV Press, 2002.

Dreze, Jean and P.V. Srinivasan. "Widowhood and Poverty in Rural India: Some Inferences from Household Survey Data". *Journal of Development Economics* 54, no. 2 (1997): 217–34.

Elbers, Chris, Jean O. Lanjouw, and Peter Lanjouw. "Welfare in Villages and Towns: Micro-Level Estimation of Poverty and Inequality". Mimeographed. Amsterdam: Vrije Universiteit, 2001.

―――. "Micro-level Estimation of Welfare". Mimeographed. Amsterdam: Vrije Universiteit, 2002.

Esping-Andersen, Gøsta. *The Three Worlds of Welfare Capitalism*. Oxford: Polity, 1990.

Feridhanusetyawan, Tubagus. "The Impact of the Crisis on the Labor Market in Indonesia". Report prepared for the Asian Development Bank. Jakarta: Centre for Strategic and International Studies, 1999.

Ferreira, Francisco, Giovanna Prennushi, and Martin Ravallion. "Protecting the Poor from Macroeconomic Shocks: An Agenda for Action in a Crisis and Beyond". World Bank Policy Research

Working Paper No. 2160. Washington DC: The World Bank, 1999.

Fields, G. and E. Ok. "The Measurement of Income Mobility: An Introduction to the Literature". In *Handbook of Income Inequality Measurement*, edited by J. Silber. New York: Kluwer Academic Publishing, 1999.

Foster, James, J. Greer and Erik Thorbecke. "A Class of Decomposable Poverty Measures". *Econometrica* 52 (1984): 761–66.

Frankenberg, Elizabeth, Duncan Thomas, and Kathleen Beegle. *The Real Costs of Indonesia's Economic Crisis: Preliminary Findings from the Indonesia Family Life Surveys*. Mimeographed. Santa Monica, CA.: Rand Corporation, 1999.

Gaiha, Raghav and Anil Deolalikar. "Persistent, Expected and Innate Poverty: Estimates for Semi-Arid Rural South India, 1975–1984". *Cambridge Journal of Economics* 17, no. 4 (1993), 409–21.

Galasso, Emanuela and Martin Ravallion. "Distributional Outcomes of a Decentralized Welfare Program". Mimeographed. Washington, DC: The World Bank, 2000.

Gardiner, Peter. "Poverty Estimation during the Economic Crisis". Mimeographed. Jakarta: Insan Hitawasana Sejahtera, 1999.

Gelbach, Jonah and Lant Pritchett. "Is More for the Poor Less for the Poor: A Political Economy of Targeting". Policy Research Working Paper No. 1523. Washington, DC: The World Bank, 1997.

———. "Indicator Targeting in a Political Economy: Leakier can be Better". *Journal of Economic Policy Reform* 4 (2000): 13–45.

Glewwe, Paul and Gillette Hall. "Are Some Groups More Vulnerable to Macroeconomic Shocks Than Others? Hypothesis Tests Based on Panel Data from Peru". *Journal of Development Economics* 56, no. 1 (1998): 181–206.

Goodin, Robert E., Bruce Headey, Ruud Muffels, and Henk-Jan Dirven. *The Real Worlds of Welfare Capitalism*. Cambridge: Cambridge University Press, 1999.

Grosh, Margaret E. *Administering Targeted Social Programs in Latin America: From Platitudes to Practice*. World Bank Regional and Sectoral Studies. Washington DC: The World Bank, 1994.

Hastuti and John Maxwell. "Rice for Poor Families (RASKIN): Did the 2002 Program Operate Effectively?" Field Report, June 2003. Jakarta: The SMERU Research Institute, 2003.

Hastuti, Nina Toyamah, Syaikhu Usman, Bambang Sulaksono, Sri Budiyati, Wenefrida Dwi Widyanti, Meuthia Rosfadhila, et al. "A Rapid Appraisal of the Implementation of the 2005 Direct Cash Transfer Program in Indonesia: A Case Study in Five *Kabupaten/Kota*". Research Report, July 2006. Jakarta: The SMERU Research Institute, 2006.

Hentschel, Jesko, Jean O. Lanjouw, Peter Lanjouw, and Javier Poggi. "Combining Census and Survey Data to Trace the Spatial Dimensions of Poverty: A Case Study of Ecuador". *The World Bank Economic Review* 14, no. 1 (2000): 147–65.

Hill, Hal. *The Indonesian Economy Since 1966: Southeast Asia's Emerging Giant*. Cambridge and Melbourne: Cambridge University Press, 1996.

———. *The Indonesian Economy in Crisis: Causes, Consequences and Lessons*. Singapore: Institute of Southeast Asian Studies, 2000.

Ikhsan, M. and U. Wikarya. *Special Study on Poverty*. Manila: Asian Development Bank, 1999.

Imawan, Wynandin and Arizal Ahnaf. *Pedoman Analisis Data Susenas Bidang Kesejahteraan Rakyat* [Guidelines for Analysis of Susenas Data on Social Welfare]. Jakarta: Biro Pusat Statistik, 1997.

Jalan, Jyotsna and Martin Ravallion. "Are the Poor Less Well Insured? Evidence on Vulnerability to Income Risk in Rural China". *Journal of Development Economics* 58, no. 1 (1999*a*): 61–81.

———. "Income Gains to the Poor from Workfare: Estimates from Argentina's Trabajar Program". Policy Research Working Paper No. 2149. Washington, DC: The World Bank, 1999*b*.

————. "Is Transient Poverty Different? Evidence from Rural China". *Journal of Development Studies* 36, no. 6 (2000): 82–99.

Johnson, Colin. "Survey of Recent Developments". *Bulletin of Indonesian Economic Studies* 34, no. 2 (1998): 3–57.

Lanjouw, Peter and Martin Ravallion. "Benefit Incidence and the Timing of Program Capture". World Bank Policy Research Paper No. 1956. Washington DC: The World Bank, 1998.

————. "Benefit Incidence, Public Spending Reforms, and the Timing of Program Capture". *The World Bank Economic Review* 13, no. 2 (1999): 257–73.

Lanjouw, Peter, Menno Pradhan, Fadia Saadah, and Haneen Sayed. "Who Benefits from Public Spending on Health and Education in Indonesia?". Mimeographed. Washington DC: The World Bank, 2000.

Lindblad, J. Thomas and Thee Kian Wie. "Survey of Recent Developments". *Bulletin of Indonesian Economic Studies* 43, no. 1 (2000): 7–33.

Luttmer, Erzo F.P. *Inequality and Poverty Dynamics in Transition Economies: Disentangling Real Events from Noisy Data*. Mimeographed. Washington DC: World Bank, 2000.

Manning, C. "Labour Market Adjustment to Indonesia's Economic Crisis: Context, Trends and Implications". *Bulletin of Indonesian Economic Studies* 36, no. 1 (2000): 105–36.

McLeod, Ross H. "Workers' Social Security Legislation". In *Indonesia Assessment 1993: Labour, Sharing in the Benefits of Growth?*, edited by Ed. C. Manning and J. Hardjono. Singapore: Institute of Southeast Asian Studies; Canberra: Australian National University, 1993.

McLeod, Ross H. "Indonesia". In *East Asia in Crisis: From Being a Miracle to Needing One?*, edited by Ross H. McLeod and Ross Garnaut. London: Routledge, 1998.

McLeod, Ross H. and Ross Garnaut, eds. *East Asia in Crisis: From Being a Miracle to Needing One?* London: Routledge, 1998.

Meerman, J. *Public Expenditure in Malaysia: Who Benefits and Why?* New York: Oxford University Press for the World Bank, 1979.

Menpangan and BULOG. *Pedoman Umum dan Petunjuk Pelaksanaan Distribusi Operasi Pasar Khusus Beras, Buku I* [General Guidelines and Directions for Implementation of Special Market Operation Rice Distribution, Book I]. Jakarta: Menteri Negara Pangan dan Hortikultura and Badan Urusan Logistik, 1999.

Muller, Christophe. "Transient Seasonal and Chronic Poverty of Peasants: Evidence from Rwanda". Working Paper No. 97–8. Centre for the Study of African Economies, Institute of Economics and Statistics, University of Oxford. Oxford, 1997.

Musgrave, R., K.E. Case, and H.B. Leonard. "The Distribution of Fiscal Costs and Benefits". *Public Finance Quarterly* 2 (1974): 269–311.

Musgrave, R. and P. Musgrave. *Public Finance in Theory and Practice.* New York: McGraw-Hill, 1989.

Olken, Benjamin A., Musriyadi Nabiu, Nina Toyamah, and Daniel Perwira. "Sharing the Wealth: How Villages Decide to Distribute OPK Rice". Working Paper, October 2001. Jakarta: The SMERU Research Institute, 2001.

Papanek, Gustav F. and Budiono Sri Handoko. "The Impact on the Poor of Growth and Crisis: Evidence from Real Wage Data". Paper presented at the Conference on the Economic Issues Facing the New Government, LPEM-FEUI: Jakarta, 18–19 August, 1999.

Poppele, Jessica, Sudarno Sumarto, and Lant Pritchett. *Social Impacts of the Indonesian Crisis: New Data and Policy Implications.* SMERU Report. Jakarta: Social Monitoring and Early Response Unit, 1999.

Pradhan, Menno, Asep Suryahadi, Sudarno Sumarto, and Lant Pritchett. "Measurements of Poverty in Indonesia: 1996, 1999, and Beyond". SMERU Working Paper. Jakarta: Social Monitoring and Early Response Unit, 2000.

————. "Eating Like Which 'Joneses'? An Iterative Solution to the Choice of Poverty Line Reference Group". *The Review of Income and Wealth* 47, no. 4 (2001): 473–87.

Pritchett, Lant, Asep Suryahadi, and Sudarno Sumarto. "Quantifying Vulnerability to Poverty: A Proposed Measure, Applied to Indonesia". Policy Research Working Paper No. 2437, September 2000. Washington DC: The World Bank, 2000.

Pritchett, Lant, Sudarno Sumarto, and Asep Suryahadi. "Targeted Programs in an Economic Crisis: Empirical Findings from the Experience of Indonesia". Working Paper. Jakarta: The SMERU Research Institute, 2002.

Rahayu, Sri Kusumastuti, Robert Sparrow, Akhmadi, Vita Febriany, and Sri Budiyati. "Special Assistance for Students (BKM): Is It a Suitable Replacement for the JPS Scholarship Program?". Newsletter No. 6. Jakarta: The SMERU Research Institute, 2003.

Ravallion, Martin. "Poverty Comparisons: A Guide to Concepts and Methods". Living Standards Measurement Study Working Paper No. 88. Washington DC: The World Bank, 1992.

————. "Poverty Comparisons". *Fundamentals of Pure and Applied Economics*. Vol. 56. Chur, Switzerland: Harwood Academic Press, 1994.

Ravallion, Martin and Benu Bidani. "How Robust is a Poverty Profile?" *World Bank Economic Review* 8, no. 1 (1994): 75–102.

Saadah, Fadia, Menno Pradhan, and Robert Sparrow. "The Effectiveness of the Healthcard as an Instrument to Ensure Access to Medical Care for the Poor during the Crisis". Mimeographed. Washington DC: The World Bank, 2000.

Sadli, Mohamad. "The Indonesian Crisis". In *Southeast Asia's Economic Crisis: Origins, Lessons, and the Way Forward*, edited by H.W. Arndt and H. Hill. Singapore: Institute of Southeast Asian Studies, 2000.

Selowsky, M. *Who Benefits from Government Expenditure? A Case Study of Columbia*. New York: Oxford University Press, 1979.

Sen, Amartya. "The Political Economy of Targeting". In *Public Spending and the Poor: Theory and Evidence*, edited by Dominique van de Walle and Kimberley Nead. Baltimore: Johns Hopkins University Press, 1995.

———. *Poverty and Famines: An Essay on Entitlement and Deprivation*. Oxford: Oxford University Press, 1981.

Skoufias, Emmanuel. "Changes In Regional Inequality and Social Welfare in Indonesia from 1996 to 1999". *Journal of International Development* 13, no. 1 (2001): 73–91.

Skoufias, Emmanuel, Asep Suryahadi and Sudarno Sumarto. "Changes in Household Welfare, Poverty and Inequality During the Crisis". *Bulletin of Indonesian Economic Studies* 36, no. 2 (2000): 97–114.

Skoufias, Emmanuel and Asep Suryahadi. "A Cohort Analysis of Wages in Indonesia". *Applied Economics* 34, no. 13 (2002): 1703–10.

SMERU. "Rapid Field Appraisal of the Implementation of BULOG's *Operasi Pasar Khusus* (OPK) in Five Provinces". Special Report, December 1998. Jakarta: Social Monitoring and Early Response Unit, 1998.

———. "Hasil Pengamatan Lapangan Kilat Tim SMERU pada Persiapan Pelaksanaan Program PDM-DKE" [The Results of Rapid Field Observations by the SMERU Team on Preparations for the Implementation of the PDM-DKE Program]. Special Report, May 1999. Jakarta: Social Monitoring and Early Response Unit, 1999*a*.

———. "Update on the Impact of the Indonesian Crisis on Consumption Expenditures and Poverty Incidence: Results from the December 1998 Round of the 100 Village Survey". Working Paper, August 1999. Jakarta: Social Monitoring and Early Response Unit, 1999*b*.

Soesastro, Hadi and M. Chatib Basri. "Survey of Recent Developments". *Bulletin of Indonesian Economic Studies* 34, no. 1 (1998), 3–54.

Strauss, John, Kathleen Beegle, Agus Dwiyanto, Yulia Herawati, Daan Pattinasarany, Elan Satriawan, Bondan Sikoki, et al. "Indonesian Living Standards Three Years after the Crisis: Evidence from the Indonesia Family Life Survey". Mimeographed. Santa Monica: RAND, 2002.

Suharyo, Widjajanti, Akhmadi, Hastuti, Rizki Fillaili, Sri Budiyati, and Wawan Munawar. "Developing a Poverty Map for Indonesia: A Tool for Better Targeting in Poverty Reduction and Social Protection Programs". Book 4: Field Verification. Research Report, February 2005. Jakarta: The SMERU Research Institute, 2005.

Suharyo, Widjajanti, Sudarno Sumarto, Hastuti, Syaikhu Usman, Nina Toyamah, Bambang Sulaksono, Sri Budiyati, et al. "A Rapid Appraisal of the PKPS-BBM Education Sector School Operational Assistance (BOS) Program 2005". Research Report. Jakarta: The SMERU Research Institute, 2006.

Sumarto, Sudarno, Anna Wetterberg, and Lant Pritchett. "The Social Impact of the Crisis in Indonesia: Results from a Nationwide *Kecamatan* Survey". Report, December 1998. Jakarta: Social Monitoring and Early Response Unit, 1998.

Sumarto, Sudarno and Asep Suryahadi. "Principles and Approaches to Targeting with Reference to the Indonesian Social Safety Net Programs". Working Paper, July 2001. Jakarta: Social Monitoring and Early Response Unit, 2001.

Sumarto, Sudarno, Asep Suryahadi, and Lant Pritchett. "Safety Nets and Safety Ropes: Comparing the Dynamic Benefit Incidence of Two Indonesian JPS Programs". Working Paper. Jakarta: Social Monitoring and Early Response Unit, 2000.

Sumarto, Sudarno, Asep Suryahadi, and Lant Pritchett. "Safety Nets or Safety Ropes? Dynamic Benefit Incidence of Two Crisis Programs in Indonesia". *World Development* 31, no. 7 (2003): 1257–77.

———. "Designs and Implementation of the Indonesian Social Safety Net Programs". *Developing Economies* 40, no. 1 (2002): 3–31.

———. "Assessing the Impact of Indonesian Social Safety Net Programmes on Household Welfare and Poverty Dynamics". *European Journal of Development Research* 17, no. 1 (2005): 155–77.

Suryadarma, Daniel, Akhmadi, Hastuti, and Nina Toyamah. "Objective Measures of Family Welfare for Individual Targeting: Results from the Pilot Project on the Community Based Monitoring System in Indonesia". Research Report, December 2005. Jakarta: The SMERU Research Institute, 2005.

Suryahadi, Asep and Sudarno Sumarto. "Update on the Impact of the Indonesian Crisis on Consumption Expenditures and Poverty Incidence: Results from the December 1998 Round of the 100 Village Survey". Working Paper. Jakarta: Social Monitoring and Early Response Unit, 1999.

———. "The Chronic Poor, the Transient Poor and the Vulnerable Before and After the Economic Crisis". Working Paper. Jakarta: The SMERU Research Institute, 2001.

———. "Poverty and Vulnerability in Indonesia Before and After the Economic Crisis". *Asian Economic Journal* 17, no. 1 (2003): 35–64.

Suryahadi, Asep, Yusuf Suharso, and Sudarno Sumarto. "Coverage and Targeting in the Indonesian Social Safety Net Programs: Evidence from 100 Village Survey". Working Paper. Jakarta: Social Monitoring and Early Response Unit, 1999.

Suryahadi, Asep, Sudarno Sumarto, Yusuf Suharso, and Lant Pritchett. "The Evolution of Poverty during the Crisis in Indonesia, 1996–1999." Policy Research Working Paper No. 2435. Washington, DC: The World Bank, 2000.

Suryahadi, Asep, Sudarno Sumarto, and Wenefrida Widyanti. "Design and Implementation of the Indonesian Social Safety Net Programs, Evidence from the JPS Module in the 1999

Susenas". Working Paper. Jakarta: Social Monitoring and Early Response Unit, 2002.

Suryahadi, Asep, Wenefrida Widyanti, Sudarno Sumarto, and Lant Pritchett. "The Impact of Indonesian Social Safety Net Programs on Household Welfare". Working Paper. Jakarta: The SMERU Research Institute, 2002.

Suryahadi, Asep, Sudarno Sumarto, and Lant Pritchett. "The Evolution of Poverty during the Crisis in Indonesia". Working Paper, March 2003. Jakarta: The SMERU Research Institute, 2003.

Suryahadi, Asep, Wenefrida Widyanti, Daniel Perwira, Sudarno Sumarto, Chris Elbers, and Menno Pradhan. "Developing a Poverty Map for Indonesia: An Initiatory Work in Three Provinces". Parts I–III. Research Report, May 2005. Jakarta: The SMERU Research Institute, 2005a.

Suryahadi, Asep, Wenefrida Widyanti, Rima Prama Artha, Daniel Perwira, and Sudarno Sumarto. "Developing a Poverty Map for Indonesia: A Tool for Better Targeting in Poverty Reduction and Social Protection Programs". Books I–III. Research Report, February 2005. Jakarta: The SMERU Research Institute, 2005b.

Sutanto, Agus, and Puguh Bodro Irawan. *Regional Dimensions of Poverty: Some Findings on the Nature of Poverty*. Paper presented at the International Conference on Poverty Measurement in Indonesia. Jakarta, 16 May, 2000.

Thee Kian Wie. "The Soeharto Era and After: Stability, Development and Crisis". In *The Emergence of a National Economy: An Economic History of Indonesia, 1800–2000*, edited by Howard Dick et al. Sydney: Allen & Unwin; Leiden: KITLV Press, 2002.

Thee Kian Wie. "The Indonesian Economic Crisis and the Long Road to Recovery". *Australian Economic History Review* 43, no. 2 (2003): 183–96.

Tim Dampak Krisis SMERU. *Laporan Perkembangan Pelaksanaan Program Operasi Pasar Khusus (OPK): Januari 1999–Maret 2000*

[Report on Development of Implementation of the Special Operation (OPK) Program: January 1999–March 2000]. Special Report. Jakarta: Social Monitoring and Early Response Unit, 2000.

Van de Walle, Dominique. "The Distribution of Subsidies through Public Health Services in Indonesia, 1978–87". *World Bank Economic Review* 8, no. 2 (1994): 279–309.

Van de Walle, Dominique and Kimberley Nead. *Public Spending and the Poor: Theory and Evidence.* Baltimore: Johns Hopkins University Press, 1995.

Varian, Hal R. *Microeconomic Analysis.* 3rd ed. New York: W.W. Norton and Company, 1992.

Warr, Peter. "Food Policy and Poverty in Indonesia: A General Equilibrium Analysis". *Australian Journal of Agricultural and Resource Economics* 49 (2005): 429–51.

Wetterberg, Anna, Sudarno Sumarto, and Lant Pritchett. "A National Snapshot of the Social Impact of Indonesia's Crisis". *Bulletin of Indonesian Economic Studies* 35, no. 3 (1999): 145–52.

World Bank. *World Development Report 1990 — Poverty.* Washington DC: The World Bank, 1990.

———. *The East Asian Economic Miracle: Economic Growth and Public Policy.* New York: Oxford University Press, 1993a.

———. *Indonesia Poverty Assessment.* Washington DC: World Development, 1993b.

———. *Indonesia: Sustaining High Growth with Equity.* Washington DC: The World Bank, 1997.

———. *Indonesia in Crisis: A Macroeconomic Update.* Washington DC: The World Bank, 1998.

———. *Indonesia: From Crisis to Opportunity.* Washington DC: The World Bank, 1999.

———. *World Development Report 2000/2001: Attacking Poverty.* New York: Oxford University Press, 2000.

————. *Indonesia: The Imperative for Reform*. Washington DC: The World Bank, 2001*a*.

————. *Poverty Reduction in Indonesia: Constructing a New Strategy*. Washington DC: The World Bank, 2001*b*.

————. *Averting an Infrastructure Crisis in Indonesia: A Framework for Policy and Action*. Washington DC: The World Bank, 2004.

————. *Indonesia: New Directions*. Washington DC: The World Bank, 2005.

————. *Making the New Indonesia Work for the Poor*. Washington DC: The World Bank, 2006.

————. *Indonesia: Economic and Social Update*. November 2007. Jakarta: The World Bank, 2007.

INDEX

A

absolute poverty
  government target for
    reduction of, 14
  steep decline, 5
agricultural growth, (1970s), 5
agricultural labourers, 71
agricultural sector, poverty rate,
  55
all non-food deflator, 85
anti-poverty strategy, pre-crisis
  period, 235
Asian Development Bank
  funding for JPS, 146
Asian economic crisis (1997–98),
  1
  currency depreciation, 7
  growth and poverty after, 7–14
  hyperinflation, 11
  onset of, 7–9
  socio-economic impact, 9–13
    capital outflows, 10
    shifts in relative prices, 10
Askeskin program, 226
  replacement by Community
    Health Insurance, 233

B

Bahan Bakar Minyak (BBM), 218
Bali, poverty line, 79
Bantuan Langsung Tunai (BLT),
  199, 227, 229
  final stages, 231
  fundamental concerns, 230,
    231
  prevention of sudden increase
    in poverty, 230
basic consumer theory, use of
  inflation rates, 97
benefit incidence, 186
bottom 30 per cent index, 22

C

Central Bureau of Statistics (BPS),
  3
Central Kalimantan, 46
Central Sulawesi, total vulnerable
  group, 47
children, supplemental food
  program, 131
China, research in rural
  households, 60
chronic poverty
  increase in, 51, 59
chronically poor, 44, 46, 75
Cibulakan, 205
  CBMS testing, 202
  characteristics of poorest and
    richest families, 206, 207
community based monitoring
  system, 200–01
  ease of data collection, 209
  entering of data into database,
    203
  enumerators, training of, 203
  family questionnaire, 203

pilot testing, 202–08
use of Principal Components
    Analysis (PCA), 201, 202
variables, 204
verification of accuracy, 208
Community Empowerment
    Program and Infrastructure,
    220
community projects, 152
compulsory education, 224
Conditional Cash Transfer (CCT)
    program, 231
consumer price index, 20
Consumer Price Index (CPI), 20,
    21, 92
    actual food share, 34
    differences in inflation rates,
        94
    increase in non-food
        components, 84
    non-food inflation, 92
consumption
    changes in, 68–72
    per capita, August (1998) to
        October (1999), 69
consumption expenditures
    deficit of, 81
    deflation of, 31
    economic crisis, 17–32
    median consumption
        expenditures, 24, 27
    regional evolution, 23–26
Consumption Module SUSENAS,
    123, 124
    comparison with Core
        SUSENAS, 143–44
consumption quintile, transition
    matrices, 70
consumption-based poverty,
    predicting, 242

construction of poverty line,
    65–66, 80
controlling variables, community
    characteristics, 42
Core SUSENAS (Survey Sosial
    Ekonomi Nasional), 19, 124
    see also National Socio-
        Economic Survey
    comparison with Consumption
        Module SUSENAS, 143–44
cumulative distribution function
    vulnerability to poverty, 45
crash programs, 115, 146

D

Dana Bantuan Operasional (DBO)
    operational grants for schools,
        223, 240
data collection
    improved real time, 244
    measurement error, 41
Demography Institute of the
    University of Indonesia, 107
development policies, after
    (1987), 6
dynamic benefit incidence,
    150–57
    definition, 154–57
    household income and
        expenditures, 153–54
    use in measuring and
        comparing programs, 183
dynamic benefit incidence of
    participation, 155

E

East Kalimantan, 79, 195
East Nusa Tenggara, 46–47, 79
economic activity, sustaining
    local, 113

economic crisis
  poor and vulnerable, 42–59
  consumption expenditures,
    17–32
  evolution of poverty, 81
  poverty estimates, consistency,
    98–104
  poverty incidence, 17–32
  social impact, 234, 235
  social welfare impact, 31
economic growth, poverty
  alleviation, New Order
  [1966–98], 1
economy, contraction of, 9
education programs´
  post-crisis, 220–21, 223–25
  social safety net program, 113,
    116
El Nino, 9
ELL methodology, 193–95
employment creation, 115–16
  budget allocation, 140
  coverage of program, 127
  nature of labour intensive
    work, 159
  social safety net program, 113
  study on targeting of program,
    157
  targeting of program, 132
employment creation program
  comparison to subsidized rice
    program, 169–72
  funding by state, 238
  lack of coordination, 159
  problem of favouritism, 159
  program participation, 161
  receipts and budget shares,
    175
  relative likelihood of benefiting,
    169

static and dynamic incidence,
    164–69
static and dynamic
    participation, 167
Engel's Law, 85, 95, 106
estimates, reconciliation of, 105
estimation model, 197
Ethiopia, panel dataset of
    households, 64
exact inflation index, 83
expenditure function, 82
expenditures, reduction in, 236

F
family workers, 11
family planning list, used for
    subsidized rice program, 158
family planning services, 120
feasible generalized least squares
    (FGLS), 39
female headed households, 58
  India, 62
  poverty rate, 58
fixed weights deflator, 85
focus group discussions (FGDs),
    196, 198–99
food, ensuring availability of, 113
food poverty line, definition, 89
food security, social safety net
    program, 113
food security sector, 237
food share
  changes, 87
  poverty line, 95
food share deflator, 85
food versus non-food process,
    methods of choosing weights,
    91
Ford Foundation, 194
formal sector, loss of jobs, 11

Fuel Subsidy Reduction
    Compensation Program,
    (PKPS-BBM), 219, 221–22
fuel subsidy reductions, 218, 246

G
Gadjah Mada University, 107
geographical information systems
    (GIS), 192
Gross Domestic Product
    per capita, (1960s), 2
    proportion for social and
        human development, 232

H
headcount poverty rate, 63, 76,
    86
    method for estimating change,
        89–98
    sensitivity to poverty line, 88
health, 116–17
    insurance for poor, 225–27
    social safety net program, 113
health cards, 120
    distribution of, 239
    unused, 130, 148
    possession of, 130
health insurance scheme
    employees of medium to large
        enterprises, 235
health program, budget
    allocation, 140
health programs
    eligibility, 120
    impact evaluation, 239
    post-crisis, 221–23
Health Service Insurance for
    Poor Families, post-crisis,
    222, 226
high vulnerability group, 60

increase in all sectors, 55
increase in numbers, 44
high-performing Asian
    economies, 2
household income, relation to
    expenditures, 153–54
household survey data, 38,
    use in ELL method, 193
household specific deflator,
    Engel's Law, 85
household-level poverty data, 226
households
    aversion to risk, 177–80
    categories of vulnerability, 39
    choice of programs, 179
    consumption, changes in, 72,
        76
    distribution by participation in
        JPS programs, 136
    female headed, 58
    head educated at tertiary level,
        56
    possession of health cards, 129
    pre-prosperous, 34, 134
hyperinflation, Asian economic
    crisis, 11

I
Ikhsan's Poverty Line index, 22
International Monetary Fund
    (IMF), 8
income
    changes in, 68–72
    per capita *see* per capita income
    per capita, August (1998) to
        October (1999), 69
    transition matrices, 70
income mobility, 154
India, panel research of
    households, 60, 62

indirect utility function, 82
Indonesia
  macroeconomic background,
    67, 68
  macroeconomic indicators,
    August (1998) to November
    (1999), 78
  official poverty line, 6
Indonesia Family Life Survey
  (IFLS), 101
Indonesian rupiah, 7
Indragiri Ilir, 23
inflation
  early (1960s), 1
  extent of, 22
  increase in, 10
inflation estimates, effect on real
    expenditures, 87
inflation index, exact, 83
inflation rates
  differences, 94
  calculation of aggregate, 106
informal coping mechanisms,
    244
informal social safety net, 236
Inpres grants, 5

J
Jabotabek, 19, 32
  100 Village Survey, 19
Jakarta, total vulnerable group,
    increase, 47
Jaminan Kesehatan Masyarakat,
    233
Java, population, (1960s), 2
JPK-Gakin program, 222, 231
JPS, *see* Social Safety Net
JPS Bidang Kesehatan (Health
    Sector JPS) programs, 117

K
Kendari, 23
Kecamatan Development Project
    (PPK), 115, 152
krismon (monetary crisis), 9, 17

L
Lampung
  poverty line, 79
  total vulnerable group, highest
    increase, 47
Laspeyres indices, 91, 97, 106
Logistics Depot (DOLOG), 188
lower secondary school
    scholarship program,
    coverage, 128

M
Malaysian ringgit, depreciation, 7
male-headed households, poverty
    rate, 58
Maluku, 47
mean food share of SUSENAS,
    85
median household real
    consumption expenditures,
    24, 27
medical services program
    coverage, 129
  coverage at district level, 138
  targeting, 131
Method 1 deflator, 92
Method II deflator, 92
Method III, 96
Mini SUSENAS, 99
  December (1998), 101
Ministry of Manpower, 115
moral economy, 236
multimodule data, 151

N

National Family Planning
 Coordinating Board (BKKBN),
 29, 32, 228, 242
classification of households, 29,
 34, 117, 147, 238
methodology, 199
National Logistics Agency
 (BULOG), 188
nutrition program, 125
targeting, 131
National Socio-Economic Survey
 (SUSENAS), 41, 65
February 1998, 11
New Order
 absolute poverty, reduction, 4
 industrialization, rapid, 2
 poverty, downward trend, 66
 poverty alleviation, 1–7, 3
 social development, 3
New Order government, 1
nominal expenditure, deflation
 of, 84
non-food allowance, 89, 90
"non-food only" deflator, 84

O

100 Village Survey, 17–19, 99
 aggregate consumption
  evolution, 26–28
 changes in incidence of
  poverty, 28–31
 changes in real consumption, 20
 consumption expenditures,
  23–26
 pure measurement error, 163
 continuous fall in real
  consumption expenditures,
  25
 coverage of areas, 19

data, 160–61
data by quintile of per capita
 household expenditure, 162
data to be treated differently,
 100
data on participation in Padat
 Karya work, 168
deflator issue, 19–23
households receiving *sembako*,
 165
introduction, 18–19
median consumption
 expenditures, changes, 27
median household real
 consumption expenditure,
 24
poverty incidence, benchmarks,
 30
price index, 20, 28
rebound in real consumption,
 25
sample size, 18
sensitivity of real consumption
 changes to deflator, 21
100 Village Survey Index, 21, 28
 increase in median real income,
  23
oil, price decline, 9
oil boom, end of, 5
Operasi Pasar Khusus (OPK,
 Special Market Operation),
 114, 157, 220, 237

P

padat karya (labour-intensive
 program), 115, 127
coverage, 128
padat karya programs, 119
Papua, chronically poor category,
 46

Parakantugu, 205
  CBMS testing, 202
per capita income, (1960s), 3
persistently poor, 74
petty traders, 71
Philippine peso, depreciation, 7
PODES (Potensi Desa), 19, 33, 41
point estimate, significance, 216
policies and programs after 2005,
  223
poor and vulnerable households,
  across gender, 58
  educational level of household
    head, 56–58
  national level, 43–46
poor households, supplementing
  purchasing of, 113
Population Census 2000, 46
population census, use in ELL
  methodology, 193
poverty
  absolute, *see* absolute poverty
  August (1998) to October
    (1999), 69
  before and after economic
    crisis, 36–62
  categories, 39, 75
  changes in, 68–72
  changes in incidence, 28–31
  dynamic nature of, 37, 64
  evolution of, 81–106
  headcount measure, 4, 13, 76
  increase in, 44
  movements, 74
  narrow definition, 81
  national headcount rate, 36
  reasons for persistence of, 6
  steady decrease, 3
  sustainable reduction, 246
  total vulnerable group, 39

poverty alleviation, 3
  long term, 245
  New Order period, 1–7
poverty basket food share, 97
poverty categories, 75
  by province, 48, 49
  by urban and rural areas, 52
  changes by province, 50
  educational level of household
    heads, 57
  gender of household heads,
    59
  occupation of household heads,
    54
  population distribution, 43
  regional variations, 51
poverty dynamics, short term,
  63–79
poverty estimates, consistency
  during economic crisis, 98
poverty incidence
  change between May (1997)
    and December (1998), 29
  decrease, between August and
    December (1998), 32
  economic crisis, 17–32
poverty level, increase, Asian
  economic crisis, 12
poverty line
  based on food consumption, 80
  construction of, 65, 66, 67, 80
  deflation of, 82
  food share, 95
  food share in, 34
  rise in, 87
  sensitivity of poverty rate, 86
poverty estimates, use of
  SUSENAS Core, 99, 101
poverty incidence studies, 151
poverty line, Riau, 79

poverty mapping, 194, 217
  advantages, 191–93
  calculation of poverty, 215
  estimating consumption model,
      213
  experience in other countries,
      217
  interpreting results, 216
  matching variables, 210
  methodology, 210
  selecting variables for
      consumption model, 211
  selection of village-level
      independent variables,
      212
  simulations on census data,
      214
  stages in process, 210
  verification, 195–97
poverty maps
  evaluation of impact of various
      interventions, 192
  use of, 209
poverty measurements, problems,
      81, 82
poverty rates
  changes, various food shares
      and prices, 93
  consistent estimates, 103
  consistent series, 98
  estimates, calculation from
      secondary data, 102
  food share at, 106
  headcount, 76
  increase, 53
  peak, 105
  pre-crisis, 98
  sensitivity of, 86
poverty status
  pattern of change, 72–76

pre-prosperous
  definition, 146
pre-prosperous households, 34,
      117
pregnant women, supplemental
      food program for, 131
primary data, reconciliation of
      estimates, 105
price inflation, measured, 87
Principal Components Analysis
      (PCA), 201–02
Program for Underdeveloped
      Villages (IDT), 115
provinces, number of, 217
proxy means test, 228
public service
  social security and health
      insurance schemes, 235

Q
quantitative method
  estimating vulnerability to
      poverty, 60

R
Raskin (rice for the poor), 220
real consumption
  changes, 20
  expenditures
  August (1998), 26
  increase, 32
real expenditures
  definition, 82–86
  nominal expenditures, deflation
      of, 82
  sensitivity of change, 85
real income, changes in, 72, 76
real wages, fall in, 36
Regional Development Planning
      Board (BAPPEDA), 203

Regional Empowerment Program to Overcome the Impact of the Economic Crisis (PDM-DKE), 115, 241
Reduced Energy Subsidy Impact Alleviation Program Health Sector, 221
Regional Autonomy Law, 199
regional development grants, 5
Regional Research Initiative on Social Protection in Asia, 194
Riau, low incidence of chronic poverty, 46
rice
  importance, 106
  subsidized
    sale of, 114–15
    social safety net program, 125
  stablization of price, 26
rice imports, ban, 12
rice price only deflator, 85
"rice-only" deflator, 84
risk mitigation programs, 150
rural areas
  poor and vulnerable, 51–53
  short term poverty dynamics, 63–79
rural development strategy, broad based, 4, 5
rural infrastructure program, 233
rural population, effect of Asian economic crisis, 10
Rwanda, chronic poverty, 64

S
Sachs, Jeffrey, 7
"safety net" guarantees, 149
safety net programs, transfer or insurance, 173–83
"safety rope" guarantees, 149

"safety rope" program, pure, 157
sale of subsidized rice
  budget allowance, 140
  coverage of program, 126
scholarships, 116, 119
  amount disbursed, 129
  budget allowance for, 140
  coverage, 126, 128
Scholarships and Block Grant program, targeting and program design, 152, 223
School Operational Assistance (*Bantuan Operasi Sekolah*, BOS), 223–25
school students, eligibility for scholarships, 120
schools
  block grants to, 116
  operational grants, 223, 240
secondary data, reconciliation of estimates, 105
self-interested voting politics, impact of, 184
sembako (basic necessities), 160
  targeting, compared to *Padat Karya*, 170
small-area estimation method, 197
small-scale credit, 113
SMERU proposal, 194
SMERU Research Institute, 200
social development, during New Order, 3
social indicators, lagging, 3
social protection post-crisis, 218–32, 245
social protection policies
  progression towards equity and efficiency, 245
social protection programs
  cost of monitoring, 232

implementation during
economic crisis, 190
importance of accurate
targeting, 209
post-crisis, unconditional cash
transfer program, 227–31
targeting households vulnerable
to poverty, 230
targeting, 190–217
targeting, small-area poverty
mapping, 191
social safety net, as metaphor,
149
social safety net programs, 33
design and implementation,
111–48
evaluation of program
targeting, 153
formal, 142
main classes of targeting, 152
targeting and budget allocation,
173–77
Social Safety Net programs
(*Jaring Pengaman Sosial*, JPS),
235
before economic crisis, 111,
112
response to crisis, 112–17
budget, 139–40
budget allocation, 140
calculation of implementation
ratio, 133
centrally drafted program
guidelines, 137
coverage, scholarship programs,
126
coverage ratio, 134, 135
coverage by quintiles of per
capita expenditure, 145
design of programs, 183

designed by central
government, 136
education program, 240
effect of regional heterogeneity,
136–39
effectiveness, 141, 243
employment creation, 127
evaluating targeting outcomes,
121
food security, 113
funding for, 146
heterogeneity of performance,
141, 142
household choice of programs,
175
implementation ratio (IR), 132
lessons learned from, 244–45
major programs, 113
medical services, 129
method of targeting, 117–20
multiple coverage, 135–36
objective, 113
per capita expenditure, 132
performance, 132–35
post-crisis, 218–33
program coverage, 125–31
targeting of two programs, 157
study, JPS module of SUSENAS,
122–25
supplemental food program,
131
targeting, 131–32, 152
targeting effectiveness, 120,
153, 243
targeting expenditure ratio,
133
targeting mechanism, 118
targeting problems, 244
use of data from 100 Village
Survey, 160–61

social security schemes,
    mandatory, 235
social services
    pre-crisis, 112
    preserving access to, 113
social welfare, 31
    maximising choice, 181–83
    voting outcomes, 181–83
South Kalimantan, low incidence
    of chronic poverty, 46
Southeast Sulawesi, poverty line,
    79
Special Assistance for Students, 221
Special Assistance to Schools
    program, 221
Special Market Operation (*Operasi
    Pasar Khusus*), 114
special regional budgetary
    allocations, 222
static benefit incidence,
    visualization, 156
static benefit incidence of
    participation, 155
Statistics Indonesia *(Badan Pusat
    Statistik*, BPS), 17, 194
subsidized rice program, 237
    comparison to employment
        creation program, 169–72
    coverage, 137
    household expenditure and
        participation in program,
        163
    household participation by
        quintiles and changes in
        per capita consumption,
        166
    likelihood of middle quintile
        households benefiting, 172
    likelihood of poorest
        households benefiting, 171

maintenance after crisis, 220
    program participation, data,
        161
    receipts and budget shares,
        175
    relative likelihood of benefiting,
        169
    static and dynamic incidence,
        164–69
    study on targeting, 157
    targeting, 131
    use of family planning list,
        158
    targeting mechanism not
        uniform, 158
supplemental food program, 148
    coverage, 131
Surabaya, 19
SUSENAS Consumption Module,
    32, 99, 101, 107
SUSENAS Core, 99
    creation of poverty estimates,
        101
    databases, 100
SUSENAS surveys, 32, 151
SUSENAS Unit Prices, differences
    in inflation rates, 94

T
targeting, definition, 156
Thai baht, depreciation, 7
The East Asian Economic Miracle,
    2
total poverty rate, 77
total vulnerable group, 39
    increase in, 52, 1999
transient poor, 75
    majority of poor category, 55
    proportion of, 44
transition matrices, 71, 154

U

Unconditional Cash Transfer
   (BLT) program, *see Bantuan
   Langsung Tunai*
unemployment rate, increase, 36
upper secondary school
   scholarship program,
   coverage, 128
urban areas
   high vulnerability group,
      increase, 53
   poor and vulnerable, 51–53
urban areas, ratio of chronic to
   transient poverty, 53
urban population
   effect of Asian economic crisis,
      10
   vulnerability due to
      consumption fluctuations,
      243

V

Village Community Resilience
   Institution, 241
vulnerability
   before and after economic
      crisis, 36–62
   categories, 39
   definition of, 37–38
   method for estimating, 38

vulnerability threshold, 45
vulnerability to poverty, 37, 59
   cumulative distribution, 45

W

wages, *see* real wages
welfare-comparable basis,
      comparisons of poverty over
      time, 82
welfare indicators, availability of
      accurate, 194
welfare score, 228
   testing robustness of, 205
West Java
   CBMS testing, 202
   poverty line, 79
   total vulnerable group, 47
West Nusa Tenggara, 47
Workers' Social Security Law, 112
World Bank
   ban on rice imports, view, 12
   classification, 2
   funding for JPS, 146
   grant for creation of poverty
      maps, 194
   poverty mapping software, 217
   study of poverty, 12